A Mexican Running Wild
ultrarunning adventures of a single mom

By Norma Bastidas

FIRST EDITION

www.normabastidas.com

ISBN: 978-0-578-67493-3

For Karl and Hans and for my Mother.

Contents

Acknowledgements

The contents of this book would not exist if it wasn't for all the people that helped me during a very difficult and ultimately significant time in my life. My siblings, Carlos, Hector, Lourdes and Muñeca thank you for your love and understanding. W.Brett Wilson, Rudi Lopez, Jerry Gamez, Charlie Engle, Leslie, Gerein, John Longarini, Peter Lubbers, Scott Dunlap, Maria Madueno , Greg Stevenson, Wayne Gaudet, Nicola Fontanesi, Mario Lacerda, Stephanie Case, Matt Cordes, Jason Glass, John McCain, Ana Sebastian, Neil Runnions, Richard Donovan, Charlie Engle, Ray Zahab, Claudia Katz, Alan Lam, iempatize team, Ken Christie and so many others that help my journey. Kevin Compayre thank you for your love, Nadia Ukrainetz thank you for the laughs and the tears. To the charities that provide essential services for individuals and their families, cnib, Foundation Fighting Blindness, International Network Of Hearts. Mom you are extraordinary. Karl and Hans, the adventures were only worth it because I got to come home to you both.

Preface

The idea for this book came after extraordinary circumstances, as most of my books ideas are born. It's 2020 and the world is amid a global COVID-19 pandemic and life came to a standstill. In a matter of a few weeks, we were forced to isolate in our homes in the hopes of flattening the curve to slow the spread of a highly contagious virus. I was in the final preparations of my running project "Border Run" and after 8 months of hard training, I was now running up to 10 hours a day. Then suddenly, I found myself indoors for most of the day except for going out to get essentials. I knew how important was to follow the experts' orders but it wasn't initially easy, you can't flip off a switch and immediately adapt to new circumstance. That's when I went to my old journals and posts from an old blog, Mexican Running Wild, named that because when I started running my mom was bombarded with advise from family members to stop me, her daughter, from running wild or Corriendo Como Loca, and that I should be putting my energy into finding a man to look after me and my kids. The name was a rebellion to my culture, one that didn't encouraged women to play sports. So now If I couldn't physically visit remote places because the world was in chaos, I could mentally visit them through my stories. What I discovered while reading my old journals was that the lessons I learned back then when I had just begun my life as an ultrarunner and adventurer are still relevant today. It reminded me why I fell in love with running and how it changed my life for the better. I hope you enjoy reading my stories as much as I did reminiscing and I wish they inspire you to seek your own adventures. I changed some names for privacy but the stories stayed the same. I edited as best I could but I want this book to be publish for the value of the stories not the quality of the grammar. So I hope you enjoy learning how I went from victim to champion.

Mexican Running Wild

Wednesday, July 25, 2007

I Thought They Were Kidding too!

I can't believe this is happening! I started inquiring about the Canadian Death Race in hopes to race it next year and next thing you know I am going to be racing it next weekend!!.The only two people I had a chance to tell in person try to talk me out of it, so I do know how crazy this is. I am excited (not about running 125K) but that I have found a way to give back to the Canadian National Institute for the Blind (cnib). When my son Karl was diagnosed with Cone Rod Dystrophy and started to go blind last year, I had a lot of questions and they took the time to help me understand what the diagnoses meant and provided the resources I needed to help Karl. There are a lot of amazing organizations that help families like mine deal with adversity and you never fully appreciate them until you need them. They never made me feel guilty for thinking," What am I going to do?" they understood that even though Karl was the one diagnosed, it affected as all. Of course, I relied on friends and family as well. So this ultramarathon is dedicated to everybody that held my hand. My kids are doing amazing now, they act like normal preteen boys and that is why I am so thankful to everybody. I am sure this is going to be quite an adventure. Talking to a few ultimate runners I had the pleasure of hearing fantastic tips on how to suffer the least. I am told the pain will never stop but they are ways of lessening the pain. So enjoy the ride is guaranteed to be a bumpy one.

Thursday, July 26, 2007

All of a Sudden I Am An Emotionally Unstable Single Mother.

You can't be serious... There must be something wrong with you... I'll give you $1000 if you don't do it...That seems to be the reaction from most of my friends. On the other hand, I have already collected $1000 in pledge money for the cnib, and my goal had been $300, I am so excited!. All of a sudden my mental health seems to be of great concern though. Sure, my kids are gone for 3 weeks and I am not the best of dealing with loneliness, this goal is tough but my expectations are realistic. I am aiming at finishing the race, that realistic right? even if I just started running a year ago. Will I be disappointed if I am a force to drop because I time of or an injury? Of course but my main priority is to be safe. Everybody is acting as they have never done anything stupid, we all do stupid things, they are doing it now during Stampede week In Calgary. DUI, unprotected sex, parties with drunk people wrestling livestock. Well, I don't drink or party so this is my own Stampede. The goal is to finish, I will push through blisters, fatigue, muscle pain and things like that. I will stop if I think I am in danger at any moment, plus it's just 24 running. Like Karl says, "is just my eyes mom, everything else works really well". It's just pain!, it's just going to be really long 24 hours. Preparations are underway, my friend John Longarini is willing to car camp with me and be my support crew and help me with bandages, change my shoes, feed me and such. Support is not allowed outside checkpoints but having a friendly face in the checkpoints specially late in the evening will be invaluable. My training now is mostly walking, my muscles are fatigue since I was training for the 5 peaks race mid-September. I had to do a forced taper (cutting back on training before a race) to let my leg muscles rest.

Top 5 songs on my iPod to get me going this week

1. La Cadena de Oro ---Cabas

2. Party Like is 1999---Prince

3. Daria ---La 5a Estacion

4. Tu Tortura--- Shakira y Alejandro Saenz

Friday, July 27, 2007

I Only Laugh When I am Nervous.

Wow! I am now screening calls. I think I have collected more pledges from people that ask me not to do it than people pledging me to go!. Yes is nuts and I am very intimidated by it. Some people seem to think it is a cry for attention. I can think of better ways of crying for attention. Being 39 years old, dressing up in animal print and hitting the bars. Now that sounds more like something that I could do this long weekend that will also give me attention. I am really doubting my ability to finish this race after all this negative pushback. When I first sign for it, I knew it was going to be crazy but there was a small part of me that thought "maybe" is not like I have been sitting in the couch and all of a sudden saying "My kids are gone for 3 weeks, let's see, should I get another cat or I should I run 125K?". The thing is, my life is getting easier, my insomnia is gone, I am looking forward to my next Athabasca University classes, the craziness of two preteen boys and their school and sports schedule. Why should I feel guilty for enjoying my now less stressed life and even set some goals. If it's not for organizations like the cnib that provides help to families like mine, I wouldn't have been looking into the possibility of going back to normal life so soon. I feel great about being able to give them 24 hours of my life so they can go ahead and do what they do and I feel great about looking forward to it too. The strangest thing is that now I almost never notice that Karl is visually impaired, that's thanks to the cnib that helped us create a new normal life. When I get a yellow box with braille writing and a book on tape I am reminded that they are only a phone call away. Before I ever considered doing the Canadian Death Race, I imagine this race being full of renegades, people who had trouble adapting to the norms of society and after talking to a few people who have done the race as a soloist, I realized they are your average white-collar corporate Calgary. Sure is unusual to spend some of your hard-earned vacation time to do something like this. John introduced me to a coworker of his that had ran the CDR before. Larry and I met for a run so I could be asked questions about this race and he never doubted my ability to do it. He has run this race for 4 straight years and he is doing it again this year. Larry never needed an excuse for racing ultras, except that he just loves running. He was however very disappointed that the 100 miles Lost Soul Ultra in Lethbridge was full and I couldn't sign for that one too. I am committed to doing this race, I hope I completed so I don't have to give it another shot next year unless just like Larry, I end up falling in love with the sport and then start to look forward to spending my long earn vacation time in Grand Cache Alberta August long weekends year after year.

Saturday, July 28, 2007

You Mean You Will Be Only In a Lot Of Pain For 24 hours?

I ran into my friend Nancy yesterday. Her husband and her were out taking their new born daughter for a walk. We were chatting about motherhood when she stopped me and said," listen, I really want ask you about your upcoming event, what is it exactly you are doing? I keep hearing something crazy about it". After trying to explain my best what this race is all about she asked me "is it dangerous?" I guess there is always risk involved, I explained, but most people drop out of injury or because you are in too much pain. Nancy didn't even blink, " You'll be fine" she added. I guess, to a mother who just experiences childbirth, pain is not something that makes you cringe anymore. There are experiences in life that stretch our boundaries of what we think is possible. That is why when I got the call from the Death Race organizers and was told there was a spot for me if I wanted I decided to go ahead and not wait until next year. After dealing with a job loss and my son's diagnoses last year expanded my boundaries of how much adversity I can withstand. I picked up all my gear now and I am ready to go, headlight for running at night, walking poles to try and use my upper body and give my legs a rest, extra pair of shoes 1 size larger for the later part since my feet will swell a full size I am told, table salt, electrolyte tablets, gels, Boost meal replacement, Smart Wool socks, moleskin, duct tape for my feet and an extra-large Camelback backpack. I went running for about 40 minutes and tried my gear, I need to know where it chaffs and where it pinches and try and be proactive. The race is exactly in a week and I am feeling anxious, there is nothing I can do to prepare myself physically, is too late to get any fitter, I have to go with what I got, and I don't want to lose my courage. I am not afraid of the race I am more afraid of the week after. Reading the stories of last year racers, it always ends the same way, it seems unbelievable how much your body can ache. Well, one thing I am looking forward to after the race is the fact that the next day meals will account for 0 calories, my body will burn so many calories that it will not matter. I am going to order that extra slice of chocolate cake.

Updated note:

Who cares, go for the slice of cake! After a few years of ultrarunning, fortunately I stopped obsessing about being thin.

Sunday, July 29, 2007

The Crying Game.

I started my taper and I am not feeling well. I have been running so much for so long that not running is making me cranky. Last time I tapered I insulted my best friend Nadia, told her " as if you would know" rather snarky when she was helping me manage my emotions because I feeling overwhelmed with my single parent life, yes she came from a privileged upbringing, but has never behaved with entitlement and is always there for me when I needed her, she deserved better from me. Lucky she is a runner and she just shrug it off, "Fuck! you are a delight when you are tapering aren't you?". Training at a certain intensity and then taking it away is like taking nicotine away from a smoker. I have been very emotional. I watched the movie "Because I Said So" and even though it was bad I couldn't stop crying. I am ready to go. I am as ready as I could be given the circumstances. I have been training for Boston so I haven't prepared for a lot of hills. I am no different than anybody else in terms of training for a marathon here in Calgary. I drive to Memorial Drive to go for a run along the river and go to the gym but hardly ever do hill sprints. Now I am wishing I had taken the stairs a bit more often. John stopped by today to go over next weekend. Here is a friend whom I hardly know that when he heard I was going to race alone volunteer to be my support crew, our kids play soccer at the same league and we both volunteer for the association but including today I have met him only a handful of times. I told him he would absolutely hate me after the race. I guess it will be like giving birth in front of a person I hardly know. John will be in my friend's list forever, next time I move I know I will be calling him first. We had a good chat until the part where he saw my equipment and then asked me why didn't I have the bear spray yet. It is wishful thinking of my part. I know I am not going to be the first in the race and I am hoping to be somewhere in the middle, bears will be long gone by the time I go by unless of course I fall so far behind the bear come out from hiding when I pass. Maybe I should get a small bear spray, I am not sure I can operate the canister properly while tired, with my luck I will probably spray myself and become peppered Mexican beef jerky. My kids called me today, talking to them eliminated any doubt in my mind. My kids had a rough time last year and now their only worry is trying to schedule play dates with their friends over the summer. I am thankful for all the support that got us there. I will try my hardest to make it as far as I can on the race, but just like John said "Don't worry, if you don't finish I guess this will be your practice run for next year".

Tuesday, July 31, 2007

I Hope Fried Green Tomatoes is on TV tonight.

I am experiencing some soreness in my quads. I am not sure it is serious but at this point, I don't want to take a chance. A healthy average runner is better off on a race than a fit injured one. I have been sitting and eating comfort food and it might seem like a great day but, beware doing this will lead to endless channel surfing to find romantic comedies and downloading terrible songs to your iPod. I feel guilty for just sitting at home and not exercising, and just like somebody going through a breakup and sees couples everywhere, I too seem to notice people jogging, on bikes, rollerblading. Sunday when I went for a walk I saw running groups everywhere, having a great time. I came home and ate more carbs. I am leaving Friday and the day doesn't come fast enough, I never thought I was going to be looking forward to driving for 7 hours to car camp on a community parking lot and sharing the general showers. Not exactly a Club Med vacation. I imagine that things would be different if I had been a single mother of girls. But would they? When I as a kid being a girl meant that I was never allowed to play sports only dance classes. Sports were too tomboyish for my mom. In Mexico a good parent will make sure daughters are marriageable, and what nice boy will want a girl that behaved like a boy, my mom always said no when I asked if I could play on a team. In my teens it didn't get any better, I was never allowed to do anything that made me too muscular, models and actresses did not look muscular so I was always discourage. I think I am finally coming on my own. I realize that the reason why I never did anything like this before was not that I don't enjoy it, but because I was never allowed. As a mother of boys, I am around sports that I always thought were for boys. I have learned to enjoy mountain biking, running marathons, I now love sports as a lifestyle, not just something you do to look a certain way. So I am sure if I had been a mother of girls I would have allowed them to get dirty, to play any sports they wanted, none of this boy sport, girl sport BS.

On my iPod this week

1.Umbrella---- Rihanna

2.Dime------Giselle

3.I Am Changing--- Jennifer Hudson

4.Sorry--- Madonna

5.Here I go again--- Whitesnake

Thursday, August 2, 2007

"Big Girls Don't Cry" Fergie

I went for a bike ride a few hours ago. Just for an hour. I haven't been feeling that well lately. Sitting at home and watching TV every evening has made me feel a bit sluggish. I had to go for a bike ride because I was experiencing stress and decided that an hour will probably be good. I had to resign from my job today. if your clients are not calling you back because is summer, or maybe because three new competitors opened their doors and you are sitting in your manager's office looking fit and tan, then she hears that you are running 125K, no amount of explaining of how you are working your hours will get you out of that one. I couldn't take her yelling at me of how I was the worse sales person she ever hired, it's not true, she started treating me different when her fiancée talked to me at a company party last week. Perception is a funny thing, people assume things just because of your clothes, hair or choice of car. I run at 5am or evenings never during work hours. I might run at lunch time sometimes with Nadia so we can catch up but I other than that I am working. I guess is human nature to try and size each other up. I stopped at Gord's running store right after my last day of work store to get my shoes and I asked to speak with him. I was told by friends that because Gord is a well know ultramarathoner he was going to be the best person to help me. Then he saw me, I looked more like Victoria Beckham than Deana Kastor, I could tell he was a bit annoyed to be disturbed, once he heard how many miles a was logging per week he was very generous with his advice. The beauty of my kids is the way they perceive themselves and I should learn. They both are so embarrassed of being seen in public because they think I am a geek because I am even if don't look like a geek. Karl who has to wear funny glasses that look like inspector gadget at school because he can't see the whiteboard and Hans that knows everything there is to know about Star Wars and wears a Clone Trooper costume at the dinner table and yet when they see me they think, "Gee mom, why do you have to be so weird!". The only thing that matter to my kids is the perception of themselves not what other say. I wish I could think as my kids and see myself not from the outside but from the inside, I judge myself so harshly from the things that are superficial, my looks, and not for the things that are really important. My kids look in the mirror and judge themselves by their characters and like themselves, I am going to learn from them and start to be gentler to the woman in the mirror. This is my last entry before the race, I leave early tomorrow. Thanks to everyone's generosity I have collected $3000.00! that is unbelievable. We are so close to finding the cure for blindness. Dr. Ells, was very positive, last time she saw Karl said we are approximately 10 years from finding a cure and even better, they are reversing the damage, she was very positive Karl was going to benefit by all the research. I don't think that my life is what fairy tales are all about, but even after all, lost jobs, flooded basements, broken heart when I hug my kids good night I feel just like a princess of a far, far away kingdom.

Monday, August 6, 2007

125K, 17,000 Feet of Elevation, Freezing Rain. What is This The Death Race?

This was no ordinary weekend. I arrived at Grand Cache Friday night to the mandatory meeting and looking around the crowd I was sure I had missed a turn somewhere and ended at Woodstock 2007. I started feeling nervous. It was pouring and I didn't bring extra clothing. John and I walked around the booths trying to find anything that was either waterproof or warmer. We did find a pair of running tights that would not keep me warm but with their crisscross design would make me look fast as John casually mention when I showed up wearing them at the start line. I suddenly felt like I was Paris Hilton and this was my Simple Life attempt. Larry was already there when I arrived.

Leg 1. Just as we were ready to start Larry looked at me and said " my wife doesn't want me to pace you" My face froze mid grin and then the gun went off. I chatted with other runners to stop myself from crying and I am glad, they all had stories of failed attempts or glorious victories, we settle into what seemed a very slow pace and kept a close eye on Larry because he had successfully finished his last 3 attempts and If I couldn't run with him I could still use him to pace me even if I had to follow him like a detective following a suspect.

Leg 2. The second hardest leg of the race gave me a true indication of what was to come, climbing Flood and Grand mountain was a hard 4-hour long test of sanity. The climb was steady and the descend was even harder, the steep terrain was made even more difficult by the slippery conditions, I had trouble keeping Larry in my sightline because he is great at using his poles to aid himself on the descend. It was still raining but the rain felt nice and cool on my body.

Leg 3. This leg was a breeze, only 19K of rolling hills, armed only with my iPod and a bottle of Gatorade in hand I knew it was my only chance to gain ground. I passed Larry in the first 15 minutes never to see him again, I was going to go ahead since I thought he was clearly going to pass me on stage 4 the hardest climb. He never did, the next day John told me he didn't finish either, he didn't say much to John when he ran into him in town, he was either too tired or to chocked to explain. From this point on I was tracking for a 22 hour finish time.

Leg 4. This leg was by far the hardest thing I had ever done physically including running a full marathon. I started the climb around 6pm since leg 4 is 8 hours long and unaided I put as much on my backpack as I could physically manage. The climb is not technical like leg 2 but the 6986 feet climb start all at once. I hiked at a pace that didn't seem fast because my lungs were screaming for air. it felt like I was hardly moving but only two racers past me and when I joked with them that I felt like I was standing still, one of them motion me to look behind me, one of them said, " No, you are moving, they are not" behind me down below I could see people everywhere lying down or bent over trying to catch their breath. I keep thinking about an advise someone gave me about running CDR, " don't worry if you feel like you are slowing down, just keep moving, never stop" What it makes this climb even harder is that as the climb progresses there are longer periods of times where you don't see anybody else. I got to the top around 9:30pm and started my descend. The rain that had felt nice around 4pm was making my descend miserable as the light started to disappear. I got to the emergency station around midnight only to find out that I had to go back up and climb other 5K before climbing down again, which is what they called the Amber Loop. It broke my heart, It was pitch dark and I was alone for most of my hike, I had a headlight but as I try to avoid the puddles that were forming everywhere, for every puddle I managed to avoid I would slip and fall in two after. Finally, around 2 am, and with only 9K to go to the next station I was stopped by the emergency crew patrolling. Hypothermia was making me disoriented and I had trouble answering their questions, I was asked to get on their ATV and relinquish my timing stick and coin, the only proof a Death Racer has of finishing. I was in a lot of pain then but as I finally sat down on the ATV the pain that I was experiencing tripled. John came to pick me up and I had only the energy to climb to the back of my minivan and I fell asleep fast. I woke up 4 hours later and amazingly felt great, it was only when I tried to walk that I realize what I had just done was not natural. At breakfast, the town was full of people who walked funny like me, after a long shower I took advantage of the complimentary massage. Make no mistake this was not Banff Spring Hotel spa, the massage felt like a torture technique to make me confess, but I knew I needed to release all the lactic acid that had built around my muscles. The woman that worked on my legs asked if I had stretched before the race, my IT band was too tight she noted. No, I reply. "That is why you are so sore" I don't have a degree in sports medicine but I know that no amount of stretching beforehand will prevent my muscles from been sore after 18 hours of continuous effort. So was it worth it? Yes! it was all worth it. I think we should all do something that seems impossible once in our lifetime, something that brings us out of our comfort zone and forces us to look hard inside and ask the hard questions. It is easy to avoid dealing with ourselves. We spend most of our time doing unimportant stuff to avoid thinking and using our families or jobs as excuses too and even when we find ourselves alone we are quick to hide behind our TVs or computers. Out there in the middle of the night, alone and with miles to go I had nowhere to turn but in. I have now found the strength to keep me strong if more challenges come into my life as I am sure they will come. From now on I will approach new challenges like I did at the Death Race, I will take it one leg at the time, some legs will be more challenging than others but they will all be part of the journey and even if I don't win the race I will learn to appreciate that at the end I have grown a little bit stronger.

Saturday, August 18, 2007

No Way...Never Again... I swear I Don't Care That I Only Had 31K to Go...

Is official, I am going back to The Canadian Death Race in 2008. I guess I am just like Joan from Lethbridge, I met her at the beginning of leg one, when she told me this was her third attempt her two previous attempts resulting in DNF, I remember thinking, "get a life" "why is it so important to finish this race?". I have been thinking about the reason why I changed my mind and I figure that in races like this where there are a lot of factors that can determine finishing or not is like winning the lottery, everybody has a chance. I watched people that looked a lot younger and fitter and why not maybe even childless giving up, the part that makes me want to go back is the people that seemed less fit and older than me that did finish. The thought that it's within my abilities to finish is intoxicating. At almost 40 I had started to think the best years were behind me, silly I know, but that's how the influential entertainment industry makes you feel when you no longer see yourself represented on TV, movies or beauty products. The only time I see a woman my age on an ad is for a cream to remedy her decaying looks. I started my new job Monday with my fingers crossed. Not that I am negative but just like the race, I might be the right person for the job and still not succeed because of other factors. I guess at this point I am just hoping I am prepared and fit for the job as well. Harold from the cnib was very happy when I called him with the pledge results, he said the money was going to be used in Calgary for a classroom they are building. I was happy, then he said the P-word. I have heard the P-word over and over the past 2 weeks since the race. " You must be really proud" it got me thinking, why don't I feel proud, I feel happy, excited, I am proud of having amazing friends and family that responded so quickly to my pledge, but I wasn't proud of me, why? I felt proud watching my kids win awards such as Karl's citizenship award. My heart sank watching some kids' names being called to the front to receive their award and watched with envy how their parents, moms, and dads stood together side by side smiling with pride. I felt guilty for not giving my kids the same advantage because I thought as a single parent my kids were probably not excelling as much as kids who have both parents dotting on them. Then when it was time to announce the winner of the citizenship award, I heard the teacher's voice cracked as she introduced Karl to the audience, I was so proud to watched everybody in the audience give Karl a standing ovation, he was so modest about it, I cried so hard I had to run to the bathroom because he had told me the day before that if he won anything not to scream like a Mexican mom. I am also proud of how Hans' classmates marched into the school's office to request being placed in the same class with him again. I am proud that my kids are very well-liked because they are good human beings and are fair to the people around them. I figure why the word proud never crossed my mind when I think about myself and it is because of how I am condition to focus on the things I haven't accomplished instead of that ones I have. Karl is a perfect example of how we should all live our lives. Karl loves hockey, he was disappointed to find out there is no league for the visually impaired. " It's a shame," he told me with sincerity " I am so good at it". I love my kids but Karl and great hockey player have never been spoken in the same sentence. Luckily for me, Karl explained himself further. This is how he remembers it. Karl never once told me that he only scored one goal in the whole season, the odds of even that happening were not in his favor, you could hear me scream so loudly (hey, Mexican Mom here) when it did because I had given up the idea that was ever going to happen. What Karl did remember were all the things he did do. He blocked the puck from going in many times, or the many times he managed to assist a team member so he could get closer to the net. By the time Karl had finished his story I was standing next to Wayne Gretzky and my little Karl was the MVP. I wish that the world saw what Karl sees. I will still have my old job. I would not have sat in that office feeling like I failed them because I failed to produce the recommended new business revenue. I, just like Karl, I did stop the biggest client on my list from going to a competitor because they were a lot cheaper than us. 80% of sales are from current customers. I was made to quit because I failed the company

20%. Karl is right if you take the amount of time is spent actually scoring and the amount of time is spent setting it up Karl excelled at the bigger part. It really is a shame that he will not be playing anymore, the hockey league will miss their MVP. So, yes, I am proud, I did raise $3500, I did try my hardest, I didn't give up when all I could think was "I want to stop badly", and as painful as it was running the CDR I do enjoy running a lot more now like Hans noticed when I came back from one of my runs last week "why do you have that creepy smile?" and best of all I am proud that I didn't sit at home feeling like a victim because something like this happened to my family. I learned that from Hans, there is nobody better than him at moving forward, he spends less time crying about what happens and more time trying to figure out how to get out a situation. I have no control over what happens, but I always have control over what I do about it. Next year when I see Joan from Lethbridge, I will tell her how proud she must make her family . Next year on her 4th try she already will be a winner to me. I get why her family was cheering from the sidelines to them she is a hero, they have seen her dedication to training day after day. Joan is somebody that works hard at a goal and enjoys her successes along the way. Maybe I will meet somebody who is running the Death Race for the first time and when I will explain the is my second attempt because I didn't finish last year with a big smile on my face that shows how proud I am, I will not be offended by the sad look of " get a life" in their face, it will be Joan's and my little secret.

Thursday, August 23, 2007

"Love, Pain and the Whole Damn Thing" Amy Sky

Trail Running magazine has an article about running addiction. The article goes deep about when a good thing goes terribly wrong. I started running seriously about a year ago and there is not a day that goes by that somebody I know doesn't tell me that there is something wrong with me. I had a good chat with my friend Joylin this morning, she is been a runner for a long time and she often wins age group races by a big margin. I don't know how old she is but we both compete on the 35-39 age group, if I didn't know her I will think she was early 20's, she also has 3 young children often on tow. I like talking to her, she is always in a good mood, and she is the kind of person that makes you feel good about yourself. We started talking about running with the same passion people talk about a good movie or a juicy gossip of a friend having an affair. The way only a runner can talk to a runner without feeling self-conscious of being weird. When is a good thing a bad thing?. We as a society we are quick to judge people around us for being different when we don't follow general rules, as we get older you are supposed to leave behind things that seem superficial such as running and concentrate on working and raising your kids. I like running, a lot, and that makes me a happy person, a happy person makes a great parent and a reliable employee. What it seems to make no sense to people around me is that I spend so much time on a hobby, something that I make no living out of, and even if I improve I will never make it to the elite ranks. Reading the article I recognize some of the danger signs, " being constantly tired" for example. Well that I am, but I am not sure that running is the single source of my fatigue, I work full time and have kids that alone will make anybody tired, I find that by exercising I have more energy, sometimes training does catch up to me but sometimes work does or kids so I am almost always tired but the source is different every time. " Missing out on social events" Well you got me there, I am known for missing out on going out and the only time I do go out I know how to clear a room because I am awful at small talk and it gets worse as the night progresses since I hardly ever drink, is hard to go out when you know you have to get up early and take care of your kids in morning, I haven't slept in since I had kids and until my kids are old enough to drive themselves that won't happen. I am not sure if I have an addiction or a passion, this is simply just something that I do that make me happy. I like talking to friends such as Joylin who is excited talking about mile repeats and lunges with the same passion people talk about the new restaurant in town. If something is enhancing your life rather than taking away from it, then is a passion not an addiction. Sure running every day and sometimes twice a day seems a bit obsessive, and I am sure that there are people that really have running addiction but we are too quick to label people with having a problem just because they behave in a different manner than us. I think we use mental stimulus like happy thoughts of running or loosing ourselves on our

Facebook accounts as an escape from the daily routine, we need a mental break every day to stop us from overstimulating ourselves at work or at home. It might seem unhealthy but is preventive medicine aimed at enhancing your life, not unlike taking vitamins when you already have a healthy diet.

Friday August 24, 2007
Happily Ever After.

How many times can you fall in love? At my age, I didn't think it was going to happen anymore and it happened when I least expected. Trail Running is my new love. I went to Ha Ling Peak, the climb was 1:10 minutes but running down was 35 minutes of pure adrenaline. I learned that I need to lean forward not back when running downhill and stay low to the grown to avoid getting too much air. I put my iPod on and I was flying and loving the burning sensation in my quads. Hiking purist be damn! I was doing everything hikers are against: Going as fast I could possibly go uphill and downhill. If running is classic music then trail running is rap music. I did stop to look at the view, at the top for a few minutes to quickly eat a banana to refuel for the way down but I couldn't wait to run the way down I arrived downtown Canmore AB 2 hrs51 minutes later, dusty and limping a bit since my knee was giving me trouble the last 2K. Just like when you are seeing a bad boy, every time I go for a trail run everybody expects me to say, that is it, is over, almost like I had finally realized that it will break my heart. So far is working out, just me and the trail, a match made in heaven.

There are a lot of running clubs that go out and train in the mountains, I am a bit selfish and have trouble sharing my love. My friend Breena wants to go next time with me, I panicked I am not sure I am ready to introduce my new love to my circle of friends. I have 5 peaks race in a couple of weeks at the Nordic Center in Canmore and I can hardly wait, 13K only, now I wish I had signed for the half marathon. Of course, I should slow down and get to know each other first, Trail Running and I just met after all. 13K then maybe half in a few months and aim for the full marathon at Powder Face in July. I need to remember that Boston is in April and I need to focus on speedwork and tempo runs as well. I am having trouble finding songs that motivate me this week, after running so much I have played the same songs to death, so no iPod songs list this week. It was touch and go for running this week, I had good days but most of it was junk mileage. Now that I have found the key to trail running I should go back to quality running again.

Tuesday, August 28, 2007

If You Don't Like Where the Story of Your Life Is Heading, Write Another Chapter.

I have been thinking about what motivates us lately. My good friend Gretcher from Venezuela stopped by Sunday night. I hadn't talked to her in a while, she dating and in love again after her divorce, she is really beautiful but she looked even more beautiful as she talked to me about her boyfriend. She definitely was glowing, passion is something that drives us to seek pleasure while risking pain. It is funny how my friend was looking at me with horror as I excitedly talked about the Death Race and my next race, the Five Peaks in Canmore in a couple of weeks, 13K in the mountains!? no way she said. The funny thing is that I was thinking the same thing about falling in love. I much rather run 125K than falling in love again. What motivates us is either seeking pleasure or avoiding pain. Sometimes it starts like one and develops and another. Running for me was a way of avoiding pain, the pain of lying in bed hour after hour crying and unable to fall asleep. As the pain slowly left, I experience pleasure, the pleasure of feeling strong, the pleasure of keeping up with my best friend Nadia, a way better runner than me. I guess we risk pain only if the reward is of value to us, Gretcher value romantic relationships more than me and that's wonderful, what matters is that we were both at a happier place now than after our divorces. My kids couldn't sleep last night, Karl woke up at 3am with a panic attack. He is starting grade 7 next week and is nervous, he worried his teacher wouldn't know about his eyesight limitations and would ask him to do something he wouldn't be able to do "Then you tell your teacher that you can't and explained why and what accommodations you need to do to be able to do it" I calmly told him. Then Hans woke up and joined in the panic attacked "What if nobody likes me" he asked, I had decided to pull him out of his school too and move both of them to a school that offered elementary school and junior high together, I feel guilty for doing that to Hans but I need him as my spy, I know Karl will never tell me if he had a bad day. I told Hans that if I could find friends he certainly could too, he looked at me and smiled , knowing that to be true. I went on a short run after dinner and they both biked with me. Karl felt great, he knows the way really well and that makes him feel really good about himself. It is hard for him to do anything new, he relies on memory to fill in the blanks. Karl and Hans are experiencing pain but with time it will turn to pleasure, the pleasure of overcoming their fears. My run today was of about only 10K, I am going to supplement my running with biking to keep my fitness level and let my legs and joints rest a bit. I am starting to feel a bit bored with having evenings off, TV was a great distraction but now is really annoying me. Dating? too bad there is no training I can do to ease into it. If I can feel the same passion that I feel about my kids, or running, in my new job or a new relationship (in time) there is really nothing that will stop me from succeeding at it anymore.

Friday, September 7, 2007

Danger is the New Black.

I still don't get why we humans behave the way we do. Buckle up when we drive but will pay money to jump out of a plane. Danger is something that we seek right next to security. Do we need both to become happier humans or is it only the brave that attempts to have their cake and eat it too? I have a strong need to belong with my usual running friends, the marathoners but I secretly dream of racing ultramarathons. I pour through my

Trail Running magazines and fantasize about all the ultras. It is the dream of doing something so daring that is driving me to want to become an ultrarunner. I haven't taken many risks since I had kids, I felt pressured to play it safe then look where it got me, I am back to where I started before having kids, broke and trying to find a way out of my problems so now I get to do what I want. So dreaming of escaping the monotony is the only thing that gets me through another meaningless yet necessary task that I have to fulfill, like doing laundry. I have decided to race the Death Race, not just to finished but to actually race it. I spend my days calculating my game plan to get me there. There is a lot of information about running marathons but not a lot about running ultramarathons. All I am going by is my experience at last Death Race. I didn't get passed on the flat stages, and very seldom on the incline, it was on the downhill where I lost most of my time so I am keeping the training to about the same distance, between 55-80 miles per week with speedwork and core training but adding hill training. It should not add to any more time than I am already committing between 10-18 hours a week depending on how early I am on the training because all I have to do is to replace one of my easy runs with hill training. Another change that I am making is reversing my plan, concentrating on speedwork now and adding mileage later as suggested by Dr.David Martin from the Elite Athlete performance lab. My favorite thing this week? My Asic Nimbus running shoes, great on the trail and the road. I definitely feel like WonderWoman when I think about doing something so daring so bold. If you come over on a Saturday night and I am doing laundry don't be a surprise if I am actually enjoying myself, I got plans of my own, plans of someday breaking out of this mold and becoming a superhero.

Sunday, September 30, 2007

"Disappointment to a Noble Soul is What Cold Water is to Burning Metal; it Strengthens, Tempers, Intensifies, But Never Destroys It." Eliza Tabor

The results from Five Peaks race are in. 3rd in age group and 6th overall female. I was happy about the results although I was hoping for 2 and third overall. I saw the woman that placed second, almost 2 minutes ahead of me, the winner I never did, she was almost 12 minutes ahead of me. I couldn't stop thinking if they were in better shape or if they could dig deeper than me. I am not sure if I need to train more or to utilize what I have and think like a racer. For 2 minutes maybe 12 minutes ahead I am thinking she was fitter than me for sure. It is funny how things have changed now, a year ago I was just trying not to be last, and now I am placing to 10 and still feel disappointed. I am ready to start my training again. I don't have any races booked until Boston so here is what my training looks like until now. I am running 6 days a week between 6 to 9 miles per day and a long day of about 12 miles. I have one tempo day of 6 X 7 minutes miles and a hill training day where I add 4X 10-second sprints at the end adding one more each week and building to up to 10. Sandwich in between are 2 or 3 core training which usually is 3 sets of single-legged exercises like walking lunges, single-leg deadlifts, single-leg squats and of course bridges, push-ups, and sit-ups. I add mileage gradually to avoid injury, only increasing 10% of total weekly mileage every 3 weeks until I am running 70 miles/ week and then cut down the mileage to 70%. The plan I took from Running Times Magazine. I am from the school of thought that more is more, I know a lot of people that run a lot less and are performing better than me. I just feel good running a race knowing that I am prepared, and my body can handle the

mileage. I am only writing my plan because I have been asked many times. I am not a coach or anything, I just simply love to

Week	Mon	Tue	Wed	Thu	Fri	Sun	Sat	total
1	4am/5pm	7	4am/6pm	9	8	12	Rest	=55Miles
2	4am/6pm	8	4am/7pm	10	8	13	Rest	=60miles
3	4am/7pm	11	5am/7pm	11	9	14	Rest	=65miles
4	6	7	8	6	7	9	Rest	=43miles

run and I read a lot of articles on the subject. This is what my training will look like in miles at the end of my cycle 3 weeks before Boston, running every day and resting on Saturday. I do adjust my schedule to fit my kids but the mileage stays the same.

I tried this training very successfully last spring but I was spent for about a month, the time commitment is big and forget about having a life. I am mentally preparing for my next year, I am excited and for the first time I am thinking winning might be a possibility since I will be in the 40-49 age group and I am not far behind the top age grouper. Not for the marathon of course! They are on a different league but for the trail running series, being small is an advantage as well when carrying yourself up a hill, I just need to work on endurance. My favorite thing this week is the band Marron 5, especially the songs " Makes me wonder" and " Wake up call" my legs get faster just listening even if I am on my 15th mile . My son Karl had been my motivation this week. I have been watching him struggle because he is doing new things that he is not used to. I watch him try hard to learn his new school grounds and joined the Cross Country team which is hard because they train outdoors and his retinas don't regulate bright lights too well, the same feeling you have after stepping out of a movie theater now imagine trying to run a race like that. I just keep thinking of Karl and how hard it is for him to just do the things we take for granted. Who am I to think my life is hard. Karl has been giving an unfair disadvantage and he doesn't complain he just deals the best with what he is given and try to adjust his life to his new condition. I think we can all learn a lot from that.

Updated Note: I am still not a coach. Consult a trainer or a coach for a training plan specific to your goals and fitness level. Back then coaching was only for the elite. Thankfully is not so anymore. I had many injuries because I tried doing it by myself.

Sunday, October 21, 2007

"Love That is Not Madness is Not Love" Pedro Calderon de la Barca

What a week it has been. I was out last night and I was amazed how hard is not to obsess. I don't think I am obsessed about running that makes me not go out anymore. I really don't like it. I enjoy an intimate dinner party, movies, theatre, music. It is just the big impersonal parties that I feel like fish out of water. What can I possibly have in common with a bunch of strangers that the when the goal of the evening is to get as drunk as possible and flirting with people we wouldn't normally even talk to when sober. Nothing wrong but I don't like drinking much and as for hooking up, I want to go home alone especially now that my kids are gone to a friend's house I am so looking forward to an interrupted night of sleep. I think I have the right priorities. My life is going great. Karl is getting all the help he needs at school. St. James is doing a lot more than they are required by law and I could not be more grateful. Karl comes home beaming every day showing me all the special books or showing me the equipment he is getting to help him be independent in school. Things like large font textbooks, extra light in his locker, a colored volleyball with a bell inside, a CCTV computer to enlarge text to any book at school. I am very grateful because he feels empowered. I don't want to sound like Oprah talking about empowerment and gratitude but that's all Karl needs in his life to be independent, very few accommodations but makes all the difference in his life and I am so grateful to them. There was a minor bump on the road, Karl has giving up riding his bike and is bothering him. I explained the best I could that even as a fully able person, we still by choice don't do everything we are physically able to do, we still choose the things that appeal to us mostly, so in the greater scope of things he still was doing as much as anybody else, the only difference is that choices were being made for him. There are a lot of things that he still could do and concentrate on that was not a less courageous, it was just practical. Karl has been so determined to show himself and everybody around him that this is not going to stop him that he was not giving himself a break. So after talking to Hans, we came up with the perfect alternative, tandem bike, Karl loved the idea, although he questions my driving skills, Hans complained that he could never beat us since it was two against one. I love my family, I love that we look after each other. Hans had an amazing week as well, he did amazing yesterday at his first swim meet and won a couple of his heats. My ex-boyfriend Greg and I sat there beaming with pride, seemed very normal until other parents came to congratulate me and my husband for Hans. "He is not my husband", I replied, "he is my ex-boyfriend", "Hans' dad? Or why would be here" " I guess you can call him the almost ex-stepdad". She was so confused and in a way I felt as glamorous as Elizabeth Taylor with a long list of ex's. I guess looking from the outside it might be a bit unconventional. There is a reason why people decide it is not working for the two of you, but how about the kids? What do they have to do with it? They have a completely different relationship with that person and that's what I see. Their relationship was working amazingly well. I asked my kids a few months ago how they were feeling about my break up and they said that their biggest fear was never been able to see Greg again. That's when I knew I was doing the right thing. Is their relationship, they decide when is enough. It seem crazy to use my kids as pawns because I want to feel right about the break up. Plus I have move on, to running and so has he, a new girlfriend, I call that even. I went trail running to Barrier lake last Sunday and I felt butterflies in my stomach, I get such a thrill to be out there in nature running on my own, It's exhilarating!. I am waiting for my Garmin 305 to come, a present to myself for my birthday in a couple of weeks. I would like to track my performance better since training it's becoming a bit trickier now after I started my University classes. I can't just endlessly run, I need to train smart and accommodate studying on top of kids, their schedule, and work. Last night I went out after some of my coworkers complained I never join them, talking to a few people I felt uncomfortable, is not my world at all. Is not where I belong. I belong here in my life, with my kids, and doing all those things that make me happy, taking care of them, spending time with them. I know they are growing and one day will they will leave home, that's why I run, that is the thing I do for me, running will be there when they leave. At this moment I enjoy being their mother and taking care of them, I wish I could put them on a tandem bike forever and take them around their life with me protecting them from all their challenges they are sure to face. But my role is to love them then let them go into the world when they are ready and be there when they need me.

Wednesday, November 14, 2007

The Secret (Whispering) It's Just Positive Thinking and Hard Work.

I just finished my last race in 2007. The last chance half marathon in 1:39:04. An improvement from my last half by almost a minute. Not bad since it was a training run, I went on it as tired as I could be, train my body to respond even when tired. When you run ultras, running tired is a normal thing, so asking my body to perform to such a level after a hard month is what it will prepare me for next summer. I have decided to add a few more races to 2008. I am looking forward to doing the Swiss Jura marathon, 175K over 7 days or a half a marathon a day for a week, I am so excited I have been reading my race package as a bedtime story. My best friend Nadia came trail running with me last month, she liked it so much we are talking about running Transrockies together in September. That is 3 ultraraces in three months for me, Swiss Jura, the Death Race, and Transrockies. I have an idea of how I plan on accomplishing this, in two words, hard work. I feel it's a possibility, only because I see myself doing the work day after day. Now, I am not a big fan of the book The Secret about just thinking your way into a goal, I am old school. If you work hard at it, you can accomplish anything. I don't want to sit at home and visualize myself on the race, I do it every time I go out for a run. Every time I do I work out, I can see myself closer to my goal. That's why The Secret is not my favorite book, a book were as part of achieving a goal asks you to keep and empty drawer for the new things to come. For inspiration, I flip through Trail Running Magazines or watch shows like Everest- Beyond The Limit, I am changing my world around me to meet my goals. My favorite thing this week is friends. I just had a birthday, I turned 40 to be exact, and its friends that make times like that special, for my birthday, Nadia took me and my kids to Canmore and we raced Winterstart together, as I looked around I couldn't think of a better way to celebrate than that, with friends, family, a race and beer afterward in a parking lot. As for not believing in the Secret, I do keep an empty drawer in my bedroom just in case.

Thursday, November 29, 2007

"Success is Getting What You Want. Happiness is Wanting What You Get". Dale Carnegie

The last 2 weeks have been really hard. I pulled a tendon on my foot and couldn't run for a couple of weeks. I did everything else to keep sane, swim, row, spin. At one point I realize that I resembled the flight attendant who is trying to quit smoking on the TV Commercial. My foot has healed enough to resume my running. I am back to just half my mileage, can't overdo it, I now run in the morning and bike in the evening, it amounts to the same mileage but with less impact. It is getting tougher to stay focus, I notice my motivation hasn't diminished, just the focus of my training. I am lacking the fire in my belly. For one thing is cold outside and I am doing a lot of indoor running on my treadmill. Which is my favorite thing this week is My True

Z. I could go out but I don't want to slip again and re-injure my foot. Second, my next race is the Frozen Ass 50K in February, I was looking forward to it and placing maybe 1st in my age group and then a saw the results. Syl Corbett won the race last year and her times are out of this world! and there are also basically only 2 ages groups categories, under 35 and over 35, that doesn't really narrow it down. I talked to a friend about it and I guess the focus of my training should be about finishing, a smart tip is given that ultras are all about insane endurance, and she is right, I didn't finish the Death Race and at the start of my training that was the focus, somewhere down the lines, as I get stronger, the lines get blurry. I have been talking to a lot of runners online and I am amazed of the different reasons people do what they do, some have been doing it for so long that they need no reason at all, is part of their life, just like going to work, or eating, other are like me, it was a way of coping with things such a divorce or an illness . It's weird that I feel so close to all these strangers, running, one common bond that keeps us close. Karl and Hans had an amazing weekend, they both had swim meets and at different pools. Somewhere around 3pm on Saturday when I was driving from one community pool to another to watch them, cloning seem like a great invention. Well, Hans' meet went as well as his previous meets, he won 3 out of 4 and on Sunday he competed against the 12-year-olds, I was lucky enough to volunteer that day, my heart was bursting out of my chest with pride, he looked so tiny compared to the other boys, he managed to place second, his arms and legs went so fast because he had to go that much faster than the other kids, parents around the pool pointed and laughed because his little arms looked like tiny windmills, but he did it, he was very determined and has been working very hard at it. I have seen him at the practices and he is always paying attention and he often begs me to leave him after practice longer and his hard work and dedication paid off this weekend. Karl's meet was a lot different but just as successful, he is in Junior Lifeguards. He has never been good at swimming, the only reason why he is there is because the values teamwork and also because is the only sport he can do at the club as a visually impaired kid. Karl's story was just like the movie Rudy, if you have seen it you know what I mean. He struggled through the events and by 5:30pm he was exhausted, he had been at the pool with bad lighting and no glasses for hours, the last competition was the 100m swim with obstacles, I was nervous watching him against the other kids and as the other kids where finishing he was only half way done, he had on more lap of the pool to go, a full 50m to go but he just kept on going. I stood up and yelled his name and so did Hans, I wanted him to know I was there since he knew I was back and forth between his brother and him, all of a sudden the whole place was calling his name and clapping in encouragement, even the men calling the heats started to call his name. When he finished, he had a standing ovation, parents around me were congratulating me and I was once again filled with pride. When went home that night laughing all the way home. I placed their new ribbons in their room. first and seconds for Hans and third for Karl, the truth is there where only 3 kids on the Junior obstacle course competition, it didn't matter, he had earned, if Karl had been too intimidated to show up he would never have gotten it. So now, once again, showing up to my races is a reason for celebrating, I know I will check the results online after my race and maybe will be a bit disappointed, but I know that thanks to Karl and Hans I will always show up, work hard, go the extra mile, and give my best no matter the outcome.

Friday, December 14, 2007

I Run Therefore I Blog.

This has been the easiest week to get up at 5am to run. Even when the weather said -25C. I couldn't wait to lace up to go out. This week instead of my usual 11 miles I was running 16miles/day. The reason? Scott Dunlap, I am a huge fan and have read his blog for a long time. I have never posted a comment, why bother I thought, I often feel like the Anna Kournikova of the ultra-world, really good at the sport but mocked for not being better. I never wanted him to know who I am I just wanted to be part of the ultrarunning world to my surprise he answered it! His words were kind and encouraging. Well unless you are a runner you probably don't know about him, but to me, it was like having Lance Armstrong replying to your fan mail and wishing you luck on your Tour of Bowness. I am amazed by how giving the ultra and trail running community are. I have talked to ultrarunners and they patiently answer my questions, wishing me luck even though our goals are vastly different. I am a finisher and they are the elite, but down the line, I feel closeness because we share the same the passion for the outdoors and running, that and the common interest in trying to figure out the exact point of how far is too far. Scott has no idea that such small act had such a positive impact on me. We need role models, we can't be what we can't imagine. In a culture where we build people up to tear them down just as fast is not something I aspire to be anyway but if it was nice to see that some people reach some level of fame and stay humble. I have been inspired and even dared to dream of finishing first at the Frozen Ass 50K. Now, the odds of that happening are pretty slim but I am proud of saying I am an ultrarunner, even though I often get the " but why?" look, it makes me happy get over it already. It is not like I need to look very far to find heroes, just looking at my kids I am reminded about the strength of the human spirit. I watched a movie of the first and only blind climber to climb Mount Everest and I called Karl to my room at the exact moment when Erik makes it to the summit, of course, I was crying hard! not just because Karl has cone dystrophy, it's a moment that would make anybody cry. Karl just looked at me and said: " What's the big deal?" "He is just blind mom" then it hit me, Karl doesn't see limitations, I do. I am just in awe of how gracefully my kids are handling the changes in our lives, our world turned upside down two years ago and they handled it with such grace if you know me well you will know I didn't. I cried myself to sleep on endless nights when I lost my job and Karl was diagnosed, I was so afraid of being alone that I begged my ex-boyfriend Greg to take me back losing the last bit of dignity I had left. But watching my kids every day has given me the strength I needed to move forward and running has brought joy to my life, out there in the mountains on my own, there is no better feeling that the quietness of my footsteps on a trail. I don't know if I am happy because I run or I run because I am happy. It doesn't really matter. It is out there where I find myself, find who I truly am. A mother, an ultrarunner, a friend, a sister, a daughter and that is good enough for me.

Updated note:

That blind mountaineer in the movie Erik Weinhenmayer became my friend and role model when I started to climb mountains.

Sunday, December 30, 2007

"There Are Some People Who Live In a Dream World, And There are Some Who Face Reality, And Then There Are Those Who Turn One Into The Other." Douglas H. Everett

It is almost New Year's Eve. Looking back at 2007 I am amazed by how fast everything seemed to happen. Here is a quick recap of my 2007.

Races

The Policeman's Half Marathon- Before that race I had never run a race longer than 10K, by then I was running enough I just didn't know if I could run it faster than my training runs.

Calgary Stampede Marathon- By now I was feeling a bit more confident, I had decided to try and qualify for Boston, I needed a 3:50:00 to do this, I was so nervous but ended up finishing at 3:39:42, I was going to Boston!

The Canadian Death Race- If I was feeling better after my half marathon then after my marathon I was feeling ecstatic! I realized I was in better shape than I gave myself credit when I got up early, run a Marathon, drove home, made lunch for my kids, took them out, drove them to their grandparents a couple of hours away, went out for dinner, all without a problem. How much potential did I have but never gave myself a chance believing what people told me. I then decided that evening to try an ultramarathon, I wanted to give back to the cnib, before I walked through their doors, running a half marathon didn't seem possible, so running and ultra-marathons and collect pledges seemed the appropriate to show gratitude. The Canadian Death Race was close enough to Calgary that I could be back to work on Monday after. This was the race that forever changed me, I remember arriving there and realizing I was home, the strangest of it all was all too familiar to me, even though it ended up in a DNF at 94K it stretched my perception of what was humanly possible. By then I was not only a runner but an ultra-runner. From then on I wanted to find my own limits.

Banff-Jasper Relay- This race was so much fun, I was in an all-female team of 13 and we kick butt, winning gold for the all-female team division, my leg was about 16K. The scenery was spectacular, it was inspiring been out there in such a beautiful part of Alberta.

Five Peaks Race- This is another race that changed the way I view running, trail running was my new passion. After this race, I was 100% sure of what I wanted to do, run trails and run ultramarathons.

Winterstart In Banff- This will be my favorite race of 2007. This race was a present from my best friend Nadia for my 40th birthday, the race fell on that weekend, she took me and my kids to Canmore where the 5 boys got to play at the water park while we raced in Banff Saturday night, the race itself was only 5 miles, to make it more exciting I climbed Ha Ling that morning then raced in the evening if at this point had any doubt about my life and priorities, they all vanished, I was surrounded by people that loved me and it felt amazing, turning 40 was not a lot of fun, but it sure helps to be with friends and family

The Last Chance Marathon- This was my last race of the year and it felt every bit like it. I finish this race tired and with a nagging injury, it was time to cut down in intensity and mileage.

My kids

Karl's vision kept deteriorating, at the last parent-teacher interview his teacher recommended teaching Karl Braille because he is having trouble keeping up with his classes. His spirit is intact, he discovered wrestling and he had a great time at his meets. Of course, I wish Karl had never been diagnosed with a progressive condition that is making him blind and has left him visually impaired, even if there where to find a cure there are things that he will never be able to do anymore, but I am thankful that he is taking it the best possible way. Karl is a perfect example of how all you need to have a great life is the right attitude.

Hans too had an amazing year, he struggled a bit at the beginning of the year, he was a bit angry because I had pulled him out of sports, I had a hard time scheduling all the activities. Once Karl's life was under control Hans was able to have more of my attention, he played soccer in the summer then he tried out for the Sea Lions Swim team and in a short time he became their little star. His bone scan was abnormal but turned out to be nothing after further testing, Hans has Osteochondroma and has to undergo testing every year. At the end of last year I was unsure of how I was going to find the strength to keep my family from falling apart when all I need was them, Hans and Karl showed me what true strength really is, not the superhero kind of superpower, but the silent, quiet strength that comes from within. It was okay to be afraid as long as you don't let that stop you. 2007 was a year of many highs and some lows, in racing, it seems like I was almost there, like a bridesmaid never the bride. The beauty of almost is that it is that much closer is all attitude and perception, half empty or half full. My life was definitely only half empty, but I am looking forward to toasting to a fuller glass next year.

Sunday, January 6, 2008

"The Starting Point of All Achievement is Desire" Napoleon Hill

2008 here I come. If the start of the year was any indication of how my year is going to be, I am fully embracing the year to come. On January first I flew to Denver Colorado to try snowshoeing. "Why" that is the question that I heard over and over. All I could think was 'Why not" is it because I am going alone? or because it is cold there? I have no idea why going snowshoeing in Colorado didn't make much sense. I guess I could have done that here in Canmore, but this was New Years', a new beginning and I found a great deal so it was decided. Going to Denver for New Year day turn out to be a fantastic adventure. Here is a quick overlook of how my trip went. I arrived in Denver January 1st and stayed at the Hyatt Tech Center, a beautiful place away from downtown, it was a lot cheaper and very accessible by light rail commuter train, 12 miles to downtown and 1.2 miles from Cherry Creek Trail. A quick google search and two of my runs were decided.

January 3rd - For my first day I decided to run downtown and do some shopping along the way. Armed with directions from Mapquest I headed North on side streets, stopping at gas stations for snacks and washrooms. The run itself was very quiet except for a couple of guys on pick-up trucks that kept following me but I managed to lose them. Arriving downtown 3 hours, 1 lunch, and 2 shopping malls stops later was worth the 12 miles, the architecture was spectacular. I walked around for 2 hours to places such as State Capitol, Civic Center Park,

Denver Performing Arts Complex the 16Th Street Mall before heading back the hotel by light rail.

January 4th-Before leaving I had schedule snowshoeing lessons with Denver Adventures. Kevin picked me at the hotel at 9am and headed to Jefferson County. We arrive at Elk Meadow Park. The snow at the bottom of the trail was packed so I didn't need my snowshoes yet, I went ahead of Kevin and started to gain some ground on him. I ran ahead and waited for him at intersections, after 30 minutes he handed me a map and told me to go ahead until the snow was too deep to run in and told me the equipment was slowing him down, I offer to carry some and he looked as insulted as if I had offered a date to change his flat tire. Halfway Bergen Peak the snow was too deep to run and I waited for Kevin again. Strapping on snowshoes for the first time felt like a kid trying to ride a bike for the first time, after 10 minutes Kevin told me to go ahead once again and to wait for him at the peak. The feeling of running on the snowshoes was of strength, I was going slower than my usual run but a lot faster than I thought I was going to be. At the peak Kevin and I exchanged some quick snacks, I didn't want to stop too long, I wanted to try running down Bergen Peak on snowshoes. At this point Kevin swallow his ego and handed me the car keys The freedom I felt running downhill! It was so much fun, I got to the bottom and instead of waiting for Kevin at the car I decided to add another 40-minute loop, and caught up to Kevin 5 minutes before he arrived to the car. Driving back to the hotel 4 hours later, you would have thought we had been friends forever.

Kevin and I talked about trail running, he has ran the mosquito marathon and that is when he got hooked on running but as a single father of 3 he doesn't have much time now working two jobs and all.

January 5th- I woke up sore in muscles I didn't know existed. My calves and quads were killing me. Running on snowshoes forced me to run more on the ball of my feet, sort of chi running, leaning forward. After breakfast, I was ready to go to Cherry Creek Trail. The trail is 17 miles of open spaces, once again strapping my snowshoes I felt giddy. I was now running significantly slower than the day before but it felt great to be out there. The weather in Denver is a lot warmer than Calgary, mid to late 30F's. about an hour after my run I stooped at the reservoir where there was a family ice fishing. Snowshoeing is such as a hard work out that at the end of my two-hour run I had only a few layers on. After 3 days in Denver, I decided that that is what I wanted for myself for 2008. Booking trips to different destinations are out of my budget but I am lucky to have it all in my backyard. The only difference is that I should book trips overnight not just for the day. It felt great not to have to worry about laundry, kids, house cleaning. After a few days away I saw a person I hadn't seen before, me. Not Norma the mother but the person that can run for hours before heading out for some shopping then dinner and drinks (I didn't know I had it in me anymore, it turns out I can be fun at parties!). I thought I might even start a new adventure, the single runner's guide to fun. Traveling alone was more fun than I thought it was going to be. Me walking to a restaurant and asking for a table for one made people nervous but I felt great. On my short trip, I got to meet some fantastic people, and yes I might never see them again but it was fun. Randy the beach volleyball player that asked me out for drinks, or Steamboat as they called him(I didn't ask him why, too afraid to ask), Laura the minister, Kevin the single father of 3 and my guide. Traveling alone taught me to live in the moment, to stop looking at my phone waiting for the call that was sure to never come and absorb my surroundings. My only regret is not adding more destinations to my trip, like Aspen and Leadville but this will be a great excuse to once again pack my bags and head to the mountains. There were moments of doubts, I did cry once in my long snowshoe run the day before I came back, I started to go over the things I needed to do once I came back home, phone the CNIB and schedule Karl's Braille lessons, phone the Children's hospital to schedule Hans bone scan, Schedule Karl's eye appointment to see how he is progressing. I somehow felt overwhelmed again. The beauty of long runs is that I have enough time to work through things. There were a lot of great things waiting for me, seeing my kids again, my new job as Marketing Director, a field I love and that will finally pay enough to pay my bills and fix my leaky basement, the 50K frozen ass race, my friends. I arrived in Calgary to a flat tire at the airport, I had taken my car there, because try and find a cab or a sober friend willing to drive you to the airport at 3am on January 1st. I made new friends at the gas station as I waited for the tow truck to arrive since the tire key was missing from my car and they had to tow my car to the dealership. Nadia pick me up and we caught up to each other's few days, once more living in the moment a skill I am determined to master. I need to focus in the positive instead of the negative. After only 5 days into the new year I was ahead of most people who were too busy writing down their goals, I was instead full-on living my goals. Living in the moment will be a skill that I will need in 2008 to make sure that my spirit keeps growing. Living in the moment teaches me to enjoy the journey until I reach my destination.

Saturday, January 19, 2008

"When Everything is Coming Your Way, You're Probably in The Wrong Lane" Tom Snyder

How are you?, where you been? I have been sick and with my new job, my kids back at school and training, I have become as mythical as Bigfoot. During Christmas, it seemed as was everywhere since my kids were gone, but now, I am most often found at home and I am happy to be home with my kids or out on a trail with my BFF Nadia snowshoeing. Nadia and I if you haven't met us, we are like Oprah and Gail without the gay rumors, at least I don't think there are any, but that might explain why I have more male friends than females and why some people will not return my call. We went last Sunday to Moose Mountain. It was a beautiful morning and we had a great time together. I hadn't been feeling well so I was glad that she was making all the talking, I was struggling just to keep up on the uphill, but after some small talk and me not responding Nadia thought maybe something was up. " I am fine you know"" the kids are great, I love my new job, it pays my bills, really for the first time, I can't complain" " really," she said still not convinced, " I guess, I am surrendering to my life after all" I guess she wanted to go deeper because she then asked me" But where do you see yourself in I don't know 10 years from now?" waiting for me to throw at her a fortune cookie wisdom phrase I guess. The problem with surrendering to your life and trusting the journey you are in is that it looks a lot like giving up and no friend wants that for a friend, certainly not giving up. I had stopped calling my best friend to tell her I missed my ex-boyfriend, I really stopped caring but she couldn't believe that to be possible. I do have to admit that even a best friend will be a concern when she will get a call from me Friday night and saying " You are going to be so jealous" " Do tell" she asked and by the tone of her voice I realized, my answers not going to be what she was expecting. Then I recalled that this weekend is Robert Kennedy's Waterkeepers Gala in Banff and a lot of celebrities are in town, she was probably thinking I had met someone famous during one of my runs and had asked me out but instead I blurted out "Well with all the snow that fell today, I can go snowshoeing here in town tonight when I take my kids swimming, no need to wait to drive to the mountains!" I said now rather embarrassed " I know I am a loser" I added " You are not a loser and yes I am jealous". The truth is hard to explain why adventures mean so much. I am sure that everybody expected things to fade by now but it doesn't work that way. It's ingrained in me and it's hard to let go. The best possible way to make you understand is to take you back to Mexico, a long time ago, when I was 7 years old, I remember asking my mom if I could try for the dance competition. My mom said yes and I am sure it was hard, we didn't have money and being in the dance show meant she had to buy me clothes, but she said yes. I did make the cut but I got a part of a boy because hardly any boy ever tried out, so she didn't have to buy me clothes anyway because my mom always dressed me as a boy since we couldn't afford new clothes and we only got hand me downs, the girl clothes were for my sisters, " you looked better as a boy anyhow" she told recently when I asked her. I remember dancing my heart out for years until one year when I was about 10 I got my first part as a girl, my mom ran to buy me a dress, I remember the feeling of wearing a dress for the first time, it was white and brand new, she couldn't afford shoes so she bought me white sandals and with white socks underneath from far away they looked like shoes. I will never forget the pride of my mom watching me and also watching my male cousin cry because until now he assumed he had been playing with a boy, he never talked to me after that. That is what I see and feel standing at a race or running a trail: I see a 10-year-old that has made the cut even though nobody thought she could or should, standing there proud with a brand new white dress. That is all I have ever know, grabbing a dream and never letting it let go. I am excited about the racing season, and

I bit disappointed, Swiss Jura Marathon might be out, the organizer couldn't wait any longer, I looked at my bank account and decided fixing my roof was a priority. " Please one more month" I begged the race director as the race entry fee deadline approached . "Absolutely not" Urs said with what I assume was a very Arnold Schwarzenegger accent on his email. $790.00 is a lot of money, I pay for my races and every cent I collect in pledges goes to the cnib so instead I signed for a new race, the Blackfoot Ultra 100K and I am thinking about racing all 7 of the Alberta Ultramarathon series. At $50.00/race they are a bargain. As for the answer of the question Nadia asked me, by the time we were on our way back I had figure it out " Here" I said," Here?" she replied rather confused " Right here on a trail" "what I am not sure is if I will be here with a boyfriend or by myself but one thing I do know for sure: I am going to be here on a trail 10 years from now".

Sunday, February 3, 2008
"Strength Does Not Come from Physical Capacity. It Comes From an Indomitable Will. " Mahatma Gandhi

This was a hard week, not from the physical aspect of it but the emotional. I am tired at the end of the day, this is my second week of being back at my 11 miles a day plan and I feel great if a little fatigued. Somehow, the emotional test seems to be a bit harder to ignore than just my tired sore legs. Everywhere I turned I heard the same comment over and over, " Is too much!!!!" my race schedule is decided and it looks a bit ambitious but in my head not impossible. The total mileage for my racing season is 583K, crazy maybe, but it is over 8 months, not impossible. Also my training is tailored for endurance and quick recovery not necessary speed. A friend suggested I should stop running when we met for coffee, he is a CEO of a company and a career mentor, "Nobody will take you seriously if they hear you run two hours a day" I was mad. I was still mad when I met my friend Nadia later that day. She laughed about it " He thinks *that* stops people from taking you seriously" then she pointed at me, there I was standing with stilettos, long hair up to my waist, black eyeliner, blue eyeshadow and a suit that takes a serious meaning of "power suit" " you know because the first impression I get when I see you is, "She must have a high IQ!".

So I spent the night reading articles of people that inspired me, like Amy Palmiero- Winters, her story is an amazing story of courage and determination, she is an amputee, welder, single mother of two that can run a marathon in 3:04 and is now trying to qualify for the Olympic trials competing against fully able athletes among other things she also holds records in triathlons and is Runners World 2007 people's choice Hero award recipient. I read her story and all the doubts about being able to finish my races vanish. I have my first race of the year soon, I am feeling excited like a child waiting for the summer holidays. I have been running 11miles/day for a couple of weeks now and my body is doing OK. I am going to go down in mileage and up in intensity by next week just before my race. I have eliminated coffee now and I understand the attraction of caffeine in

Hollywood, I am so hungry all the time, all I think is about my next meal, but that is a better way for me to get my energy and also by eliminating coffee now it will be more effective when I need it for my longer races, I only introduced it early to get my stomach used to the acids, I haven't felt that awake in a long time and I was never very hungry. My favorite thing this week is Wynclef Jean's Song " The Sweetest Thing" that will be the song I will play when I take my first step in the Frozen Ass 50K on Feb 18th, I am looking forward to wearing that t-shirt to my next board meeting while humming away Wyclef Jean's song. Take that CEOs of the world, one day it will be you calling me looking for advice and that's a promise.

Thursday, February 21, 2008

"It'll Work Itself Out Fine. All We Need is Just a Little Patience " Guns N Roses

This is the longest I have stared at a blank screen trying to make out all the words in my head so I could write them. The Frozen Ass 50K was this Monday, the race went as I had planned, I held back until 30k then I started to pick up the pace feeling strong just to finish 3rd as predicted, wait that was my dream the night before, what really happened was completely different. The race itself started long before Monday, my kids were gone so I had the chance to just stay home and try and make sense of how I was going to attack this beast. My sister who is the most spiritual person I know offers great advice, "You have done the job, now you have to prepare mentally.

Pray, visualize yourself finishing strong in third place, taste the air, smell the sweat of people around you, you need to make it as real as possible, tell as many people you know what you want to accomplish, that will help you push through the last leg because you are not going to want to disappoint them" I had decided to try and place 3rd for this race, after looking at last year's results, third place finished was 4:55:50 and I knew I could do that, so I planned and practice for a 4:55 finish. Nadia and I chatted several times and she walked me through the race, " be patient, do not attack until after 30K, if you go to fast to soon you will just fade to the back, if you exercise self-control, then you are only racing the last 10K in pain, you are prepared to do that" sounds reasonable. Shane, a guy that I met thought a blind date when mutual friends set us up offered to support me, it was only a 50k race but he said he was coming anyway so I might as well put him to work. No sparks flew when we met but we continue our relationships as friends. And as you guess it, I have zero chemistry with anybody right now unless you are a trail or a mountain I am not thinking about you. The night before I paced up and down several times, I decided to try and find a song that was going to motivate me when things got tough, I poured over my song list, Alanis Morrissette? too angry, Keith Urban? too lonely, then I found the perfect song, Daughtry, hopeful, that was me. Race day was just unbelievable, the weather a fantastic 9C ,with the weather so mild nobody stayed home, there were about 200 people, some whom were there for the 25K race, the half race. Just before the start Shane pointed to my race number " three, that is an omen" he grinned, then he handed me tiny little boxing gloves, " just in case" and he smiled some more. At 9 am we started, my legs where happy to be running again, the excitement around me made me run faster than I needed, a fellow runner alerted me I was going to fast by yelling after he notices in my race number I was doing the full. I slowed to my decided finish time pace. The path was icy, and bumpy, running on it made it very tricky and painful since it was an uneven surface. Shane was waiting on aid stations and I handed him layers as I warmed up. I was running light using only aid stations for water and food. At the turn around point that is where I could fully see how many women were ahead of me and how far. Three I counted, first and second too fast for me to catch as I had predicted but third was close enough for me to catch, the word patience lost its meaning once I turned and got a clearer picture of who was I really racing against: everybody in front of me was now a competitor. I caught and passed third after 20 minutes and left her behind, I could hear her trying to catch up to me, I was now running faster than I was supposed to, "is ok" I told myself, once she is far behind me I'll slow down. Shane was screaming in excitement every time I came to an aid station. I started to go over all the things my sister told me, 40K and I was still third, I was hurting but the outcome matched the effort I was putting. I was not going to look back so I decided not to slow down; make sure the 4th was way behind me. "It works," I told myself, "The Secret Book thing my sister talks about all the time, it works!, I am going to read it when I get home, heck I am going to write one when I get home". Then out of nowhere, a lady in a funny hat passed me like I was standing still, Third!. I was beaten, I slowed way down enough to fight the tears, then 4th and 5th passed me, twin sisters with matching Boston Marathon jackets " the Barbie twins as Shane called them because they were so beautiful in an impossible way. It didn't matter anymore, I try picking up the pace but my legs refuse to go faster, it felt so good to walk, it was like asking your mouth to stop eating after a bite of your favorite dessert, finally, they got going but not at the same speed. I saw Shane around the next corner" you can catch the twins, I saw them walking, they are hurting" how exactly he thinks we all been feeling!" I thought not in such a nice way though. "8 more k to go" announce the guy in the aid station, "6 you mean" I replied, no 8 is 52K not 50," sick people, calling it the Frozen Ass 50K, why not called it the Frozen Ass 52K!. My legs finally started doing its thing again, I keep my place 6th, the twins keep looking back to make sure I was not going to attack, I was close enough to see the logo of the Boston marathon on their jackets. I was flatter but I was beaten, I hurt all over, all I could think was " this is only half the distance of my next race" then I could see the finish line, Nadia and Shane where there, they could see the disappointment in my face, at that very moment, like a twisted joke, Daughtry's song started playing in my iPod, "shut up" was all I could think, somehow the Rocky theme doesn't have the same effect if Rocky is not standing on top of the stars victorious, but instead he is midway the stairs sucking wind, the theme song playing doesn't have the same dramatic effect. Then I heard Nadia and Shane "Congratulations you are 5th!". "6th you mean". "No 5th the lady in the funny hat was a relay", "the twins were 3rd and 4th. The next 24 hours where not a walk in the park, my body was hurting but not as bad as my morale, I had forgotten everything I had learned, I didn't race my own race, my watch read 4:47:48, I had beaten the time I was set out to do, but I was too angry to enjoy it. I avoided the phone as it rang and rang, "Me and my stupid mouth, how many people did I talk to the last two days?"" Fuck the Secret", I kept screening calls for the rest of the day. I was feeling terrible and cried most of the afternoon and didn't feel better until I picked up my kids that evening, I offered my ex-husband to drive halfway from his parents so he didn't come all the way just to turn right around. My youngest son arms around my neck felt good, I know it was his arms and not his words because the first thing he said to me was " What happened to your hair? you look like a poodle" after the race I had no strength to straighten my hair. There is where I found peace, at an Alberta highway surrounded by farmland looking like a Bon Jovi 80's music video with two tiny arms around my neck, Karl didn't hug me until we got home, 70K away from the city was still too close to your friends, you never know, you might be seeing hugging your mom. I spend the evening watching TV with my kids, I was quiet but they are used to see me sad when they leave for a few days to see their dad, I have built my life around them, they are the pillars of my existence and when they leave, well, the foundation gets a bit shaky. Then, Jerry the subway guy's commercial came on TV, he was standing on a stage and everybody was clapping because he had lost 240lb," maybe I should do that instead, I should put a lot of weight and then lose it all" I thought to myself. I wanted to be standing there on a stage holding a big pair of pants and have everybody clapping. My ego had gotten the best of me, with my attitude I would never be that person on stage either because I had not learned the lesson yet, losing weight, races, managing an addiction and such is all about managing our emotions, the negative ones to be exact, the ones that tell us we are never going to accomplished what we set out to do so we might as well quit. I needed to allow myself to continue on this journey and that it was okay to fall short of a plan and keep going. Never told my kids anything about what happened. I had shown the worst possible display of sportsmanship. I did congratulate everybody at the finish line, but I had not smiled when I did that. I had asked Shane to drive me home without mingling with the other runners. Of course, I couldn't avoid returning calls forever, so I picked up. Everybody tried to make me feel better, there was the funny "So you are not the Mexican running wild after all?" the poetic "The principle is competing against yourself. It's about self-improvement, about being better than you were the day before." which it made me even angrier, after all, I am still top 10 after a year of training, The best came from a friend of mine who said something true, although it made me even angrier when I heard it." it will all make sense later". It's funny how everybody had a story about the time that they almost made it to the podium, Clayton from the office was half a second from making it to the Commonwealth games a few years ago" stupid goggles" he said, the emotion was so vivid that he went back to the pool the next day after our conversation, the last time he had set foot on a pool was three years ago, he and now he is starting a triathlon relay team at the office. That evening things somehow started to make sense, Greg my ex- boyfriend called to see how I was making up, he is the only person that except my family really knows who I am, he is used to me calling frantically because I got a B on Business Law while I attended SAIT with a workload of 9 classes a semester that made the school counselor shiver every time he saw me down the halls, I had always gotten A's in Business Law. Greg listen patiently to me, then I realized this is a lot more about me pursuing this races that even if I said the races were about Karl, Hans and the CNIB it is about believing I have a chance of winning this thing, this is not about the races but about me, about this crazy dream of completing a series so difficult only a handful of people who enter don't even finish them. if I can set my goals so high and truly believe I can accomplish them, then the sky is the limit, I couldn't believe how much it matters to me to finish." you are different now" " I have never seen you this cocky" he said, is almost like you are a different person" he added, it made me smile. Last year I wanted to be invisible and now I was angry because I wanted the world to see me for the first time, truly see me. I have always been very focused and believed in myself, people only call you cocky when they don't believe its within your abilities, when you prove them wrong they call you talented .It was nice to be back setting goals, the last few years with the job loss, the break up and Karl's diagnoses I became so insecure that I didn't give myself permission of dreaming big anymore. I eventually stop sulking and focused on what was important, I wish I could tell you that the moment it all came to me, was the moment I talked to my friends that it was among friends when I remembered why I was there in the first place, but it wasn't, it was the moment Greg mention the word " What is your plan for the next race on the series" and I went to check the results for the Ultra Series 4th in line, only 3 points behind the twins. I was so caught up in the results that I forgot this is not just a race but series of races of this thing call the Alberta Ultra Series. I called Nadia to get the training schedule for Boston, my next race " After today I thought maybe you would cancel Boston" she said surprised, " are you kidding, I want the jacket" I said, I want to be wearing the jacket when I cross the finish line at the Blackfoot Ultra, I want people to yell," Look at the triplets" when I come around. It was nice to be called cocky, I'll take that rather than pity any day.

To be continued.....

Monday, March 24, 2008

"What Lies Behind Us And What Lies Before Us Are Tiny Matters Compared To What Lies Within Us." Ralph Waldo Emerson

I am very excited to be writing today. Even though I promised my family that this years was going to be the last year I was going to be doing ultramarathons, I am secretly planning my 2009 race calendar. I am scheduled to do Brazil 135 Ultra in 2009, I had my interview with the race organizer Dr. Mario Lacerda, usually, I am fighting very hard to let people know there is nothing wrong with me, with Dr. Mario it was the opposite, I had to convince him that I was crazy enough to do the race. Brazil 135 is fantastic and well organized I am not sure why is not more popular with other ultrarunners, but that will be to my advantage of course. Dr. Mario was a bit concern with my lack of experience, this is my first year after all, but I have the passion and that seems to make up for the other. Preparation is paramount but after 60 hours of running is the mental toughness that will get the runner though it. After I explained how I was found wandering in the mountains with hypothermia and yet I signed to do not one but 7 this year he was convinced I was motivated to get through the race next year. Is hard to explain to somebody who isn't into extreme running why a passage like the one in the race report will be so exciting to somebody like me. "Joao Sacks was found by his wife, on the Serra do Cacador Mountain, a little way before Consolacao. He had been telling all the other runners that he had already finished the race and would be having a celebration BBQ at a house he had found in a darkened alleyway near Consolacao: Pure Hallucination!". After reading this paragraph my mind was made, I wanted to be there next year. My excitement is also part of being able to meet fantastic people because I have my kids full time with me I usually train alone, races are the only time where I can meet other runners. I have been pouring every race account from this year's race and I am looking forward to meeting people at next year's race. Passion fuels the soul, I am a passionate person by nature, it shows in everything I do, the way I raise my kids, do my job, with my family. Ultrarunning is giving me a tangible outlet to express that side in a way that it matches the way I feel on the inside. This is for real, this time I have found the real thing and I am not about to let it go anytime soon.

Monday, April 14, 2008

"Do the Right Thing Baby Do the Right Thing. Go with Your Heart and Do the Right Thing" George Strait

This is been an interesting and challenging week, not in a physical way but in an emotional sense. Where do I start, well I guess Tuesday, April the 8th is a good place to begin. You probably know about the controversy surrounding the Olympic Torch in San Francisco. Protesting the Olympics because of China's record on human rights violations. I am torn. I sympathized with both sides, not sure I agree on violence but I am sure glad this issue is being reviewed. I also feel sad about the athletes that have spent years of their lives training. Hans and I had our usual conversation on the way to his swim practice on Tuesday, on how he was going to ask me to watch the Olympics on the TV when he makes it to the Olympic swim team instead of allowing me to come to the events. " Mom, you will sure to embarrass me by calling me sweetie, honey, or worse when you yell really loud in Spanish, THAT is even worse" I always welcome this opportunity to tease and torture him further on how I could make it much worse than that, this time I ponder on what the right thing to do was. Boycott the Olympics or support the Athletes? Being raised Catholic my mom's sermons where on how she expected us to do the right thing, in my mind I always assume the choices were going to be clear, " to steal or not to steal?" but as I got older the choices become less clear. "What if I need to steal for my family to eat? What will be the right thing to do? Luckily I have never had to make that decision. But life offers many choices some small and some big. As I am preparing to go to Boston and planning future races I am bombarded with choices of what the right thing to do will be. "Settle down, is better for your kids." "Running too much is not healthy" "Can't you just enter 10K races like other normal people!". " Haven't you run away from your problems enough?". After much anguish over, I decided that to continue to run long-distance events is the right thing for me, at least for now. I am sure most people have the best intentions for me and my kids when suggesting this. Scott Dunlap talks about running addictions and avoiding real issues in his blog. This is the kind of news and information that most people rely on when they offer advice. I understand that to most people is strange to hear me be excited about the opportunity of putting my body thought so much stress. But my decision on whether to do some race or not is never based on how much pain I will be in, but in what person I will become after. I had a hard time just getting through my day without breaking down over the simples things when Karl was first diagnosed and that's why I started to run. I see the difference that the running has made in my life and fundraising for organizations that help kids like my son makes me feel better. I have absolutely no control on the rate of progression of Karl's condition but doing something about it feels damn right. I get that this is not your usual partnership, ultrarunning and fundraising, at least not in my community but this relationship has strengthened the bonds I have with my kids by creating new opportunities for them. My ex-husband is bringing my kids to Boston to watch me race the marathon, although we have always put the kids first, this is truly the first time we are all looking forward to spending a weekend together. Looking at my kids face when they heard about us hanging out together erased any doubts I had if I was indeed doing the right thing. Here doing the right thing was not thinking directly related to me, doing the right thing meant for my kids. If increasing the rate and difficulty of my races results in more opportunities for my kids to be with both parents and new programs being offered for visually impaired kids because of the extra funds or exposure, well, keep the races coming. But sometimes doing the right thing is a very difficult decision to take, even though it affects a very small number of people or because it affects a very particular member of the family. My youngest cat Bella was hit by a car yesterday, she managed to make it home but she was in bad shape, it was hard to tell what happened just by looking at her, she looked OK, but I could tell she was in pain and she had hard time breathing. Bella was only gone for 10 minutes; she wanted to be outside while Jake, Lukas, Noah, Hans, and Karl played in the snow. (Yes, I have 5 boys on the weekends, but that is the other story that needs to be discussed and analyzed on its own later).The vet at the animal emergency services took x-rays, the news was not good, she needed extensive surgery if she was to survive, "all her organs are in her ribcage" "It will be expensive surgery, 2 maybe 4 grand" at this moment I had no idea of what to do, I had told my kids she was going to be OK, that she was a fighter, if she had crawled all the way home she was sure not ready to go. I had 5 boys that were looking for my reassurance that she was going to be OK. I couldn't believe what came out of my mind next; I have always made fun of people that spend a lot of money on their pets, but I found myself saying this "Can you do it for 2 grand? I don't have 4, I can try to find 2; I can probably eat PB&J sandwiches for the next month" "Are you sure? That might not be a great idea" said the Vet. Nadia was listening; she walked to my room and without judgment offer to pay half. "you can't do that" I said both touched by her offer and embarrassed that she realized I wanted to pay 2 thousand to save my cat" is a lot of money for a cat" I continued, "Plus she is no even your cat" I told her with tears, still not believing what she was offering "it is a lot of money, but if it means so much to you and your kids I will pay half, plus she is my cat too, we are family remember" she said with as much grace as anybody can say trying to spear the other person's feelings of humiliation while offering money. Listening to those words I couldn't help but realize that I might not be sure what the right thing to do is sometimes, but I might be doing something right if I found myself surrounded by friends like her. My mom was not that supporting, "No. this is a cat, not a child, plus there are no guarantees she will survive, and if she did, what kind of life will she have?". The drive to the animal hospital was a long painful one, I still had doubts on what the right thing to do was, I mean Bella had crawled all the way home in pain. Bella trusted me to do the right thing, but I still didn't know what that was. When we arrive, they brought Bella to a room to say our goodbyes. She was in a lot of pain; a lot of hours had passed since the accident and I knew at this moment I couldn't afford to pay for the surgery. Especially if there were no guarantees she was going to be OK, I am sure that if she lived it was just going to turn into a dinner story of how this friend of a friend once pay 2 thousand dollars to save a cat she had found on a shelter. But if she died, it will just mean I will paying interest on a credit card bill for a bad decision I made, even if well intended. Bella stopped crying shortly when she heard my voice because the injuries where only internal on the outside she looked perfect. Nadia held my hand as I requested the injection, the right thing to do at this time was to make her pain stop. In the next few hours, I reflected a lot about the importance of decisions that I take or help take that might seem small gestures at the moment but have long-lasting consequences. Like going to the shelter to adopt Bella. There is no such thing as small gestures; I am convinced that doing the right thing is not always easy, sometimes it might not be what we want to do, or we are not sure what that might be. I am not always going to get it right and just the same, I will never please everybody, but looking around the room in my house yesterday I realize I am surrounded but people that cared for each other, mom was there comforting my kids and if I have a friend that is willing to mortgage her home to save my small cat Bella, then I might be making some right choices after all.

Thursday, April 17, 2008

"The Greatest Barrier to Success is the Fear of Failure."
Sven Goran Eriksson

I am so nervous. I am leaving for Boston tomorrow and I am still undecided about a lot of things but is too late now to change any game plan. This is the first time that people I know is excited about my race. Nadia was right when she told me that because I qualified on my first try I didn't understand the importance of qualifying for Boston and she was right. I watched the documentary " The Spirit Of the Marathon" last week, it definitely set the mood. After the movie everybody lingered in the lobby, we all caught up with each other lives and of course running. The documentary touches on qualifying for Boston and that is where the conversation turned afterward, "are you going? " "Is it your first time?" "I remember my first...." There a realized Boston is special because you have to earn your entry either by qualifying or trough collecting pledges. A few people asked me about my upcoming races, when I told them Boston was a speed work for me, that I had a 100K race a few weeks after; there is no better way of clearing a room I became, one of those people, an outcast, simply because in long-distance running, ultra-runners are still considered social misfits. I don't understand it, to me running long distance doesn't feel much different than wanting to run a sub 3 marathon, the training and dedication are just as intense but the focus is on endurance not necessarily on speed. It is hard to explain to nonrunners why you run, it is just as hard to explain to a runner why you run that much longer. For Boston, I am going to aim for 3hr 30min as a dream goal, 3:39 as realistic and expecting to do worse than that maybe even a 3:45 or worse who cares!. I can't possibly focus my efforts on all the races, I have a different focus in all of them, some I am just hoping to finish, such as the Lost Souls 100mile race. Boston is a bit of a mixed bag, I could have trained to improve my time, but after I learned about Brazil 135 mile race, I decided that the focus should be to increase endurance, I just had my first 200K training week a couple of weeks ago and it was not pretty, but I got it done but my legs feel heavy now. After the documentary I came home feeling like I am letting everybody down because I didn't train for Boston and I feel nervous every time I get a phone call that says" I will be tracking you online" I feel like saying " not on this race, please". Karl asked me about Boston this morning, he wanted to know more about it then he got the courage to ask me if it's true that I am an "extra runner". "you mean ultrarunner" I replied with a smile" yes, it's true" Karl thought for a second "is it true you are the first Canadian to be invited to Brazil 135 Ultra?" at this point I realized Karl was trying really hard to understand what this all mean. "True, is not a race a lot of Canadians want to do" I joked. "The race can last up to 60 hours" at this point I think he was really confused " why do you want to do it?" He asked just like a lot of people asked me when I tell them about my races, this time however I was not embarrassed, or defensive, this time I felt great to be asked that questions. "For you"" I want to do it for you and all the kids like you," I said looking straight at him "Every time I do a race like that I collect money for the cnib and I bring awareness to what it feels to be you, and that honey, is worth running for as long as is humanly possible" my answer was good enough explanation, he was happier to find out I was not really as crazy as people were saying than to know I was doing it for him. I am learning a lot about myself, about why trail running and long distance is such a passion. I just don't get why it threatens some people that I could possible love running this much? A year and a half ago I couldn't stop crying and had trouble getting out of bed, then through running every day got a bit easier and now my days are spent more laughing than crying, why it this feeling that I am feeling wrong?. One passage of Dean Karnazes book " Ultramarathon Man" touches on what it means to be to be a runner, specifically an ultrarunner, "The body has boundaries, the human spirit is boundless" "Don't run with your body, run with your heart" and that is exactly what I plan to do, no matter the distance, I will run with my heart.

Saturday, April 26, 2008

And the Oscar Goes To...

I am back from Boston and the excitement is still making me wake earlier than usual. I have heard so many times about the Boston experience and unless you go yourself is hard to really know what this all means. Nadia and I arrived night in Boston the Friday before the race, when she picked me up it was hard to tell why we were friends, she looked hot in her high heels boots and tight jeans and I showed up in a turtleneck, mom jeans and trail runners. "Great" I thought " We look like Madonna and Rosie O'Donnell: people are probably wondering what we could possibly have in common. We argued all the way, I kept defending my position on how I was not going to push for any specific time and to just run for the fun of it. Nadia has been in Boston before so she knew how high profile the race was. Imagining that people I knew were going to be following my progress online made me wish I had done some speedwork. When we arrive in Boston my luggage didn't make it, it was only Friday so I didn't panic much, plenty of time to get my race stuff before Monday. On Saturday we went to the expo to pick up our race packages and to check the sponsor's booths. Here I realize the magnitude of Boston marathon, to a runner, Boston is what The Oscars' are to actors. I was feeling under the weather, but the excitement around me keep me going. We picked up our package and Nadia explained to me the meaning of first and second waves. She got a blue bib number first wave and I got a red bib number, the fastest runners where on the first wave and the slowest runners where on the second wave. I stopped to say hi to David Willey the editor in chief of Runner's World Magazine, we had talked a couple of times regarding an article I liked then I notice an unusually quiet and blushing Nadia, I had found her Achilles heel: cute runners. Nadia and I had somehow transformed into giggling teenage girls, spending the day picking up race packages, posing with cute editors and grabbing lunch at fantastic restaurant patios, so different to how we usually spend our days, looking after smelly teen boys often knee deep in laundry and dirty dishes. By now our speech resembled more a dolphin call because we were talking in such a high pitch voice. Back to the brownstone we had rented for the week we ate and talked some more until the wee hours. Sunday we woke up early to watch the Women's Olympic trials, Nadia was not so sure, little sleep and standing all day before a big race is not what you should do. But watching in awe the best female runners in the US only got us more excited to be there in Boston, Just before the final lap out of the crowd in comes Scott

Dunlap and stood right next to me I mean what are the odds!!!, if by now I was taking like a dolphin, my voice got so high that only dogs and matting wales could hear when I introduced myself to Scott. All I remember saying when he agreed to pose for a picture was that I was disappointed on not having any makeup on, Scott just told me to Photoshop myself later, after listening to him I realize that his wife had only asked him " does this pants make my butt look big? " once. When Scott asked me if I was trying for a specific time I lied trying to impress him and blurted out 3 hrs. and 20 min even though I had just said not to Nadia about trying for a specific time. Scott told us he was going to stay way back and party with a bunch of friends. Damn I didn't need to lie since he obviously didn't care, mental note "be yourself Norma". Magdalena Lewy Boulet led the race until 23.5 miles before Deena Kastor caught up to her in Cambridge to place first in 2:29:35, Magdalena Lewy Boulet and Blake Russell will be joining Deena in Beijing. Joan Benoit Samuelson set a record for women over 50 at 2:49:08. After the trials I went shopping for stuff for the race because my suitcase hadn't arrived. I was now extremely nervous to be wearing brand new shoes for a marathon and clothing I dint know where it was going to chafe. I joined my kids for dinner until now they couldn't meet up because they were having a lot of fun with their father, they had been too busy to see me until now with museums, tours and Science Centers to attend. We all went for a walk, my usually, "too cool to hug mom", kids were now fighting to hold my hand while we walked. Sadly I left them early because I was in desperate need to go to bed, the late nights and being sick was catching up. I got back to the brownstone, Nadia was getting her race stuff together. She is a pro at races, I had been copying her since we arrived in Boston doing what she did and eating everything she ate. She laughed and called me a single white female referring to the 90's movie where Bridget Fonda's roommate becomes her stalker. One more time we went over our race plan, since I had said 3:20 to Scott she was now holding me to it. I didn't want to disappoint her but I still doubted I could do it, I wasn't sure I could do 3:30 to be honest. My luggage arrived at 10:30pm that evening with just enough time for me to pull my runners out before I fell fast asleep. Monday morning Nadia and I got up at 5:45am. I wanted to go to the bus loading park with her, not knowing the city well, I didn't want to take chances and miss my bus. When we got there, it seemed that all 25,000 people were standing in line waiting for the bus. The wait was long and the bus ride was even longer, after driving for what it seemed hours I couldn't help but think " We need to run all the way back!" We got there in time for Nadia to go to the start line for the first wave start, we kissed ,hugged and said our good lucks. I still had a half-hour, so I decided to use the porta-potty one more time. Here in line, I got the chance to talk to other runners, I had a wonderful opportunity to meet a lady who was celebrating her 55th birthday that day, another runner was celebrating her engagement, the beauty of being in the second wave was that people are usually just glad to be here, no expectations, most just managed to make it to Boston so in a sense, they were there to celebrate. The second wave also hosted the charity runners, these runners were experiencing high anxiety since they didn't want to disappoint the people that pledge them. There I was standing in the number 16 corral, wearing a plastic garbage bag to keep me warm we started at 10:30am, I had trouble keeping the pace that Nadia had set for me because of all the people that were in front of me. When I got to the top of one of the hills I could see the sea of people in front. I was able to make it through what it seemed thousands of people and finally, I set on my pace group. I was trying to keep pace with my watch while watching the mile markings but I got confused because I been training in kilometers and the US uses miles, I couldn't figure out why I sometimes seemed to go just the right pace and other I seem to go blistering fast. What I decided to do instead was to use people around me as pacers, I quickly found people that were running at a pace that I found comfortably fast and tagged along. This was a lot easier to do and I could take my surroundings and quickly glance on my "pacer to see if I was lagging behind or going to fast" I also played the- if you are wearing- animal print, tutu, backpack, I randomly pick a theme you should be behind me- game to motivate me to speed up. I then checked my times on the 5K 10K half marathon and found out I was right on target, I was happy because I found it manageable to run that pace while zigzagging to high five kids along the way, or eat oranges, brownies, candy or anything I was being offered. We run past a biker pub that was playing "I am Running From Hell" and it made me smile, I also heard the Rocky theme song, and there were so many live entertainment bands playing along the way to mention. I found pleasure of running past the timers along the way and mentally said hi to my siblings knowing they were probably going to be checking online, unfortunately for me after the third mat I run out of people to thank, so I started to say hi to all the people that had made fun of me in high school. I found it easy to run at Boston, not because the course is easy but because of how much is happening around you, the signs, the people cheering you on at this moment I felt what they refer as the runners high. I saw my kids at mile 17 right after the Wesley girls, I know that they are famous for being boy crazy but I high five and hug a few that called me strong and sexy runner. It was sure nice seeing my kids, I got close enough for Karl to see me but was afraid to stop with them and not wanting to keep going. Around this time is when my legs started to feel heavy and I got a sharp pain in my left knee. I slowed enough to take salt tablets and Tylenol, the runner's high was wearing fast and I still had 9 miles to go. I was still feeling good enough to keep running but slowed down enough to a more manageable pace, I tough of Nadia, I didn't want to disappoint her, I thought of Bella, on how she had been in a lot of pain but managed to make it home. I picked up the pace a bit after the knee pain subsided around mile 20, my legs were a bit heavy, and didn't what to cooperate. It seemed that here is where a lot of people were falling apart, I saw things I didn't what to see , people shitting their pants and puking and all I could think was "that might be me at my 100 milers". I felt great when I realized that I had caught up to the blue numbers, they had left a full 30 minutes ahead of me so I started to estimate my time. I knew I couldn't possibly finish at 3:20 but 3:30 was a possibility, I picked up the pace once more and made a run for it. Nadia always talks about digging deep and I have never fully understood what it means, what if I feel I am digging deep but I am just a wimp? All of a sudden everything bothered me, my Nike band pacer, the half a gel left in my back pocket, I couldn't take enough off. The last 6 miles where the hardest for sure, I run 6 miles twice a day, so I kept telling myself that, " It's just a run around house remember" my battle was more mental than physical. Once I reached the last 2 miles I knew that making it to 3:30 was all going to come down to these last miles. Once more picked up my pace and I had 17 minutes to make it there for 3:30, by now I started to know what digging deep really means until now I had been scanning around watching the crowd but now I couldn't do it, I got dizzy just looking side to side, I decided to look ahead and not move my head at all. I couldn't see the finish line even though the last marker said one mile to go, It was not until I turned around a sharp corner that I finally saw the finish line, I was shocked that I was actually going to finish sub 3:30, I " sprinted", to the finish line, people looking at me certainly didn't think I was sprinting it look more like a steady jog. I crossed the finish time at 3:28:40, good enough for a 6288 place, there were 25,000+ runners, Nadia finish time was 3:26:58, she fought her way to

5800 place I will find this out later when Nadia's husband Magnus called us later with the news. I tried making my way to the buses to pick up my stuff, ahead of me looked like a battlefield, people were laying on the floor everywhere, being carried by stretchers, wheelchairs and saw more people getting sick, my legs were tired but by the time I saw my kids 20 minutes later my legs were OK. I have been training hard to recuperate quickly and it showed. It is hard to explain to you how amazing running Boston feels. Even amazing doesn't quite explain it properly. Watching everybody around me limping and me being able to squat down to untie my shoes to change into flip flops made me truly believe that I am making progress towards my first 100 miler and at the moment I felt invincible. I know that long-distance races are about endurance but speed also matters, the sooner I get thought the course the better I am off, The Canadian Death Race thought me that, the sooner I can cover the course the higher the chances of finishing. Nadia and I joined my kids and my ex-husband at the Four Seasons Hotel for a bite to eat. There at the Fours season, I saw Scott Dunlap again with a group of women, he was busy typing on his Blackberry and didn't see us when we walked in. Nadia noticed a beautiful blond in the group " isn't that Kirstin Armstrong?" I was trying really hard not to stare, I didn't want to turn into Scott's stalker but he has a more exiting life than us I couldn't wait to say hi again hoping he would ask for my time and I would fake modesty even though I was over the moon because I had just become a Boston Marathon Finisher!. Scott is extremely classy, I knew he was busy, and with friends yet he still took the time to ask about my race. There in that group where two people that I admire a lot, Scott's life is simple and he makes it look extraordinary, Kristin has an extraordinary life and makes it look simple. Kristin's interview with her husband Lance is hilarious as you might know Lance famously ran Boston as his first marathon. Later that night I joined my kids for supper and a walk through Quincy's Market. The next day I woke up feeling great, I was only uncomfortable because I sunburned. " I am on a witness protection program, I am really not Mexican," I told Nadia since she didn't sunburn but I did. We went shopping to the Nike store where we run into Askale Tafa Magarsa who placed fifth the day before, she was tiny and sweet, we saw Jelena Prokopcuka, just as we were leaving the Nike store. By now Nadia was fading and went home, I toured around for a bit before I went for a quick 50 minute run by the river. In our last night, Nadia and I went for a fantastic dinner at Piattini's and then for beers at a bar nearby to watch the hockey game , the Flames was in the battle for their lives in game 7 against the Sharks. The flames, our home team lost that night but Nadia and I had won. We found deeper respect and admiration for each other strengthening our bond. We secretly planned on not returning home, both of us loving the carefree feeling of the last 5 days. " Let's pretend we lose our memory and we don't know that we have families and responsibilities waiting for us back home" she said and it made us laughed hard " Let's do it!, I can totally blame my stretch marks to yo-yo dieting" I added and sent Nadia and I into a total laughing attack. But you must wake up sooner or later. When we got home we were both on cloud nine, her phone didn't stop ringing after the race, here I understood why it matters so much to her, she is surrounded by family and friends that encourage each other. Me? My phone rung twice, once from work and the other was from the roofing guy fixing my leaky roof. But that didn't matter, my reasons to be here had just left the day before on plane. I have no doubt I will finish Blackfoot Ultra, and the Death Race, The Lost souls 100-mile race still intimidate me but it will not stop me from trying.

And the Oscar goes to...

I didn't win the Oscar but It didn't matter. My 3:28 was like not winning for the Oscar in the best lighting category, you know those awards where most people watching use as bathroom break. My footsteps walked behind the footsteps of great legends that day, my kids watch me do something that I never thought it was possible a few years ago. I told my kids that they too one day will run their own Boston, maybe not the actual marathon but something just as inspiring, that the best thing they could take from seeing me run Boston is that dreams are possible if you are willing to work hard at it. The truth is when you are chasing a dream it hardly feels like hard work. And yes, it's true what they say, being nominated and not winning is still an amazing feeling.

Friday, May 16, 2008

"The Future Depends on What We Do in the Present". - Mahatma Gandhi

It is hard for me to write today. After much thinking about I decided to go ahead and blog after all my running is a way for me to bring awareness, I owe it to all the parents that I connect that are dealing with blindness and visual impairment, like my online friend blind swan who is a mother of two children both who have the same condition as my son and she is dealing with the same things except is affecting both of her kids as well as her. When there is a high there is a low, trail running has shown me that, Karl's condition is progressing and every day when I wake up I feel like I can hear a loud ticking sound, I am unable to stop it and it takes a lot of effort to try and find the strength to answer truly when he asks if I think he will be able to drive someday. Last week I dropped him at school and a teacher asked me to come in for what I thought was a quick meeting about the school family dance or something like that, instead, his teacher and aids were waiting for me, they thought it might be better to talk to me in person instead of sending a note. They are all worried because he is struggling with the things he was OK a few months ago, they order more equipment for him to be proactive but I needed to get him to the Children's Hospital again to see where he is at, the truth is, is hard not to notice, I had made the appointment already, I have seen him climb imaginary stairs when he misjudges the distance of where they truly are. I have the sense that things aren't good, but I always want to think that I am just being overprotective; talking to his teachers I realize that I am not. In the big spectrum he is still OK, he still has a decent amount of his vision left, but every time things change, it becomes apparent that the beast is very much alive. Now, there are a lot of emotions that one must go through, I feel embarrassed because this is not as serious as an illness where people must battle with their lives, but he is my son and it hurts tremendously. For mother's day we all run the Forzani's Mother Day Run 5K together, when we got to the start line the sun was so strong and bright Karl had trouble walking so I tied my arm to his to guide him with motion as well as my voice, it worked, at about 1K he got into a rhythm and we managed to finish at 41 minutes and Hans finished at 32 minutes. I was so proud of my kids, I felt a lot better, and I know that even though everything will continue to change we will always find a way. Things are much better now, it takes a lot of digging deep to put things into perspective, I would love to sit and cry and think, why? But that is not going to help us is better to put my energy on trying to find a way to deal with situations in a positive way than to dwell out how unfair life is. I believe we all have the lives we deserve. What I mean when I say that is not that we deserve divorces, sick kids, or unsatisfying jobs. What I mean is that we are all given challenges along the way, is how we choose to deal with them that separate us all; I am going to make sure that I take ownership of my actions moving forward. Is it hard? You bet!, as a single parent I feel that if my life was a movie, I will spend half of the movie on a raft in the middle of the ocean trying to get my kids and me to shore while paddling frantically with a spoon, when Karl was diagnosed, well, I felt my spoon turned into a fork. But don't feel sorry, Karl is doing fantastic, he is a bit sad when things change, but he always manages to be happy and isn't that what is all about? I want my kids to be happy. As for me, I find happiness as long as I know I am positively dealing with things, what once intimidated me now is not a big deal, I am ready for my first 100 milers, and Brazil? I am only sorry it is not happening sooner. I was invited to the luncheon for the cnib, I am starting to put my son on the map as well as linking the business affluent community about what low vision and blindness is, standing there I vowed to help find a cure, I often hear kind words from people who I know that are not dealing with this, on how I have to be realistic, they haven't found the cure to AIDS or cancer after all, but none of that matter, I am determined that my son will see the face of the woman he will fall in love until he loses his sight completely that will be my focus. Is no accident that I chose ultrarunning to bring awareness to this, I remember reading about Brazil 135, the race takes place in an area is called "The Path of Faith", the answer to my question on how was I going to deal with this positively was never more obvious.

Updated note: We are so close to finding a cure to conditions that causes blindness, gene therapy research has made amazing strides. I don't fundraise anymore because Karl's perception changed. He is 100% comfortable with is condition, he is happy with who he is, limitations and all and I don't want to continue trying to find a cure and make him feel he needs to be fixed. If he is happy so am I.

Sunday, May 25, 2008
Blackfoot Ultra 100K
"Only Those Who Risk Going Too Far Can Possibly Find Out How Far They Can Go" T. S. Eliot

On the weekend I had the pleasure of running the Blackfoot Ultra 100 Kilometer race. I knew it was going to be a great race the moment I kept asking the locals for directions to the race site and nobody knew what trail I was talking about. That told me it must be a relatively unknown trail. The directions I printed from the website said that the estimated travel time from Sherwood Park, East of Edmonton was about 30 minutes. I decided to leave my hotel about an hour ahead. I was driving slower than usual on the quiet highway at 4:10am just to make sure I didn't miss the turn, about 40 minutes I saw the Blackfoot Park turn sign and I was relieved I still had 10 minutes to go, when I got to the gate of the park I was surprised to find out that the park was dark and empty except for a single-vehicle parked, the windows were foggy, not a great sign, but I was lost, it was so early in the morning and I hadn't seen other cars on the road nearby so I had to bite the bullet and got out of my car to ask for help with directions, when I got I approached the vehicle I could see that it was a young couple and they were finishing dressing to my relief. I tried not to make too much eye contact while I explained that I was lost and I needed their help, hey, they were consenting adults so good for them! After the initial shock of being disturbed in such isolated park at that time while they were getting it on, they were very kind and gave me directions. What they told me was that I was at the right park but the wrong entrance " This is the north entrance you need to be on the south, go back to the highway and keep going for about 15 more minutes". Not good, I was now for sure going to be late. I got the race and it was already underway, the worst part is explaining that you are a participant, and yes, I am late and by the way I also need my race package. Well, is not what a race director wants to hear, I think what ticked her the most was to hear that I had never done it before " Well, you better run hard, you can't be alone and risk you getting lost" I tried lightening the mood," well, is a 100K, how fast can they be running anyway?" Well, apparently fast enough, It took me about 10 minutes to catch up to them. I quickly found a group that was running a pace that I found comfortable to keep. I had a great time meeting new people and the loop seemed to go fast because of the conversation and the scenery were great. That work for about the first 25K then I hit the proverbial wall. The course was designed on a 25K loop, the 100K runners did 4 loops, the 50 milers 3 loops, and so forth, The next 25K was not good, I started to fall behind for no apparent reason, I just simply couldn't keep up. I slowed down because I knew it was the only way I was going to survive and everybody started to pass me, a lady caught up to me and slowed down to my pace to chat. She was a nice lady from Edmonton, 52 years old and looked very fit, the sun was now peaking and it was getting warmer, " I am getting too hot now" she said, "It seems to be the story of my life recently" She added "I know" I replied. " " you are too young dear" " Well, I am not that young, I am 40 but because I have been overtraining I am hot all the time, sometimes I wake up and I feel like I am feverish" I replied, thinking it was a banter of overtraining between ultra-athletes out of nowhere she said "That could be early menopause" without a hint of sarcasm " I was in my 40's when it started, 46 to be exact" at that moment I stopped and pretended to tie my shoelaces to let her pass me because I could go any faster. Running had made me feel that 40 was not over the hill and now she just told me I might be hitting early menopause so my life is on the downhill, so why bother?. I ended up running alone for most of the loop after that, 25K at a slow pace can be a long time, which can be good or bad depending on your spirit. There I figure that ultras are a lot like a marriage, you need a strong foundation and an even stronger commitment to be successful at it. Luckily for me I had both, so quitting was really not what I thought but it was more on the lines of does it really matter that I am here giving it all when I am so far back from the real race? It was on this lap that I hear that Jack Cook the leader was clocking 1hr 20min/loop, I couldn't shake that though, all I could hope for was a 2hr 45min/loop, even on a perfect day!. If ultras are like a marriage the honeymoon phase was over and I was knee-deep on raising a toddler. Listening to my inner voice that now resembled more a child in its terrible twos, " I am hungry",' I am thirsty", "I need to go to the bathroom" " Are we there yet?" still, I just kept placing one foot in front of the other. Then something wonderful happen, I just simply felt better, I remembered that I didn't have to be here, I *wanted* to be here to be exact, after all, it hasn't been easy to find the time or energy to train but I want to do it badly enough that I always managed, as for not being fast enough, who really cares? even at a 5K, I will never have a chance of winning anyways so why was I making such a big deal out of it here? and that is not what I treat my kids, why was I treating my inner child like that. The only reason why this even crossed my mind was my ego taking a beating because it was a loop course and eventually, I was going to be lapped by the winners. I took this time to really take in my surroundings and take some pictures then the joy started to sink in, I remembered that I had never run 100K before, that alone was a celebration. I finish my second lap and I was feeling fantastic, I rushed to my car to refuel since I missed the bag drop the aid station I had to go to my car for extra food and gels and to change shoes since my La Sportiva Fireblades were not working that day, I put on my Montrail Vitesse on and it was like magic, is amazing what the right shoes and a bit of caffeine will do after 50K. The next two loops where the easiest, I decide to drink less fluid and eat only at the aid stations, since I was alone on the race, the volunteers became my family, every time I came around they all cheer me on, they knew my name because I was the infamous late runner, but by now they weren't mad at me anymore. I was having so much fun, I decided to run my own race and enjoy it. Just like you should never compare your marriage to anybody else you should never compare your race to other runners. I used *me* to gauge how fast or slow I should go and instead of relying on salt tablets or electrolyte replacements, I used the aid station snacks to provide the salt and calories I needed and It worked like a charm. Sometimes what we need to make things work is something simple like a warm cup of coffee, some chicken noodle soup or the right words spoken at the right moment. I just finished reading Pam Reed's autobiography "The Extra Mile" and I can tell you one thing, if I were to write a memoir it will never be like hers, there will be no glory, no podium no TV interviews no article on a running magazine, but that doesn't matter, all I ever aspire to be in this sport is to run for the love of it. I can't tell you my finish time or what place I took at Blackfoot Ultra, but it didn't matter to me, I enjoyed myself I talked to a lot of great people, I had a chance of meeting Leslie Gerein, one of the coolest girls on the planet because she was so confident and sure of herself, I fail to tell her that how amazing she really is when she introduced herself, I was just savoring the moment, I had accomplished what a had set to do that day and that was to finish my first 100k. I felt great and that matter too, I don't know how many times I hear- that can't be good for you - comment and as long I am healthy I get to enjoy what I am doing guilt-free. If running ultras was like a marriage, I am ready to renew my vows.

Driving back home that evening, I realize that sometimes the best thing we can do is to not quit, to forgo expectations and to enjoy life for what it truly: a journey, not a destination.

Friday, June 20, 2008

"It is Only In Adventure That Some People Succeed in Knowing Themselves - In Finding Themselves." André Gide

Well, it been almost a week since I participated in The Fast Trax Ultra last Saturday. I decided to wait until they posted the results to give a proper race result. Usually, I am aware of how my race went, or sometimes I don't even care. This time I decided to stick around to the end. First I should tell you more about the days leading up to, if only because I like talking and second because I truly believe it had everything to do with the race results. Days leading to the race I decided to buy a GPS Garmin Street Pilot c550 just to avoid being late again. Also, I found a participant for the 50K that wanted to carpool from Calgary, he posted on the race's Facebook account that was looking for a ride. I was a bit worry since I was concerned about my eclectic music taste, to say the least, not all Latin music is sexy, especially if it is mariachi music. Zoltan a young guy on his way to Edmonton on what it was his first-ever ultra and I drove on Friday around noon. I had told him to bring his ipod to take turns with the music. When it was his turn I quickly realized his taste was around elevator ambiance music (think Enya, waterfalls and wind chimes) his turn never came, and it reinforced why I am still single, I am bad a compromising. We arrived at the campground 5 hours later. I was not feeling well, I didn't taper for the race since I am supposed to get stronger, I also found out I was registered on the 50 milers, not the 50K as I originally intended. I didn't have money to book a hotel room so I just camped in my car at the race start and it was so cold that night and my legs cramped right out when I got up to go to the bathroom and the remaining few hours before the start were distant memories of fever and painkillers. I woke up three hours later not sure if I was going to be able to run. When I checked for the race I decided to keep the 50 miles instead of changing it to the 50K, in my mind as long as I took it easy and aimed to finish, I was going to be OK. The race was at Godlbar Park and it was a 10K loop, we were supposed to do 8 loops and a bit since 50 miles it's a bit more than 80K. At 6 am we all started, I stayed behind, for most of the race, Petra Graen lapped me twice to win the 50K race first overall at 3:43:34, Wayne Gaudet was second and fist male at 4:08:16. At 45K I was still third last overall and even Rick Webb and Carmen Pavelich who would eventually win the 100k race at 8:07:55 and 9:59:44 lapped me. This is the first time on a race were the words of encouraging "come on, pick it up", "show us what you got", were more in the lines of "Jesus you are too slow". I kept a pretty conservative pace for the first 45K. Then something amazing happened, I started to gain on the people ahead of me, I was going slow enough that I didn't need walking breaks, by the time I crossed the checkpoint at 50K I feel good enough to pick up the pace, my hamstring was tight but not hurting. Armed with Tylenol, I decided to kick my pace and avoid stopping at the aid stations, the next 30K I barely slowed just enough to grab a bottle of water or Perpetuum that was conveniently mixed in a bottle. By the time I reached 57K, I passed the female lead of the 50 miler and I managed to unlap myself from Carmen. At this point, there were a lot of people slowing down but I was feeling just fine. I miraculously finish top female at 8:38:27 and second overall behind Logan Beaulieu whose winning time was 7:35:11.The moral of the story? Run your own race. I don't know if the outcome would have been the same if I had speed up ahead with everybody else not when I was ready but when I felt the sting of humiliation. I do have to say it's hard on the ego to stay behind, especially since it was a loop course and I got to see everybody that was ahead of me each time they turned around. Sure they high five me, at one point I decided to play my mariachi music loud enough for me to just tune out and listen to my body. Jack Cook of Fast Trax did a wonderful job at his second Ultra. It was perfect weather and the flat course meant 5 times where improved over last year's times included mine.

Saturday, July 5, 2008

Racing the Planet

"If You Want To Make Something Happen, You Have to Be Outrageous. You Have To Go Beyond What Is Acceptable.

Unwillingness To Do That Is The Biggest Risk Of All." Mike Vance

As I am getting ready for The Sinister 7 but also I will be competing at the Sahara Race October 26- Nov 1, which coincidentally is my birthday. Can't imagine a better way to spend my birthday than to run 250K. I am now talking to a few people about sponsorship since this is not a race I can just car camp, is looking promising but I am crossing my fingers just in case. The race is a bit ahead of schedule, OK a lot, but this is how I am going to accomplish it. I am going to keep running my usual mileage, 60-80 miles per week while adding hiking and power walking with 22 lbs. backpack, and/ or biking for about an hour. This way I am increasing my endurance while avoiding injuries, I am already exercising about 4 hours a day. Good news, I am still feeling pretty good, bad news I still don't look like Penelope Cruz, worse news, my house is a mess. But how cares!!!. I can't imagine living my life any other way. The thrill, the adventure, the adrenaline, the pain, they all remind me I am alive. I have found myself on this journey that when I go to bed at night I am excited for the next day to come. The sacrifices are big but I am convinced these next few years will bring inner peace and self-acceptance that is only found when you are enlightened. Phew, kind of heavy, time to phone Oprah. Seriously, if there's ever a time that you were so certain of something you forget your inhibitions and your perception of what is possible stretches so far you feel that if you raise your arms you can almost touch the sky you are on the right path. If you don't feel like that it might be time to do something that intimidates you. Sinister 7 race is just around the corner, I will be running 135K and I think I will finish it in around 25 1/5 hours giving the terrain. Rachel a coworker of mine and her boyfriend will be my support. They are hardcore mountain bikers and they will just move my race bag from checkpoint to checkpoint while they bike in the nearby area. All I ask from them is a nice cup of coffee around 4am!. The race is located in Crossness Pass by Blairmore. Until next week, now move away from the computer and go try something new.

Updated note: Seriously, put this book down and go try something new that scares you.

Wednesday, July 16, 2008

Sinister 7 Ultra

Courage Is Not the Absence Of Fear, But Rather The Judgment That Something Else Is More Important Than Fear. Ambrose Redmoon

I am back from the Sinister 7 135K ultra, held in beautiful Crowsnest Pass. The race went better than I expected given that it was promoted as the toughest ultra in the Alberta Ultra Series. The race lived up to its reputation, of the 52 soloists only 21 finished. Rachel and Craig dropped me off at Blairmore for the start while they took my car to go mountain biking. At 9 am sharp we all started the first leg and easy 15k with only 740" of elevation. This is where I usually catch up with other runners, I stayed behind admiring the beautiful surroundings, it was hard for me to speed up because of the spectacular scenery.

Leg two was a grueling climb, the scenery at the top of Hastings Ridge was worth the effort, with a 457m of elevation gain and 607m of elevation loss, it made for a very fast run to the transition area. I am good at running downhill, I am more coordinated than most runners, I think is my dancing background. By the time I got to transition I was considerably ahead. I checked my watched and wondered how Nadia was doing, she was running Powderface half a very difficult and technical trail run, she was the second female last year and she had trained very hard this year and was hoping for a top female, I found out later is that she DNF because of an injury.

 Leg three has the most elevation gain, at 838m I keep thinking I suck at climbing even though hardly anybody passed me, the leg crosses through the remains of the 2003 Lost Creek fire, by now my body was warm and I was making really good time though each leg I started to get faster and faster. Rachel and Craig met me at the end of leg 3, they wanted to say goodnight, they were tired from mountain biking and I told them that I felt fine alone so they could go back to the hotel to sleep (a decision I would almost later regret, but just keep reading to find out), They were relieved to hear that and promised to be back in the morning in time to greet me at the finish line, they told me I was the second female just before they left, WTF! You just throw that information at me?!

Leg four was the longest leg at 31.5K, I ditched my poles in transition 3 (a decision I would later regret) to be faster and put as much distance between Anne the female lead and I, we left transition at the same time and she was quickly falling behind. By the time I finish this leg I was in the lead, I came into transition and was greeted by a complete stranger holding a cup with mash potatoes " I heard you are here alone, I thought you might need this" the first thing that came out of my mouth was " marry me" he blushed and giggle a bit. As I was leaving transition 4 I realize that leaving my hiking polls behind was not the best decision, at the rate, I was going I was tracking for 22 hrs., which meant I would be running in the dark for the next 5 hours.

"Well I know sometimes it's hard to see the light, Shinin' at the tunnel's end

And though the road just goes on and on for miles, Faith lives just around the bend". Keith Urban

Leg 5 was the toughest for sure, it was hard to run through creeks and mud without poles, I slipped and fell on a couple of creeks around 2am. For the next 3 hours, my pace dropped significantly and I started to feel really cold, this leg has a hard climb and I had a hard time coordinating my legs. 3 runners passed me including Annie who would go on to finish top female and 4th overall at 22:23:21. Darren Froese was a top male at 17:13:53. the fast Trax Team won the top team at 12:26:38. When I got to the top, the wind was howling, and I had a strong urged to lay down and sleep. *Just 20 Minutes*, that is what I thought myself, I remember I had chocolate covered coffee beans and warming packs in my backpack. The warmers worked but not the coffee beans, I immediately started to throw up, and continued to do so for the next hour and a half. Walking in the dark was aerie but, I felt peaceful and focused. I could hear whistles everywhere from racers that needed help. Calling for help never crossed my mind. I realized I am both my best asset and worst enemy. I take some bad decisions, like leaving my poles behind knowing I would need them later, just to gain ground during the day, but there in the evening, I remained calm, I knew all I needed to do at that moment was to reach transition safely, I was not going to be first, and I was OK with it, finishing was my next focus and that was still a very strong possibility. Just like with every race I get stronger physically, I also get stronger emotionally, I am also in the best place of my life currently and that helps me be less emotional and more rational. The sound of whistles were all around me but I didn't see anybody else for hours, later I heard somebody stole marking sings and a lot of people got lost, I did have to wait for other races to figure out where to turn several times because they would be no markings, at night it just got really tough to figure out where to go. I thought I was close to transitions after I started hallucinating, I was so sure I even heard laughter and the campfire and tents, walking for 10 minutes just to find it was just a glow stick. when I finally got to transition 5 I was in bad shape, shivering and a bit delirious and showing signs of hypothermia, the medical team did a good job of bringing me back to life. I had stopped drinking because I kept throwing up every time I tried to do, so their main priority after warming me up was fluids. The race allowed a drop bag per leg, especially for soloists without help, the trick was to know where to send what. To my delight, I did have a change of shoes at that aid station and somebody gave me a dry t-shirt and within 30 minutes, I was back in the game. As soon as I started running I started to get sick again, and it was coming from everywhere, I remembered I had ginger chews and medication on my backpack, that helped and by the time I finished leg 6 the vomiting and diarrhea had stopped. I probably ran an extra 2K at leg six just running into the bushes. I was wearing my running skit but it wasn't exactly ladylike squatting down behind bushes puking and shitting at the same time.

Leg 7 was a brutal climb and equally challenging descent before turning into a beautiful and fast stretch to the finish line. I reached the finish line at 24:43:09, 2nd female and 8th overall. As I crossed the line, Brian the race director put a medal around my neck then informed me my boyfriend Brett had been calling to follow my progress, being frustrated because of the results of each leg were too late, so he used his fame to convince the race director to give him updates personally, I both blushed and cried at the same time when Brian told me. Knowing that for the first time there was somebody awake thinking of me while I stubbornly pushed through the night made all the pain and discomfort immediately seem smaller. Brett and I had started seeing each other recently and things are getting comfortable, well, It seems dating again is possible after all. In ultrarunning, running is 50%, determination, endurance, toughness, or just plain stubbornness account for the rest. Kids have a natural tendency to follow through, just watch a child learning to walk, I have yet to meet grown-up that crawls because it took him or her too long to learn to walk and just decided to quit. The Japanese have a proverb *"Nana Korobi Ya Oki" "Fall Down Seven times Get up Eight"*. I get asked often how can running such distance is possible, physically is easy, with the right training; mentally is the hardest part. When you fall in love with the process, the working hard, the endless hours of preparing for something then you will be successful. Don't cut corners if it's important, it will come to haunt you later trust me, and if you fall, just get up and try again.

Tuesday, August 5, 2008

The World is Round and The Place Which May Seem Like The End May Also Be Only The Beginning. ~Ivy Baker Priest

I am back from the Canadian Death Race 2008, I joined 223 soloist and 182 teams for what it turned out to be the hardest race I have done to date. To downplay the race to seem modest is a disrespect to those who finished and also to all the racers who tried but had to drop out of the race because of injuries or missing cutout times. Of the 223 soloists only 81 finished, and out of the 81 only 8 where female. Jack Cook from Edmonton smoked the course again, he is the course record holder and he finished first overall at 13:56:13, the fastest female was Diane Van Deren from Sedalia USA, her finish time was 17:16:22. To my surprise and delight, I finished 30th overall, 4th female and first on my age group at 20:44:14. I was nervous coming into the race after all this is the race that started it all, exactly one year ago I came home from Grand Cache sore, beaten, but in love with ultrarunning. Last year I didn't finish, but I went a lot farther I had ever gone before. It seems so long ago when Karl was first diagnoses and I started running because of the stress and pain I felt, I remember wanting to run until my skin came off. In less than a year I had a son who was diagnosed with an incurable condition, I had lost my job, and I was single and heartbroken. One evening at home unable to sleep, I came upon an article about ultrarunner Mimi Anderson of the UK, she was part of a small group of female ultrarunners that the media calls "Brave Girls" feeling vulnerable at that moment, is exactly what I wanted to be, brave, to face the challenges that lay ahead. After just one more year I am pleased to tell you that things have changed significantly, while there is still no cure for cone dystrophy, I just saw an article about medication being used for macular degeneration, is in the same family of the disease so I am very hopeful. I have a great job and everybody is very supportive, my family and best friend are there for me and of course, I am dating an amazing men, Brett Wilson, before you go and google him let me save you the trouble. He is the new Dragon on CBC's TV Show Dragon's Den. I have known of Brett for quite some time, and in Calgary who doesn't, I was apprehensive about going out with him after we met at his Garden Party, he is the Canadian version of Richard Branson and he can be quite polarizing but the Brett I fell for was the one who on our first date took me to the children's hospital to visit Eugene, a friend of his son Russell. Eugene is battling cancer, Brett himself being a prostate cancer survivor wanted to stop by and see him and his mom, there in the hospital, talking about soccer with this bald teenage and making him smile, I watched his mom's face relax for a second, I could see the exhaustion on her face, but she was at that moment delighted to see her son smile and talked about something he loved, sports. when we left the hospital my doubts where gone, sure I might see him on the paper jumping off a hot air balloon wearing a wedding gown in protest of domestic violence but that is part of who he is and I love it. Brett also emailed John Bobenic CEO of Maxim Power, he contacted the local power plant in Grand Cache Milner Power and before long I had a support crew for the Death Race. Alta Ball of Milner Power turned out to be amazing, she was thorough and meticulous. I drove with my nieces Karla and Brenda whom are visiting from Mexico and by the time I arrived in Grand Cache 7 hrs. later she had everything organized for me. We met after picking up my race package to go over the details, basically told her to treat me like a spoiled child who won't eat her veggies, to prevent hypothermia I needed to make sure I ate during transitions. As it turned out we had a lot in common, she had been a runner but because of arthritis she had to quit running, her ex-husband also happens to be legally blind with the same condition as my son, well, I know my sister Muñeca is going to have a field day with this one, even I can't just write it off as a mere coincidence. We had a heart to heart talk, she worries about her kids who don't have any symptoms but since it is a disorder that is passed down on the genes they are all aware of the risks. I was glad to tell her that *even if*, her kids would be OK, with the support of friends, family, the community and organizations that cater to the blind and visually impaired, kids like my son, have the same opportunities as fully sighted kids. Harder? sure but not impossible. Race day I stood there at the start line, chatting with Neil Runnions, Logan Beaulieu, Jack Cook, John Postoluk, I was part of the group, the tough guys knew me and accepted me. Then out of nowhere strangers started approaching me to wish me good luck, they all called me the Mexican running Wild, referring to my blog telling me they were fans of it. It was a bit overwhelming and humbling. At 8am the gun went off, the first leg was an easy 19k with amazing and breathtaking scenery, it was a relatively cool day so running felt great.

Leg 2 was a lot trickier, 27K of very technical and very slippery. I spent more time on my butt going downhills trying not to break my legs than I did running, by now it started to rain so it got more and more complicated as it when along.

Leg 3 is the easiest since it is the flattest of all the legs, this is where I tried to make most of my time, I am terrible at climbing but decent at running downhill.

Leg 4 is what nightmares are made off, the net elevation is well over 6,500 feet. This is where Neil Runinion caught up to me, we have a friendly competition since he is better than I am at climbing so it depends on the design and elevation of the course he might or might not finish ahead of me, this race proved to be on his favor. He managed to finished at 19:08;28, loved when the next morning over breakfast he told me he had run scared the last leg, he was a worry I was going to eventually catch up to him and the end he thank me because he ended up besting his personal time.

At leg 5 my spirits were still high but I was feeling exhausted, I came into the last transition area before the finish line at 12 midnight, Alta, her kids, and my nieces were there to cheer me on, Brett tried calling from Nashville but coverage was sporadic. Last year I was pulled out of the race because of hypothermia just before transition 5 and he remembered so he called to check and see if I was okay this time. I was very tired but I only had 25K to go, I used "I got this" as my mantra for leg 5! I never expected this leg to be as hard as it was, I thought after leg 4 we were going to be treated to an easy jog into town to roll in with some dignity, instead, I stared over and over again to yet another climb *"How many mountains and hills Grand Cache has anyways?'* I took me over 4 and half hours to finished leg 5, quitting never crossed my mind but I wanted to be done badly, I kept straining my eyes to find a light, any light something that might resemble town lights, instead of except for a few team racers that passed me it was complete darkness. I was so happy to spot the grim ripper standing by the river and handle him my silver coin, the fee for taking the boat to the other side and onto the finish line, you are given the coin in your race package and I was never happier to pay for a service in my life!. Tough at it was, I loved the race, the whole town of Grand Cache came to cheer us, most of the ultras I go to, might be a couple hundred of racers and their families only, here people came to cheer on complete strangers. I greatly recommend this race, especially if you are a female. I heard that the brave girls club was looking for more members...

I came home with the silver Death Race coin, it was awarded back to me because I placed first in my age group and a small plaque engraved with my name, time and place, this is the only thing I displayed openly in my house, on top of the mantelpiece there are numerous awards my kids have received but mine are tucked away in a box in my closet. This award doesn't just mean I finished a 125K, that itself is amazing, but what it really means is that the human spirit is amazing about coping with adversity if you overcome your fears and keep placing one foot in front of the other you will eventually reach the finish line, trust me on this, I might know a bit about this subject ☺

Monday, August 11, 2008

"Life is Either a Great Adventure or Nothing." Helen Keller
I am back training for my first 100 miler, I am feeling a bit tired but my legs are not hurting anymore. Because of the Sahara Race, I am also doing weights especially upper body since I will be running 250K with a 22lb backpack. In other news, I am currently the female leader at the Alberta Ultra Series and second, overall behind Neil Runnions, the awards ceremony will be held after the Lost Souls 100 mile race, I am 230 points

ahead of the closest female, even if I don't finish Lost Souls I still have the lead. This has been the most amazing 6 months, I am running because I love the positive influence it has in my life, winning top female of the series will be just the icing on the cake. The only drawback I am never going to be able to watch a full movie without falling asleep from now on, ultrarunning will be part of my life forever.

Sunday, September 7, 2008

"Leadership has been defined as the ability to hide your panic from others" Unknow

6 days and 18hrs until Lost Souls 100 mile ultra. I haven't felt well for the last week or so and I am sure my body is in a panic mode. Bolt Supply House is sponsoring my race so I should be in less of a panic, I was going to be running alone with no support crew but then John McCann president of Bolt Supply House offered his help, I was thrilled when John emailed me, I started working part-time last month and I was a bit stressed about the expense of going to Lethbridge. is only a few hours away but I have to book a room at the local hotel for 3 days plus meals and gas, and you get the picture, I told my kids I was clairvoyant, I could see tuna sandwiches for supper for the next few weeks. In a few short emails, he put me in contact with Brent West.

Brent had a lot of questions, *"what exactly is the crew supposed to do?"* Well, I am sure he is still scratching his head after he read my email. The crew's main responsibility is to make sure I am safe and I don't end up being disqualified for losing more than 7% of my body weight at any time. I will be weighted a few times during the race before being allowed to continue. If I end up sick again, I can end up with dehydration, dehydration means losing weight and that could lead to being pulled out of the race. I also told Brent that if it looks like I am dying but my eyes *aren't* rolling backward, I am OK, I just need more electrolytes. I will proudly be wearing Bolt Supply House logo, I am sure if John had asked me I would have run the whole race as their mascot "Top Nut", I almost canceled the race because I didn't think was smart to spend that much on a race especially after paying for school supplies for my kids and their after school activities this month, thanks to John I don't have to, it's only a few hundred but to a single parent it might as well be a million. Lost Souls race course is a 53.7k loop done 3 times. I am hoping a sub-29hr finish but 30hrs is not hard to see as a final result. I couldn't find a pacer for my last loop so I will be running it alone. I am nervous and it's only because it means so much to me, I love that I still get butterflies before a race even though I have been running a race a month for the last 7 months, the best part of all, after Lost Souls I have to get ready for Sahara 250k Race. I get chills just typing this! all of a sudden, my friends and acquaintances are thinking, being a single struggling parent isn't so bad after all.

Thursday September 11, 2008

Murphy's Law. Noun. The Facetious Proposition That if Something Can Go Wrong, It Will.

10 hours until Lost Souls 100 Mile Ultra and all I have to say is that *it* can get worse. I am so sick with IG issues and vomiting. On a good note, at least I am not pregnant so it could always be worse. My first 100-mile run will be most interesting.

Sunday, September 14, 2008

"Mock Not the Fallen, For Slippery is The road Ahead of You." Russian Proverb

I am back from the Lost Souls; the race was canceled about 10:30pm Friday due to bad weather. I was about 45 miles into the course when I crawled into the aid station drenched, shaking badly from being out in the rain for hours and full of mud. Even before I heard the news of the race being canceled I was in trouble already , it had been raining for hours and had nothing dry to change into, I did, however, try to see if I could make a running suit out of garbage bags. I have a lot of mixed feelings about the race being canceled, I was not feeling well so it should have been great news for me when they called it off, yet, I was disappointed but deep down maybe it was a blessing in disguise. Both Brett and Nadia felt relief when they heard the news, they thought it was a crazy idea for me to try and run the race that sick, they knew how much I wanted so they never told me until later. I learned so much in such a short time, even though I didn't get to finish my first 100-mile race, I am glad I went. I woke up on race day and felt terrible, having to take anti-nausea medication and Pepto- Bismol to deal with GI issues even before the race start is not exactly the best way to start a 100 miler. At 8am we were off everybody notice I was sick because I was trying hard not to vomit and they offered words on encouragement, Wayne Gaudet from Edmonton told a fellow runner that I had never meet " she is tough as nails, she will finish no doubt, my money is on her' *Great* I thought, *no pressure here, why don't we also call everybody that picked on me in high school and tell them how they made a mistake and I was not a loser.* The course started right from the parking lot of the Lethbridge Lodge and into the coulees. Eric and his wife Lisa were there to see me off. The race aid stations were well stocked with everything I needed so I told them to go home and that I would call if I needed help. I was feeling better already but could not pick up the pace and fell way back, at the beginning I was feeling okay but the fact that I had trouble picking up the pace I started to doubt my ability to finish. Negative thoughts race through my head. What if I time out? What if I just reach the point where I can't go anymore and will want to quit? I will usually talk myself out of these situations with positive self-talk, this time, however, I was armed with a cell phone and called Nadia for words of encouragement when I reached the darkest moment when I arrived at what I thought was the end of loop one, only to find out it was the aid station and I still had 11K to go. I had run 42K, a marathon in 7hrs! Nadia and I talked for a few minutes. " snap out of it" she said sounding a lot like me when I talk to my teen sons. "Falling behind It isn't the end" she told me, " I was on the lead at Powderface marathon and ended up in an ambulance from a fall before reaching the finish line, being in the lead doesn't mean anything unless you finish, is not over until the fat lady sings" and just like that I found my mantra. *"Is not over until the fat lady sings"* When I reached Head Quarters , the end of loop one, I could see how far people were ahead of me. There was a 6K loop that went south and you came back to HQ before heading north. When I got there most people were finishing the 6K loop and were heading north, some of the runners were surprised to find me there; they thought I was ahead of them. *I am not that fast*, I remember thinking. When they checked my weight I had hardly lost any, I was 50.8 Kilos at the start and my weight was 50.2Kilos, I was delighted and feeling better and better. Some of the late group runners that were with me decided that they had enough and surrender their numbers; I left quickly just in case I got discouraged like them and quit. I headed south as it started to rain. When I got to the next aid station it was hailing and then the rain turned into a downpour. So many people started to come back to surrender their numbers as I was getting ready to leave the aid station. "It's too slippery out there," some said "Is way too windy" where the typical responses. *Now, that's healthy*, I thought, nothing to prove. When it was time to quit they did without punishing themselves the irony is that it's not what I did! so I guess I felt I had something to prove. I changed into some dry clothes put on every layer I had with me, grabbed Ziploc bags to cover my hands because my gloves were socked and useless now and took off into the night. It was at this moment when I realized...*OMG, they are right, there IS something wrong with me.* The coolies where slippery, going uphill was almost impossible unless you climbed like a snake on your belly. Going downhill was the most fun, even with poles there was no traction so I just sat down and tobogganed down on my butt using my poles to slow me down. About an hour and a half into it, I came across a group of several guys and was delighted to be in a group. "Having fun in the mud yet?" somebody asked, without replying I just turned around and asked them if they thought the tights I was wearing made my butt look big...They all became quiet and unsure of what to reply they all looked at each other, then I told them I had been sliding on my butt for the last hour and my pants were now full of mud, I felt like I was running with a diaper on. They all laughed off and for the next few hours, we all did the Spiderman and walked the hills sideways hanging on the grass to avoid falling down. When we reached Penaquin aid station around 10:45pm, the aid station resembled a homeless shelter full of people draped in garbage bags, emergency blankets hoovering a space heater. The rain had penetrated all of my layers so I was sure I was done, I had told the guys unless I found dry clothes I couldn't continue, I couldn't risk hypothermia. In the tent, I was asking around to those going home if I could borrow their dry clothes if any. Then they informed us the race had been canceled 15 minutes earlier. There were a lot of emotions rushing in the tent, we were almost halfway into the race, some people were relieved but I was disappointed but I could hardly complained, I had been whining about not going fast enough and now all I wanted was to finish. Life comes fast at you. Canceling the race was the right decision, there were already people in the hospital suffering from hypothermia and sprained ankles, and the coolies are protected area and we were damaging them by thrashing around, now I felt shame for focusing so much on my wants that it stopped me from seeing the bigger picture. Eric and Lisa where nearby waiting for me, in spite of me calling them earlier to tell them I was continuing they decided to wait and they spent the last 2 1/2 hrs. watching movies on their iPod's tiny screen waiting for me to come through to see if I needed anything. I was glad to see them and even happier when I saw they had sweats and t-shirts for me to change into, the dry layers felt heavenly against my skin. The next day in the lobby, everybody gather around talking about the race, some had stories of injuries they saw; everybody wanted to know how far you made it. The awards ceremony was still held Sunday morning, I didn't attend because I just wanted to come home to my kids. I am sorry I missed the awards, I placed top female and second overall behind Neil Runnions, not bad for a woman he once thought was too arrogant to think she could run an ultra, so new to running, I am glad we are friends now. It's in the darkest moments when we find out what we are truly made of, and sometimes the best way to find out how much something means to us to take it away. This is not going to be my last 100 mile race for sure.

Saturday, October 11, 2008

"Freedom Means the Opportunity To Be What We Never Thought We Would Be." Daniel J. Boorstin

I have less than 2 weeks before Sahara and so much has changed. I quit my job last week, I have been having trouble keeping a job especially now that I am on a high profile relationship, the saddest part is that I haven't changed at all, just the perception of people about me. I know I should just suck it up but it feels like high school and I am exhausted fighting the mean girls. This idea came two weeks ago when I met Ray Zahab, I had emailed him to see if he could coach me. I had my doubts I could afford him, but I would never know if I didn't try. He was in Calgary giving a talk so he agreed to meet that Friday evening, after I told him my story and how I had the dream of running 7 of the toughest ultras in the world he just looked at me and said " How come I have never heard of you!" and offered to train me and the position of athletic ambassador for impossible2possible. I immediately feel dizzy, Ray is my ultrarunning hero, my kids laughed when I try and play it cool when he called me to confirmed our meeting, I screamed after hanging up and my kids high-fived me. Now here I was sitting across Ray and he was asking me to join him, to be part of the team. A team is so elite Matt Damon was making personal calls to them when they were on their record-setting journey of crossing the Sahara in 111 days to raise awareness of the water situation on Africa. Running The Sahara expedition is chronicled in a documentary film, narrated and executive produced by Matt Damon and directed by Oscar™-winner James Moll. The choice was never so easy, it's a leap of faith but I tried normal already and normal doesn't love me back. I have been preparing for Sahara but it was too late for any training from Ray so at this point, I just need to make sure my gear is ready and to keep the level of my fitness. Training for warm weather has been a challenge, It is very cold in Calgary so I try to run indoors with as many layers as I can. I have also received almost every shot there is. I assumed that because I was born in Mexico I was immune to anything but no such luck. After a few rounds of shots, I feel like I can pretty much wrestle rabid dogs, step on sharp objects and be OK. The doctor also gave me a bunch of pills in case I get " traveler's diarrhea" " I want you to take this pills and withdraw from your race if you have any of the following symptoms" she said " Nausea, vomiting, diarrhea, cramping, chills, or you feel your gut is rotten" I couldn't help but smile when I told her "That's how I feel on every race, how will I know if its E-coli or just and another day at the office?" She looked pale for a second, she stuttered and asked " how about a fever? do you get that as well" I just nodded. " well, she said, if they all come at once and you don't feel better after a while, then you'll know" I couldn't help thinking when I left the office that I hadn't sold her on ultrarunning. I decided to run for Operation Eyesight Universal

(OEU),Foundation Fighting Blindness (FFB) as well as the cnib next year, the choice of charity is a very difficult decision, There are many amazing organizations such as FFB that has funded dozens of research discoveries to identify the causes of genetic forms of blindness. Operation Eyesight Universal focuses on preventable blindness due to the lack of clean water in developing countries. My son has a genetic condition, I do wish a cure with all my heart but as a mother, I can't ignore that there are kids and people all over the world going blind when they don't have to.

"The joy of giving sight to the blind is one of the most beautiful gifts a human being can give to another. So keep up the joy of giving — for gifts of love are gifts of peace." Mother Teresa

I feel enormous gratitude to have the opportunity to devote myself to a cause so important to me. I hope my kids will learn that kindness will transcend languages and boundaries. The tough part now is that as I go along to bring awareness I must become the face of the cause. The Calgary Herald ran an article that made me feel like a Rockstar. For 30 seconds I forgot that I drive a minivan and that for the last 2 years I have barely slept. I feel a duty to reach out to all those parents and kids that feel no hope. I look around me and can't help but to feel fortunate, my kids are doing great, there are some great advances in gene therapy and the cure for blindness really seems close, my family and my best friend Nadia are there for me and my kids when I need them. Quite a difference from a few years ago, I will never forget after Karl's diagnoses and I lost my job when my kid's school call me to offer me a food hamper, I had slipped so fast that it was obvious I was having trouble making ends meet. People always asked me why I decided to run ultras, my response always confuses them, *I dislike statistics,* the odds of kids from a single parent home of being successful in life are very small. The odds of a kid with a disability from an immigrant single parent home, well, the odds of being successful are a lot smaller, luckily for me I was never good at statistics. Ultrarunning was a metaphor of our lives that I could teach my kids: hard doesn't mean impossible.

"Man can live about forty days without food, about three days without water, about eight minutes without air, but only for one second without hope "Unknown

Sunday, October 26, 2008

Sahara Race Update 1

Hi everybody, I am Carlos the older brother of Norma and a fan of her since she was born (she was good at cheating on cards when she was 4, Sorry Norma, enough embarrassment for a day). Anyway, I am commissioned with the task of posting what she is sending me via e-mail because she is currently running the Sahara Race and she is only allowed one e-mail a day, so in the next days I will be updating you and copy-pasting her e-mails. My website, in case you are wondering my credentials as a blogger, is Powerpymes. Here is her first post:

Now is the evening before the race and I am ready to go, I have met amazing people and made so many friendships that I am sure will last forever.However I am tired of traveling, I feel like in the movie "Planes, Trains and Automobiles". Egypt is a lot rockier than I ever imagine, in my mind the sand dunes were a lot smoother but in reality, there is a variety of landscapes. Because of recent events of the kidnappings, we endured so many checkpoints just to make the 258K to the middle of nowhere to then run around and run back where we started. The race is actually longer than 250K between 258 and 268 I am told, but I guess after your feet are hamburger it does really matter. I Missing being home and is not what I expected, I have been at home working and looking after my kids for so long I assume I was just going to jump into this new life and love it, but this as amazing and exotic as it is not home. My tent mates are fantastic, there are two Canadians, John is a physiotherapist and Lynn is an artist from Canmore, there is also Kumiko from Japan and I had a great chance to talk to her and practice my Japanese. Most important, the Korean blind runner and the Korean TV crew are also in my tent, is hard for me to watch him struggle and not want to look after him because I keep going back to my mom mode so I have to remind myself he is no Karl and to leave him alone. I am sure that as the race progresses he will teach me that he doesn't need me to look after him and neither does my son. Well, I better go back to my tent and sleep, tomorrow's stage isn't long only 38K, I am looking forward to moving again after sitting on trucks and busses for the last 4 days. Good night

Salam Alaikum

Norma

Monday, October 27, 2008

Sahara Race Update 2

Hi, this is Carlos again and this is what Norma told me to post:

Day one

What a day it was, I was excited today when I realized that it was going to be the only 36K, I forgot about the heat!. There where 3 legs in this stage, leg 1 and 2 I found hot but manageable since I was able to run and the running gave a nice breeze. Leg 3 was a nightmare, the sand was too deep to run so I walked almost the last 14K, walking is harder since you still break up a sweat but there is no breeze to cool off. I still managed to come in 5 hrs. and 18 min. as for placing I was told it was around to 50, so not bad at all. I hope I manage to sleep tonight, I didn't sleep at all last night, the ground is hard and there are 9 other smelly people on a crowded tent, I hope I am tired enough to fall asleep first before the snoring and farting start. As right now, I am taking it day by day, results mean nothing since there are a lot of other factors that come to play. Ryan Sandes won stage one at a blistering 3hrs and 5 min, Dean Karnazes is here as well, I talked to him only once, but he mostly keeps to himself on the tent. One of my tent mates was his roommate back at the hotel and he said he is fantastic but obviously really busy. Time for me to run back tent and see if I can fall asleep before everybody. Good night

Salam Alaikum

Tuesday, October 28, 2008

Sahara Race Update 3

Norma is well into the third day of the run but she made the time yesterday to send us an e-mail. In case you are wondering she's alive and kicking and the spirits are running high. Here's what she wrote:

Today was stage 38K and hot, we woke up to "Walking on Sunshine" at least the race directors have a sense of humor. The course had 3 legs with what I though the first leg hard and the other two moderate, it turns out to be the other way around. I am taking it one day at a time. Most people found it harder today, I felt better than since for the first time had a full night sleep. I am still not sure how I am going to do 4 more days. the next 3 are supposed to be 100% harder than the first two. Spirits around me are fading, the first day when we started we were told that if we got bitten by anything we were going to be pulled out immediately that night we all slept afraid of scorpions and snakes. Now we are all walking around barefooted and kicking rocks hoping to be bitten by something so we can go home with our dignity intact. Good night.

Salam Alaikum

Wednesday, October 29, 2008

Sahara Race Update 4

Well, I think Norma is suffering from delusion because she is thinking about taking a bath when returning home from her last stint: The Sahara Race. I proudly announce you she is very much alive, but no kicking, she's just too tired to do that and looking forward to two more days at the races (sorry the lame pun, used to be a Queen fan), so anyway here is what She emailed me yesterday:

Day 3 and I am still smiling, I love it. We started an hour earlier to beat the heat and it made such a difference. I ran solid for the first two stages then took it easy on the last since it was getting hotter. For scenery, it was flat and boring for the first 4 hrs. then we made it to the sand dunes and it was a quad-burning climb for the last stage but it is so beautiful to see. I don't know how I did for placing today but I was faster than the last two days, the reason being that my pack is getting lighter as we start to eat our food, I am also learning how much water I need for each stage, too much water is heavy not enough is deadly. The spirits around camp are high, the last two days have been so hard we all felt demoralized we still have two hard days coming but as long as we are still here we have a chance to finish. Good night

Salam Alaikum

Thursday, October 30, 2008

Sahara Race Update 5

Did you think Norma was on vacation?. Think twice because she is running 100K in the scorching sand of the Sahara. Do you think she had enough and running this race will turn her into a good stay at home mom, you know the ones that bake and the only time they think of the Sahara is when they watch

Brendan Fraser in "The Mummy", I am no betting on it! this is what she emailed me yesterday:

Wow, I guess they call it Sahara desert for a reason, after a wonderful day like yesterday I assumed I was climatizing but I guess not. Today it was supposed to be an easy 38K but the temperature raised to 41 Celsius, I had trouble coordinating my legs and I felt dizzy like I was drunk most of the time. As usual, there were 3 legs on this stage but this time I had a hard time running from the get-go. I know you are supposed to take it one day at a time but all I could think was that tomorrow is two and a half longer than any previous day. I am not worried about the distance but on these conditions: hot and on soft sand is definitely hard to run. Mario Lacerda from Brazil and welcome me to the race officially!!! There are two of his friends running Sahara and we are keeping each other company while talking about Brazil 135 which we are now all doing in January. I will not send an email tomorrow, I have my 100K which will test the human limits, I will be thinking of all of you that helped me get here if I am here it's because of all of you and I am so grateful to you. Good night.

Salam Alaikum

Saturday, November 1, 2008

Sahara Race Update 6

Well, Norma has made It, at this hour of the morning (I am writing this from Mexico) The Sahara Race is officially over and she did amazingly and in one piece. So she will be at home and posting next week in the meantime I will copypaste what she sent me:

I made it at 2:30am!. It was the longest 18hrs of my life, well excluding childbirth but really it was hard! the course was 100K and the sand makes it that much harder, I have had enough of gels and power bars for the rest of my life I ate them on this stage until I couldn't anymore. I am amazed at the level of difficulty, the race itself is hard with the heat and the sand, on top of that having to run with all your supplies on your back is just simply a test of endurance. I did really well the 3rd day but then on I had a harder time going. This stage was 9 legs with a distance ranging between legs from 7K to 14K. We started at 8am and the top 25 racers started two hours later, I felt fantastic the first stage and I got increasingly weaker and weaker. I have run 100K races before so I knew not to get emotional and to run my own race so that it's what I did and I am glad, in the end, I had absolutely nothing left. but I finished and that was my first and most important goal. I rest today since there are people still on the course, there was the option to sleep around halfway or go all the way, of course, I decided to do it on one go. I am not sure why I didn't do better, I think 12:30am would have been possible but I just couldn't run anymore so I walked for most of the course and if you think that is easier, It is not, I was out there in the elements, heat and later the cold with hardly any food and walking on soft sand, what Simon my tent mate described is equal to trying to run on ice. I saw Ryan and Dean round leg 3, it was amazing to see how fast they were running,

Nina the top female finisher from Germany also passed me around Leg 4, she was looking strong as well. We have only 6K to go tomorrow so this is it, they will load up in a bus at 2am tomorrow to the start line which is by the Giza Pyramids to have friends and family watch the finish of the race. I am proud that I gave it 100% and sometimes especially last night when walking on soft sand, tired, hungry, cold and with 10 more hours to go it felt like 150%.I have also met wonderful people this week, some are athletes that came to win, some are like me that come to represent a charity and some are just plain nuts, but we all have one thing in common, we came here to give it our best and that is exactly what we did, some won, some finished and some didn't but at the end that didn't matter, we accomplished what we set out to do this week. To me pushing more and more each time I think I can't possibly give me an insight of what it is to face a challenge like a disability, I would never pretend to understand how tough it really is, it just makes me have more respect for kids like my son Karl or any other human facing a disability knowing that I had a choice every day to say this is too hard and chose the easy way, not for my son, he can't take that choice. I go back to a normal life, but he can't do that, this is his life always. I am also learning about not taking things for granted, I miss having a shower, a nice meal, clean clothes, seeing my loved ones, having a cup of coffee. We have built our life with excesses and conveniences that we forget that all we really need human beings is the simple things in life.

Salam Alaikum

Tuesday, November 4, 2008

"A Journey Of a Thousand Miles Must Begin With a Single Step." Lao Tzu

Wow. what intense 10 days. Thanks to my brother Carlos in Mexico who did an amazing job of posting for me. I arrived yesterday and the memories of pain and discomfort are already distant, instead of memories of the amazing people I met, the fantastic racecourse, the feeling of pride after finishing the race remains. Just like Simon and Yukako said back at our tent when I called them "idiots" because we were all in pain and trying to settle for the night after the 100K, they both had run a similar race in the past. " unfortunately Norma you too will forget the pain tonight and remember only the fun stuff". I ended up finishing 46th overall, 6th female and 1st in my age group, I really didn't say much when they gave me my trophy. I really wasn't expecting to win anything, I was more in a survival mode. So, how tough it really was? It was tough for many reasons, one being the distance itself was daunting, the heat made it very tough as well but to me, the hardest part was the isolation. I talked to my kids only once on the phone, the time change and the fact that the areas are so remote and we had no access to phone lines or the Internet made it impossible to keep in touch with loved ones. Except for the daily email I sent, I had no way of communicating at all. Food was a major issue as well, dehydrated food isn't exactly a delicacy, every day we will lay in our tents and talk about food cravings " food porn" as one of the guys used to describe it. The course itself was hard as well, running on the sand was incredibly tiring and every day we weren't sure what to expect, the race course changes every year so even the runners who had done it before had no idea of what to expect day to day and even after the morning briefing we found out that an easy leg wasn't easy or a hard one wasn't hard so it was emotionally hard because it made you feel isolated, I remember thinking *if this is supposed to be easy and I am struggling, I might not have what it takes.* But in the end, all that matters is the amazing way it changed my life. I got to be in one of the most remote and beautiful areas in the world, every day waking up to a different majestic landscape. I got to spend one week with a select group of individuals that are inspiring and motivating. When I arrived I couldn't wait to meet Dean Karnazes, and it was amazing for sure, he is every bit what I imagine him to be, classy, graceful, positive, amazing but when looked around so where the other 155 runners. I had to honor to talk to some amazing individuals. Ryan and Nina the overall winners were amazing and inspiring to watch, such amazing athletes, others had amazing stories, mothers lost to cancer, husbands that were living with brain injuries, people that wanted to help complete strangers because they felt a duty to make a difference in the world. Looking around I couldn't help to feel blessed to have known this individuals and to have the honor to share a week of my life with them. All I remember now are the laughs in our tent, hugging each other after a tough day, waking up to a beautiful sunset, the first time a saw a majestic sand dune, the kids from the villages that came to our cheer us and ultimately sell us sodas and chips on our last night in our camp, watching Onoh the blind runner cross the finish line, finishing by the pyramids, my first bite of pizza after the race, the sensation of water on my first shower after 7 days in the desert, my first latte' at the airport in Cairo... the list will go on and on. I will start training for Brazil Monday, Ray is sending me the training plan for the next couple of weeks. He told me not to exercise this week and to eat as much as I want to which is good because I am tired and don't feel like going for a run yet and I am so hungry all the time so it works for me.

Friday, December 19, 2008

"Though We Travel The World Over To Find The Beautiful, We Must Carry It With Us Or We Find It Not." Ralph Waldo Emerson

It's been a couple of months since I quit my job to pursue running and fundraising and I have been really busy. I have finalized my schedule for next year. I will be running 7 ultras in 7 continents in 7 months, right now I am concentrating on Brazil because it's my first race, I will start running with a sleigh next week. It has been incredibly rewarding working on the schedule and a lot of fun working with the race directors to find the best possible race on each continent. Other races are not part of the schedule that I am looking forward, I still would love to run Badwater one day. Ray who is still in Antarctica is writing my training, I have to say that I was really upset when I first saw the training schedule, I have track workouts and tempo runs, I have never attempted to run both long and fast but thankfully I am doing great if ever so tired. I have graduated to a triple Latte in the last month. So while I have quit working to run it's really difficult to answer the question " What do you do?" I don't know how to answer, is not like I am an athlete. The reason why I am sponsored right now is because I am running a successful fundraising campaign, not because I am a gifted athlete. Don't worry, I am hardly complaining. N.Murray Edwards asked me Monday at a party the question that often gets asked to all ultrarunners: " Why?" "I understand your son, but besides that why do it?" Murray and his wife Heather are big patrons of cnib. I, of course, listed all the great things about participating in endurance sports, but I just couldn't convince him. Much later at home, I kept asking myself the same question, if my son were to all of a sudden be cured, would I stop running and the answer was NO. Somewhere, somehow, it became my passion. Murray and successful people like him (just in case you don't know, Murray Edwards is one of Canada's wealthiest individuals) understands passion and hard work. However, his passion and hard work makes him very wealthy, while mine makes me really happy and fit. So to society, a passion that makes you wealthy is something that is easier to understand than a passion that makes you happy. Looking at each other that evening we wouldn't have traded places for anything in the world, but each in our own way had

found what drives us to the point where most people think is
impossible, and that is what dreams are made off.

Thursday, January 15, 2009

**"It's 3am and I Can't Sleep, Well I Can't Help But be
Scared of it All Sometimes, She Says the Rain's Gonna
Wash Away I Believe It" Matchbox Twenty**

I am having trouble sleeping, I leave for Brazil in a few days
and things are far from being ready. I am still waiting on my
visa, Mario told me that I can fly to Argentina and get it at the
border but it's still stressing me out because I don't like the
uncertainty of it. I have Antarctica and Brazil are back to back.
Brazil is Jan 23 to the 25th, I need to finish Brazi135 in under
48 hrs. to make my flight from Sao Paolo to Cape Town Jan
26th to get on a Russian cargo plane the 28th to go to
Novolazarevskaya base in Antarctica and I will be running
100K as soon as I land. No wonder I can't sleep. Richard
Donovan is marking the course and officiating the race to make
it official, we have never met in person but I feel like I know
him so well having been talking to him so much. Richard was a
key part of making it possible in 7 months, the amazing thing is
that he is the first person in the world to run 7 races in 7
continents in a single calendar year, so it will be an honor
meeting him finally. Thankfully everything else seem to be
going well, my mom arrived from Mexico and my niece
Marianna arrived from Spain to look after my kids so I am not
worried about them, they will be so loved that will hardly miss

me. All the charities, cnib, OEU and FFB are all behind me, Bolt Supply House my sponsor has been amazing and decided to sponsor me for this year as well so I am not left scrambling trying to find the funds and I feel my training has been right for this kind of challenge especially now that Ray overlooks my training, I mean, he just broke the world record to the South Pole!, who better than him to overlook my training. My head is in the right space, I have worked on this project for so long I feel ready, so why am I awake? Karl went for testing yesterday, he went to see a specialist in genetic disorders that affect the vision. After all, the reason to be as involved as I am is to find the best possible care and options. I have heard that there are going to start human testing on a cure for Cone Rod Dystrophy. First, they needed to determine all the history of the illness to see what is available to him. What happened next I am still trying to figure out. " Your son has a very rare disease, Bardet-Biedl Syndrome, BBS for short, his vision is a by-product of it as where his extra digits (he was born with 1 extra finger and two extra toes) .This illness affects other organs, the good news is that his vision will stay stable until much later in life (he did say good news) my colleague and I agree in this diagnosis but we need to do more testing to see where he fits in until recently they were only a few types of this disorder, now there are twelve, we don't feel there is much concern but to avoid unnecessary stress we will hold the diagnosis until we can properly know which type he has"

" *She's got a little bit of something, God it's better than nothing*

And in her color portrait world, she believes that she's got it all
She swears the moon don't hang quite as high as it used to
And she only sleeps when it's raining
And she screams and her voice is straining" 3AM song Matchbox Twenty"

" This is a genetic disorder is nothing you did, mom and dad have to both carry this very rare gene to pass it down" all I could think at this point was the play that I listen to at Dining in the Dark, a fundraising event for FFB where you eat blindfolded and listen to a play. In the play the man explained his genetic condition as his both of his parents bringing bread to the picnic and no sandwich meat. My ex and I, we both brought bread to the party I though. I left the office to confused, is it good?, after all his vision has been of concern for me for the last 3 years and it will be stable for the most part of? he will qualify for extra aid at school enabling him to stay at a regular school a concern that came up at the last parent-teacher interview that despite the special accommodations his grades are still slipping. I was left feeling like I been building a castles and it was actually made out of glass and it just shattered in front of me. is it too soon to push the panic button? Talking to Nadia I told her I felt like I open door number 3 just to find door number 4 behind "Honey" Nadia said " I think you open door number 87" " you been doing this for a long time". Somebody said to me that I somehow attract trouble when explaining my past relationships. I am pretty mellow but my life is anything but, ironic isn't? So here I am, exactly where I found myself a few years ago, unable to fall back asleep, the reason why I started running is that I couldn't sleep, I am so grateful to have some races coming up, I am sorry that I will be gone for long but I need to be out there alone in nature to figure out what is my purpose in life is ; I find is through the pain that we find ourselves. And with hope this is somehow a way the universe reminding me the is not over, and that I still have a lot of work to do. We repeat the lessons in life we haven't learned. Oh, by the way, I peeked behind door number 87, I saw door number 88. Clearly, I haven't learned this lesson yet.

Monday, January 19, 2009

"Life's Challenges Are Not supposed to Paralyze you, They're Supposed to Help You Discover Who You Are". Bernice Johnson Reagon

WOW. I am overwhelmed by the amount of press **777 Run For Sight** is generating, is just unbelievable. This is beyond my wildest dreams! I get hugged by complete strangers now. Only an hour after the press release went out, I was already doing TV, Radio and newspaper interviews. Impact Magazine is also running an article on about my quest in the summer issue I can't believe it. My favorite part is that I get to hear from a lot of people that are being affected by blindness or vision loss either themselves or a family member, It is hard to feel alone anymore. I also received a lot support from my friends and family about Karl's new diagnosis my favorite is my friend Alan's text. "As long as you are moving forward and opening doors, it doesn't matter if it's door #284. But if the doors are not working out the way you like, try to look for a window"

I have decided to take it one day at a time and that this is just a minor bump in the road to greatness. I am off to Brazil tomorrow but before I go I met Robert Kennedy Jr, and his wife Mary Richardson Kennedy at Waterkeepers Gala in Lake Louise and they offered their support, I was worry that when they found out I was a crazy runner they would just look at me and feel sorry, but to my surprise, they are incredibly down to earth and we had a lot in common since they too are passionate about leaving a better world for their kids and they happen to have lots of friends that are adventurers. This is it!!!! 777 Run For Sight her I come!

Thursday, January 22, 2009

Running Wild in the Amazon Part I

Hi everybody, this is Carlos posting on behalf of my younger sister Norma. In case you haven't heard of me It is not too late to start reading my musings in my blog Powerpymes (It is in Spanish but I have a handy translator in situ), anyway I will be feeding you the next weeks what Norma send me to post here because She is having so much fun running in the rain and developing blisters (ughhh!) What causes a young woman of good looks to leave it all behind and expose yourself gratuitously to anacondas and piranhas is beyond me but I think maybe Norma should start spiking her morning coffee with

Ritalin and hopefully she will mellow out a bit, she making all of us look bad. Enough, down below is what she sent us:

Only a few hours to the race and I am so nervous I am not sure where to begin. Brazil is a wonderful country, I was surprised by the infrastructure, at least the highway from the airport to Pocos de Caldas where is the start to the race. I haven't slept much, a bit jet lag and a bit nervous, I haven't had much chance to think about the enormous challenge I am about to take on until I jumped on the plane, and it all came at once. To be an ultrarunner you need short term memory, after the pain and the sleep deprivation all it will remain will be the memories of majestic trails, fantastic positive people (you have to be a positive person to think "only 80K to go") but the best of all is the feeling of having accomplished something that makes you grow as a person, and ultra is a lifetime in a day. I have mixed feelings, I know I have trained hard and that I belong here, but since I have never done this race is hard to predict if I can finish it in under 50 hours to make my flight, that makes me a bit nervous. To make matter worse is raining hard and it will make the course unsteady and it will be impossible to avoid blisters, I will need every ounce of mental strength to tell my body to keep running under such pain. I could have rescheduled this race and choose a different race in North America a bit later, not so close to Antarctica but I had committed to this race a few months ago and had a school for the blind waiting for me. I told them I will bring a donation of $1000 dollars from my sponsors .I know that I could have chosen to just mail the donation to

AADV (Associacao de Assistencia Aos Deficientes Visuales) but the main message would have been lost, I wanted to empower other racers to be more involved on the places we visit, I wanted the representative of the school for the blind to stand proud in the auditorium, to know that we are a very small world. I do promise everybody that I will run hard tomorrow,. Matt Cordes and Jason Glass, two Calgary young men who happen to be in Brazil on holidays will be my support crew. I want to dedicate Brazil 135 Ultramarathon to a very special person in Calgary, nine-month-old Hayden who is legally blind due to optic Nerve Atrophy and CVI. Hayden's mom and dad send me an email to thank me because Hayden was born blind and they have been heartbroken thinking they failed their son, seeing the article in the paper with the photo of my son Karl and I made them realized, they are going to be okay.

Monday, January 26, 2009

I Am Alive!!

Hi, this is Carlos again, Norma is currently sleeping in Cape Town, South Africa waiting to be on a vessel to the Russian base in Antarctica to run 100 Km more. By the way J. M Coetzee one of my favorite writers was born there and He used to teach at the University of Cape Town before moving to Australia. You should read " Disgrace" just to feel the loneliness of being a man in a modern world. Anyway, Norma sent us the next post about what happened in Brazil. Curious?:

I survived Brazil! when I was first told about Brazil 135 ultramarathon I believed it but you never know how true it is until you are there. The race took place Friday the 23rd at 8:30 am and I finish the crossing line 50 hours and 20 minutes according to my watch. What happened in those 50 hours would have shown me a lot about real strength comes from within. I was so worried about rain but thankfully stayed dry for the three days of the race. The temperature was hot around 32 degrees centigrade but because it was overcast it was bearable. Matt and Jason drove me to the start line, it felt a lot more like a high school field trip than an endurance event, all the runners and crew hanging around waiting for the gun go off, Brazilian music playing in the background. there was a lot of picture taking and hugging as well. My favorite part of any ultra-race is the beginning when I get to talk to other runners when we all still have the energy or the focus to listen. The first 18 hours where OK, I saw my crew every 15K or so, I tried to keep a steady pace, something that I thought I could maintain for a long time, I felt just fine, there were a lot of casualties and injuries at the beginning, this is where most of the 10 runners that didn't finish dropped out, most of the them because they go out too fast and just crash and burn. At about 4:30 am after 20 hours of running I could barely stand up, fatigue just overtook me, It was hard to be motivated to keep going when I knew I still had longways to go. At 4am I was negotiating an hour nap with my crew, their role was to remind me I had to make my flight and they took their job very seriously, I quickly did calculations in my head to show them I had a window for sleeping for 30 minutes, and they asked me If I was going to be able to run after and I said absolutely but in reality I had no idea, fortunately I was able to. The next 10 hours where an absolute nightmare. The race is long and the elevation gain and loss have your lungs burning because is hard to breathe or you quad burns from running downhill. Matt and Jason took a turn running/walking during the night to keep me awake and to also keep me safe because I was delirious. The next day was a lot harder knowing I still had another night to go through, I hit many highs and lows each peak higher than the last one. There were times where I didn't think I was going to find the strength to continue, especially after tone of my toenails started coming off from the pounding, some parts of the course were so steep you couldn't run any other way but on your tiptoe. I hit my first major low when I reached 100 miles, my toenail just ripped from my toe and I thought I was going to pass out from the excruciating pain. Isn't that what they do to torture you? ripping the toenails. The following night I learned the meaning of digging deep, there is no way I was quitting but that didn't make the pain go away, Matt and Jason where amazing on trying to do their best to keep me on time, they took turns pacing me again the second night, not a small thing considering they had never run more than 12K in their life, their approach to crewing me was very nonsense, if I stopped I wouldn't make my flight, plain and simple so no matter what I had to keep going even when I begged them to stop. I started to hallucinate like I was on mushrooms. I saw soldiers hiding behind bushes waiting to attack, alligators in the middle of the road and even though I kept telling myself that they couldn't be real I went around them trying not to step on my imaginary friends. After 46 hours of running and in excruciating pain I finally collapsed on a park bench, my support car was not there because of a misunderstanding of the meeting point so I just lay there and slept for about 40 minutes. With 17K to go, I sent the guys to sleep since none of us had slept much, and I needed them to drive me back to Sao Paolo to get on my flight as soon as I crossed the finish line, this is the leg of the race that I really took the time to admire my surrounding, I was still very tired but something had changed, but now It was really that I was going to finish and that gave me enough energy to keep running, also the Brazilian pacers for other runners left their runner to pace me, all because they heard that I had brought a donation to the local charity, one more proof that kindness attracts kindness. I crossed the finish line holding hands with Matt and Jason, I am forever grateful for the kind words and the arm that they offered when I had a hard time walking on a straight line. Next is an account of what NOT to do after a race, after a quick visit with the media and gently refusing a marriage proposal from a 12-year-old boy, I showered just before jumping on a car then a long 11 hour flight to Capetown. I am now waiting for my plane to Antarctica, thankfully It was delayed for two days, so I have time to heal before my next 100K. Thanks to the articles being published in my hometown, I have received a lot of support, people that I don't even know are emailing me to tell me they are cheering for me and my family. Three years ago when my son was diagnosed I felt so alone, now I know I wasn't, just like Karl said on his first day in preschool, "Look, mom, look at all the friends I haven't met" I wasn't alone. I just hope I can somehow make somebody out there who is feeling alone know that I am a friend that they haven't met yet.

Saturday, January 31, 2009

Two Continents Conquered, Five to Go.

I am back in Cape Town after being in Antarctica for three days and it all seems like a dream. I met Richard Donovan in Cape Town South Africa to make our journey to Antarctica. Richard is the organizer of the Antarctic Ice Marathon and the North Pole Marathon. He has the credentials to measure the course and officiate it for me. He is well known in the ultrarunning community because of his racing history but it was his long running feud with none other than Dean Karnazes that he is more famous for. Richard claims he beat Dean in Antarctica at the first ever run in the continent but North Face decided to declare Dean the winner because it was their athlete, scandalous, I know!, It sounded a lot like Richard Hatch and Susan Hawk rivalry to me!!!. We entered Antarctica by flying to Novolazarevska Station a Russian, formerly Soviet Antarctic research station. The station is located at Schirmacher Oasis, Queen Maud Land, 75 km from the Antarctic coast. The reason for choosing this place is that it has the best statistics on a plane leaving and arriving on time if there are delays the delays are usually of only a couple of days. We left for Antarctica Jan 28th, in the plane there were also 30 other scientists making their way to different research facilities, most of them belong to the first zero-emission research station Princess Queen Antarctica that is opening soon. We arrived in Novo runway at 4 pm, the weather was a balmy -3C but word got out that the weather was about to turn, so Richard hurried to mark the course so I could get going as soon as possible. For safety reasons I was to run a 2.5K stretch going north and come back for what it will be a 5K loop. Because of the snow on the ground and the incline, the loop was energy zapping. So at 8pm Jan 28th, the race officially began. I wanted to make it in under 24hrs, the finish cut of time of the official Antarctica marathon race that Richard marshals' every year. I have run a 100K before in less than 13 hours but this was right after Brazil and I couldn't bear wearing shoes because my toe was now exposed after the toenail came off in Brazil. Richard lent me his 10 1/2 size Salomon trail runners because I couldn't stand any friction on my toes. At about 2am the weather got worse, poor visibility due to the snow falling and blowing and it dipped to about -15C not really cold but cold enough for me to cover from head to toe since the wind felt bitterly cold. By 6am I had done only 45K, I was tired and cold when Richard told me to take a break because the course had become too difficult to monitor and he needed to find an alternative route. I went to bed feeling guilty but I also knew that there was still a chance to do it in less than 24 hours. So a few hours later after breakfast, I started running again around 11am. It sure felt like a Club Med race considering in Brazil I only managed an hour and a half sleep and a few bites here and there over 50 hours but I also understood that this was about safety. The next 55K went fast if a bit boring, I ran back and forth along the airport runway, my ankle had now become swollen due to the fact I was wearing horribly ill-fitted shoes. Despite it all, 23 hours 35 minutes and 02 seconds later I finished Antarctica Marathon 100K Race. It was right after I finished running that I got to really get to know Antarctica, I walked into the cafeteria to find out a group of individuals that were clearly not a scientist just by looking at their badly frostbitten faces and fingers, that and the fact that they smell a lot worse than me and I just finished running 100K that told me there were there for similar reason. It turned out, these where the competitors of the first-ever South Pole Race, six teams battled for 6 weeks on cross country skis to be the first team to the Pole, among the competitors there were UK TV personality Ben Fogle, UK Olympic gold medalist in rowing James Cracknell, but there was one person that captivated us all, also competing Mark Pollock an Irish blind adventurer and author of the book " Making it Happen". Mark is very well known in the endurance sports circuit, having gone blind in the space of two weeks in 1998 Mark rapidly learned how to adapt to changing circumstances, that made him, incredibly though and delightful to be around. He is witty and very modest, I spent the next day getting to know more about all the competitors, I listen to their pain and suffering hey had endured in the last 6 weeks, most of the participants were there in the name of a charity. Sitting there I couldn't help but feel amazed and incredibly lucky to be sharing a meal with such an amazing and intimidating group. I mean these 6 teams endured so much the last 6 weeks all in the name of a charity of their choice. I felt a bit humbled by them, Rachel one of the two females competitors notice I was a bit uncomfortable when they asked me to share my story, it seemed silly to tell them how hard it had been for me in Brazil, and how tired I felt to run 100K more in Antarctica, how I for the first time since I started running, I had not enjoyed running. Rachel looked at me and said, in my opinion, what you are doing is more difficult, you are running a greater distance we had done, and basically, we just walked for 6 weeks. Looking at all of them, frostbitten faces and fingers, sunken eyes, gaunt bodies, it was really obvious that they had done more than just go for a walk, but I appreciated that they included me as one of them. That night I called home, I wanted to talk to my kids, I was thrilled to tell them all about how cool it was to be standing in Antarctica, the research stations, the South Pole races, but just as they answer the phone, Hans, my 10 year- old son told me very excitedly that he had shaved 3 seconds off his swim time on freestyle, just like that, nothing mattered, not Brazil, not Antarctica, nothing mattered more at that moment than to hear my kids talk about their triumphs and dreams. I have been going all over the world just to reinforce what I already know, the best place in the world for me is home. Just like Nelson Mandela once said, the world is truly round and it seemed to start and end with those we love.

Sunday, March 1, 2009

A Love Story.

My niece Marianna and I finished building my sled for 6633 Ultra and I took it for a four-hour run. We struggle with the design for days arguing since it fails to work several times. I joked with her that if we had been the group WHAM today at around 2pm it would have been when George Michael and Andrew Ridgeley disbanded. Finally, around 4pm it was finished and I was happy to go for a test, I think my niece was happy to see me leave for a few hours as well. As I was leaving I waved and yelled: *"Can you believe I never remarried?" "Such a catch"*. After a few adjustments, the sled worked just fine, considering I used whatever materials I could use from a bike child carrier and an ice fishing sled. Today was my long run and I couldn't be any happier. There has been a lot on my mind lately, from just the regular challenges of a single parent who travels a lot, to the races itself, to dealing with Karl's new diagnosis. When I run I can hear the silence, it's like there is nothing there but the road and me, very cleansing. 6633 is proven to be a very difficult race to plan and I am sure it will be to execute as well. I am consumed with details on what to wear, eat and race plan such as when to sleep, I am trying to work every possible scenario since it's such a difficult race, the wrong kind of sleeping bag can mean the difference between finishing or not finishing. I am feeling a bit better about it, I am getting to the point where I think that I can only do my best and see what that means. The training that Ray has me on makes me feel like a drunken Koala, I am incoherent by 7pm! This is where my fingers have a hard time typing on the keyboard right now, Karl was diagnosed with Bardet-Biedl Syndrome or BBS for short, the specialist doesn't think I have much to worry about but the truth is that it's hard not to. in short, this is what BBS prognosis is:

Growth and development: Mental and growth retardation

Behavior and performance: Poor visual acuity and blindness

Eyes: Rod-cone dystrophy (sometimes called atypical retinitis pigmentosa), myopia, strabismus, and cataracts

Hand and foot: Polydactyly, syndactyly or brachydactyly

Cardiovascular system: Hypertrophy of interventricular septum and left ventricle and dilated cardiomyopathy

Gastrointestinal system: Hepatic fibrosis, central obesity and diabetes mellitus

Urogenital system: Hypogonadism, renal failure,4 urogenital sinuses, ectopic urethra, uterus duplex, septate vagina, and hypoplasia of the uterus, ovaries, and fallopian tubes.

In short, there is a high risk of renal failure. Karl is still going for further testing to determine which of the 12 kinds of BBS he has since he is not obese or mentally challenged the prognosis is good, most likely is a mild case. This, however, was brought a new range of feeling, I felt silly running for Karl's vision after finding out that that was going to be the least of my worries. My niece Marianna joked to get charities logos on Velcro to put in my running jersey, blind!, kidney failure! Hear disease! My family has a ready dark humor!!. Running brought a bit of clarity and peace, I am running for the love of my kids no matter what they call what he has, it is still for them. I also feel blessed to think that if it wasn't for all my crazy quest to find a cure I wouldn't have met the doctor that wanted to know, the "why" this was happening. Now the doctors can monitor his health. I just make me feel that the purpose just got a bit deeper so it's not likely that I am going to go away anytime soon. I plan on making as much noise as possible. It is strange how my journey is going in a completely different direction than I anticipated, I went to church today for the first time in a really long time. While I hadn't become an atheist, I just didn't go to church anymore. In Brazil at a very tough time, I asked God to help me get past the pain, I was also scared of running alone on the deserted roads, I never thought I was going to find my way back to a pew on an ultrarace but this is my journey and I intend to follow it no matter where it takes me. On my run I also reflected about the whole generic lottery, the odds of Karl being born with BBS are infinite, both his father and I have to be carriers and of course this is something that my kids have to take into consideration when choosing a spouse, there is always a risk of passing the gene, I imagine my choice if I had knowledge of this, would I have gone and married their father? and the truth is that how could I not, my kids are perfect in every way, I feel terrible and wish that this was happening to me and not Karl but he is the most amazing kid in the world. I just watched Slumdog Millionaire and it reminded me that powerful love stories happen in many different forms and sometimes under amazing circumstances. Maybe this is how my love story was supposed to unfold. I am the kid covered in shit smiling because I felt so lucky.

Friday, March 13, 2009

"Wish You Were Here"

As you are reading this Norma is off to compete in one of her most daunting races to date. She sent me an email to post it here for you to know what is going on in that part of the world. She has the company of Claudia Katz an excellent photographer and they will try to keep us updated if there is a cybercafe on her route thru the wilderness of the Arctic Circle :). She is running the 6633Ultra and fearing it. So as you may, or not, remember my name is Carlos and I am a Tech Blogger from Mexico and Norma's brother. Before I post It I must tell you that I received truncated because of the tech limitations of writing from that part of the world, but you can understand the spirit of what she is telling us, so here it is:

There are 9 competitors in total, all male except for me. As it also turns out, I am the first Canadian to ever participate in the race, where the majority of the competitors are British and one American. This is the third year the race has been held, with the first year having only 3 finishers and last year only one. Both years won by a female, so overnight I went from being the underdog to favorite. We had a long discussion on the reason why females historically perform better at this race even though they represent a very small number. I have said that to be successful on extreme ultras you need to have no common sense and short term memory. The reason why the failure to finish the race is so high is the fact that is 100% self-supported, I will be running pulling a sled with all my survival gear and isolation will be a major issue as well as the high wind, we will be running through Wright Pass where the highest winds in the world have been recorded. There will be two checkpoints in between of nothing more than a wind shelter and a couple of parked cars where we will be allowed to sit to escape the wind. I had to make my own sled since I couldn't locate one of the specialized sleds that are commonly used on this type of Arctic race, that and the fact that they are almost as much as my mortgage payment to purchase. So I took a hard look at it and fabricated one with part of ice fishing sled, a bike child carrier, and plumbing pipes. I felt silly when I arrived with my homemade sled, sort of like what a Rolling Stones cover band would feel if invited to perform with the real Rolling Stones, but after we took it for a test drive yesterday the guys were feeling a bit embarrassed to have a handywoman on the team. While I wouldn't t say I am looking forward to the race or that you would enjoy it if you were here, I Wish you were here. I arrived at the Yukon Monday for 6633 Ultra, after spending 3 days in Whitehorse for gear testing and course briefing we made an overnight stop in Dawson City and finally to Eagle Plains for the start of the race. If you ever find yourself in Dawson City, don't miss the opportunity to try the Sourtoe Cocktail where you drink a cocktail with a real frostbitten toe in it, it was the worst thing I have ever done but being part of a hardcore group is hard to set limits on how crazy you really are, crazy enough to run 120 miles in the Arctic while pulling a sled but not enough to try a drink with a mutilated body part, is an argument I sure to lose so I just bottoms up the shot when it was my turn to drink it. The story on how this bizarre celebration can be found on Ripley' s Believe It Or Not. There are less than two days to the start of the race and I am still overwhelmed with doubt, I am not going to lie, I am completely unsure if I have what it takes and there is absolutely nothing about this race that will motivate me enough to want to do it if I was not doing it for the reasons that I am. Running (or mostly power walking) 120 miles, pulling a sled half my weight, on extreme weather is enough to make me want to cry. But this race is also going to teach me a lot about courage, determination and overcoming fear. The race will start Friday at 8am in Dawson City and finish Monday at 8am in Fort McPherson following predominately the Dempster Highway. Giving me 71 hours to finish since we lose an hour when we enter the North West Territories. The race is mostly run on the Arctic Circle giving the name 6633 after the latitude where the race takes place. There are 2 categories in the race 120 miles and 350 miles. There is three of us in the 120-mile distance, and 6 on the 350-

mile distance this race, I have made peace with the fact that I am here, it will be incredibly hard and I have done this race since it will be one of the races that I will refer to if I am ever to speak about overcoming challenges and fear. And that was the biggest obstacle I had to overcome fear, Hans my son had a hard time letting me come to this race saying he was afraid that something might happen, he asked me why if I was afraid I was doing it, the truth is that even though I am afraid of this race, I am more afraid of watching my son Karl go blind he is not afraid of his condition progressing but I am and I need to find a way to deal with this situation and not make it my own. What I am doing now might not mean a cure but I much rather live my life knowing I have done anything in my power to contribute. Motivation is temporary, inspiration is infinite.

Sunday, March 15, 2009

6633 Ultra Update

I am home and sad about the outcome. At about 4 am on Friday and after only 70K I decided to pull from the race. The main reason why I decided it was time to go home was that I didn't think I could continue the race safely. This very serious races and they should be taken as such. I hurt my back when the wheels on my sled froze. 6633 Ultra is a truly a self-supported race, continuing under such circumstances would have been irresponsible. The temperature had dipped to minus 50C if you take into account the windshield and my sleeping bag had frozen. I discovered that if I used heat packs on my baklava and mitts I was still warm I was safe but for how long? checkpoints where usually 43K apart, that is a long way is you are running with a sled and add slowing down because I was running injured it could take a long time to make it to each checkpoint. At around 20 hours into the race I was once more experiencing pain and getting worse, the first time, I took ibuprofen and sat at a car at the first checkpoint for about 45 minutes while they brought a new sled for me because some participants had dropped out already and they wanted to lent me a sled that wasn't frozen. I felt great when I started to run again but about 8 hours later the pain returned and I failed to make the next checkpoint and had to be helped. This is what it crossed my mind, I was only one-third of the race done, getting weaker and weaker since eating and drinking on the course was impossible at night, I already had frostbite on the tip of my nose from exposure, and I wasn't sure that spending three more evenings battling the elements unable to move fast was a smart decision. I got a ride to the checkpoint two and got my back checked, I left the sled to mark the course something that it's mandatory if you want to continue, you are allowed to leave the course at any time as long as you return to your same location to continue after. I didn't think that it was fair that I was forcing them to babysit me, the minimum expected for an athlete is to make it checkpoint and I had failed to make it safely. It was time to pull the plug. Andrew and Douglas both finish the 120-mile race and there are still two other competitors on the course for the 350-mile race. Am I sad because I quit? not really, although I did learn a lot, I have to be very responsible and I had 5 other races to finish so I had that too to think about. While there is always a risk when competing in endurance events but I have a responsibility to my kids that I would not do something stupid, crazy yes stupid never. I didn't feel disappointed when I finished the race, I was exhausted and I was somewhat relieved to be in a warm car resting. It was not until much later that regret hit. I am looking into other North American races to continue with the quest, I am excited once more with the anticipation on what other race I will be adding to my list, I do hope this time is going to be on a warmer location, after Antarctica and the Arctic I think I deserve it. So it won't be long before I will be back doing what I do best, running wild.

Tuesday, March 24, 2009

Mea Culpa.

Boy did I ever get in trouble, Martin the race director of 6633 Ultra wants me to clarify somethings from my last post. I really didn't want to sensationalize 6633 Ultra while I wanted to reflect on the internal struggles that happen in the race I want to make sure that everybody knows I was never in danger of dying. I failed to make it checkpoints and that is the minimum expected when you sign for that race, Martin and his crew did a great job of helping his athletes it was me that after all had a hard time on the race. There re somethings that I need to clarify. I hurt my back and had my sled switched and everything was fine. When they checked on my during at night I was fine, it was not until I undid my sled harness that the sharp pain came, I tried to sleep on the course and that is the reason why the left me, I never told that my back was hurting, they had already left thinking I was going to be down for a couple of hours. It was when I strapped my sled again to continue because I was getting colder in my bivvy that the pain became too much so I set out again with my arms behind my back holding the sled underneath to relieve the pain. I would have made it checkpoint on my own for sure but when I saw the car passing I decided to ask for help because I knew it was over by then. The frostbite was not visible until the morning light when I had already left the course that we notice the bridge of my nose was black. My apologies again to Martin and his team, they were great and I am sorry that it came across as whining. I have been thinking a lot about the race and regret hit a few days ago, I think the only way I can make peace is to return and run it once more, there are no guarantees that next time will be better, I know of athletes that have returned and they are a force to quit even sooner than the time before but I will never know if I can do better if I don't return. A lot of people asked me about my equipment, I did try it beforehand but it was always from warm to cold, I took my gear out to try out but it had been nicely stored at home warm, next time I will leave it out for a couple of days then try it.

Updated note:

In 2019 tried the Yukon Ultra 400 mile race, a similar race in the Arctic Circle and once again came short. This time however when I had to quit I cried when I was in my warm hotel bed, not wanting to quit but knowing it was the right decision. I will be returning for sure and finishing this race will be my quest for as many tries as it will take me.

Saturday, March 28, 2009

Australia

I am writing on the plane. Leslie and I are on our way to Australia. This time I am traveling with a crew. Leslie Gerein and experienced ultrarunner and adventurer from Banff and Jason Glass who also supported me in Brazil is waiting in Sydney for us. From Sydney, we will board a Plane to Albury then a two-hour drive to our final destination Harrietville, Victoria. I will be arriving Friday evening in time for the mandatory meeting and I will be ready to start the race at 4:30am on Saturday, it will not give me any time to write the pre-race report. I can tell you however what I know about the race. 17 people are running the race in total, two teams of 7 people each and 3 soloists, one male and two females including me. The race starts at 4:30am on Saturday 28th and ends 48 hours later on Monday 30th at 4:30am. I am as nervous going into this race as I was going into my race in Brazil, not completing the 3366 Ultra Race has made me feel unsure that I might not have what it takes after all to finish what I started. But I have to try, I don't want to live my life with regret, that and the fact that my attitude is being observed by mi kids. I want them to never give up hope that impossible things can be achieved with the right attitude and determination. And what I am bringing to the table on this race, is something that my son has taught me the last two years of him dealing with his disability, an indomitable will. Alpine Skyrun is a 100 mile race in the Australian Alps,, in Bogong National Park, last year was the first year the race was held, with three people out of five finishing in about 42 hours. The race major obstacle for me will be course navigation, I lack navigation skills, I will need to learn to follow the course with a map and compass. The second obstacle will be terrain, according to the race road book, the 100-mile course features six major ascents, including Victoria's three higher peaks. The course is designed with six stages and a mandatory overnight camp. The first aid kit is similar to other races except for the mandatory elastic band for snake bites. I have read the race manual guide several times before, it was not until now that all of a sudden I am filled with why did I think I could do this? Not finishing Yukon has been terrible for my confidence but it did also thought me something very valuable, to be in the moment, ever since I started this journey I have been consuming with the preparation for the races if Ray asked me to run 5 hills I did 7, I read everything available about the races but I the end of the day, it's not all up to me, since I return, I have enjoyed the company of those around me, my mind no longer drifts to far away places or to the next few training sessions, while I am not taking the races lightly, I am giving myself a break and allowing myself to even enjoy the journey. Looking around my life, driving my kids to practices, having coffee with my best friend Nadia, going out to dinner with my boyfriend, it's all there waiting for me when I get back. I already know my destination, climbing mountains, running deserts, jungles and tundra is the icing on the cake.

Wednesday, April 1, 2009

The Race from Down Under

Here is my race report from Alpine Skyrun 100 mile race in Australia, I can cross Australia off the list now!. Just as I thought navigation did proved to be a major issue for me at the race. During the first stage, I got lost three times, because it was the beginning of the race I was able to find my way back to the right trail by following the headlamps. For safety reason I decided to buddy up with other runners, by the time I made it back to the trail that would take me to the top of Mt Feathertop, I had found my running buddies for the rest of the race. Elm Tree men's relay team from Melbourne was armed with a Garmin GPS so they became my pacers for the rest of the race. Safety wasn't my concern even if we got lost, each runner was equipped with EPIRB (a tracking beacon) and my cell had coverage, so the major concern was lost time and snakes of course, but we did learn that it takes about four hours for the venom of a deadly snake to kill you, so there was plenty of time to rescue. At the meeting the other racers made fun me when they watch me squirmed every time they showed the snakes slides, I don't like snakes or frogs, I am not afraid just repulsed by them. Leslie in exchange reminded them in Canada we have bears to deal with, and with bears especially the Grizzly kind there is no 4 hours window to protect you. They left me alone after that, they realized I wasn't really a wuss. On ultrarunning there are three types of competitors, the frontrunners, who usually run most of the race and win the top spots, the mid-packers are usually competing for the age group brackets and usually do a combination of running and fast walking, most of the time this is where I find myself, competing for the 40-49 age group, and the third group is the late group, these are the competitors that speed walks the race mostly and do a bit of running if any, this is where Elm Tree Relay team fit, the range of fitness of the eight members vary from somewhat fitting to very fit but as a team, you must finish each stage together so you are only as fast as you slowest member. And sometimes especially at 1am and because I was had been running each and every leg of the race until I paired with them, the slow member of the group was me. At first, the pace seemed a bit slow but I knew that I had a better chance of finishing the race if stay with the team that if I went on my own. After the 6633 Ultra, my focus had shifted more toward surviving a race rather than setting course records, even of the age group kind. As I am also finding out, racing so often has affected my speed dramatically, last year I run Boston Marathon in 3:28:42, this year I would be surprised if I can run in under 5 hours. After a few hours on the course, their speed became my speed. We struggled through the first 21 hours of the race, they because of an injured member and I fought fatigue and the effects of jet lag, we missed the cut off time at the end of stage three so Paul Ashton the race organizer decided to allow us to continue on an alternative shorter distance, the 120-kilometer distance. We camped on top of Mt. Bogong, and continue the rest of the race at 9am the next morning. I woke up to spectacular scenery and discovered that coffee, even the instant kind is infinite better on a mountain top. If you think we Canadians are the friendlies people, then you haven't been to Australia yet. This is by far the race that I have enjoyed the most, I usually run races alone and ultras can be so long that there are times I would run for up to seven hours before I would see somebody again. The next day facing a much shorter course and after a few hours of sleep my pace become a bit faster, Team Elm also put their fittest members on day two since they could replace team members so we successfully finished the new 120-kilometer race in about 42 hours. At the end of the race, three different distances would continue to be an option for next year, 100K, 120K and 160K, Paul and Jessica and team one won the 100-mile distance, Paul Ashton, Elm Tree team and I won the 120K and Andrew a soloist runner who also couldn't navigate successfully either finished the 100K distance. Alpine Skyrun's course was breathtaking, also the participant's attitudes of no man left behind made it a unique experience, this was no picnic, the course is truly challenging, but in a true Aussie fashion the race environment was very laid back. So even though I did successfully finish the race, there was a possibility of not finishing if the rules had been enforced and ended up being disqualified for timing out. I did a lot of thinking during the race, my next race is 100 miles and the time limit is 30 hours, I wondered if this is still realistic giving the fact that I am slowing down, I played with the idea of finding a 100-kilometer race somewhere in North America and running that instead after all 100K is no laughing matter. But just a few hours, a nice shower and pizza, I wondered if it was not fear talking instead, the fear of making a fool of myself. There are certain risks I am willing to take, and making a fool of myself because I am stepping out of my comfort zone is one of them, where would humankind be if it's not for that wonderful willingness of being ridiculed for the sake of following your dreams. So after much thought, I decided to run the Iron Horse 100-mile race in St Paul, Alberta on Mother's day weekend as my replacement race. The good news is that I have a few weeks to prepare for it, as I am finding out my quest to run 7 ultraraces in 7 months is as much to do overcoming the limits of the body as of the mind.

Friday, May 8, 2009

Iron Horse Ultra

I am ready for race number 4. Iron Horse ultra in St Paul AB promise to be challenging and beautiful. The route will cover the beautiful farmlands, lakeshores, riverside of the county of St Paul while incorporating the old abandon CNR railroad. The race starts Saturday 9th at 6am and it ends Mother's day at 1pm giving me 31 hours to finish. I am looking forward to this race; I can bring my kids for at least part of the way. My sister

Muñeca and my nephew Taylor are flying from Vancouver to meet us in Edmonton, my kids and my mom will be celebrating Mother's Day weekend with them while I run the race. I am also looking forward to running with some of my ultrarunning friends. I only started ultrarunning last year and in a short time I had a wonderful opportunity of meeting fantastic people from all over the province. Iron Horse Ultra is part of the Alberta Ultra Series which attracts a group of runners from elite to recreational. Alan Lam is coming as a support crew, he is an accomplished runner and very knowledgeable about endurance sports since he has crew for Badwater135 Ultra which is considered the thoughest ultra race in the world. This last few weeks I had off were sure interesting, it was fun to watch my body experience withdrawal from the highs of running, after Australia I had to cut down my training to let my body rest and it was harder than I thought, all of a sudden I was behaving like I had a broken heart, watching endless bad movies and eating Mac and Cheese. During this time I also had a chance to get more involved with the charities I am representing. Cnib, FFB, and OEU had their annual fundraising events and I had a chance to volunteer .Last night Operation Eyesight presented me with a guide stick as a thank you for my fundraising effort. In villages in Africa when somebody goes blind, they are giving a guide stick to navigate, this is as much help as it's offered. The saddest part is that these types of blindness are avoidable but in developing countries are very common; the cost of restoring their sight it's as low as 30 dollars a lot of money to someone that that their yearly income is 20 dollars a month. The guide stick was presented to me because this person, in particular, doesn't need anymore, Operation Eyesight made that possible, so the stick is a symbol of what an amazing impact a small gesture such a running a race for pledges can make on someone's life. It sure helps put things into perspective about why I am doing this.

 It is, unfortunately, that because I am in the spotlight at the moment I get credit for the work I do, but these charities had been doing amazing work and changing people's lives way before I started to help. Standing there on these events being thanked was an overwhelming moment, I don't feel I should be thanked for doing what's right. Albert Einstein said it best with these words, "The world is a dangerous place, not because of those who do evil, but because of those who look on and do nothing." So as long as there is a reason to and an open road I will keep running wild for sure.

Monday, May 11, 2009

North America- Done!

Well, let me tell you about the Iron Horse Ultra, I ran a strong race, kept with the lead group until the end, gave them a run for their money, oh wait, that was my dream the night *before* the race, what really happened was that I *survived* my first 100-mile race. I finished the race at a little after 10am, around the 28-hour mark, it felt so good to be done. the weather was fantastic if a bit cold at around 3am. Of the 12 runners that ran the race

11 finished. It was nice to see familiar faces, I run the first stage with most of the group, except for the top 3 guys who finished the race at around 19 hours, they took off strong from the beginning and I never saw them again. On the second leg of the race, I got lost for about 45 minutes, I was busy trying to decide between a Stinger Energy Bar or Sharkies and missed my turn. By the time I figure out I was on the wrong path I had to backtrack for a while since the race is long enough without adding more distance I decide to focus hard on the markers and concentrated on following the fluorescent orange ribbons that were on the course, so much that at one point I found myself standing on a farmers backyard on a sandbox, I had to blink several times to figure out that the fluorescent orange I had followed was a kid's sandbox shovel!. By the end of this stage, I had fallen back behind so much that I was the last runner on the course, I was OK since I was still hitting my times so it wasn't likely to time out and be disqualified since the 6633 Ultra race I learned a valuable lesson, being last is never bad, my focus was on finishing the race this time. By the third stage I started to catch up to the group of runners, although I was enjoying having the sweepers behind me, (the sweepers are the people who are checking on the last runner on the course and also picking up garbage left behind as well as taking the markers down), I could hear them behind me and it was kind of nice to know they were there. By the end of the five-stage, I had ended up catching up Selena, I know her from last year's races so it was great to run together, Selena ended up falling behind

and eventually dropping out of the race unfortunately but just before she stopped she did tell me she was happy since she had made it past 100K, farther than she had ever gone before, I loved the positive attitude of the ultrarunning community. On stage six I backtracked to ask the sweepers if I was going the right way since I didn't see any markers on the course, nighttime now made it even more difficult to find any markers on the road anyway, after an hour of back and forth I found Don running backwards like me to find help. Don and I decided to stay together for the rest of stage six. We were confused that it was not marked just like other stages, there were no orange ribbons on the course, the only thing we saw once in a while was wooden sticks with red tape on top, Don joked that maybe we were following the sticks that the farmers use to remind them where the ditch is. It's a terrible feeling when you find yourself running the wrong direction. We decided to trust that this was the right way since we couldn't keep running back and forth to ask for help anymore and kept moving forward instead, Don and I made it to the end of the stage at 6am and found out that we were going the right direction for sure and locals had stolen the markers because they hated strangers in their area. I was cold and hungry, I hadn't planned on stopping since we only had 17K to go but I decided to stop for a half-hour and warm-up and Don caught a quick nap too. On the last stage, Don told me to go ahead if I wanted to since there was light out now but I decided to cross the finish line with him. We had stuck together through the night so it was the right thing to do, he couldn't run anymore so we power walked, Don is a tall man with long legs so he can power walk very fast, and after running for so long my running resembled more a newborn baby giraffe, felt really good to walk. It was at the edge of town his wife joined us for the last two kilometers to the finish line. When we finally crossed the finish line, there were only a few people left since Don and I were the last to finish. The race organizer Anna and her brothers and their 70-year-old something mom were there. Ana's mom was so sweet, cheering us and manning some of the aid stations and instead of finishing medals we received an engraved bracelet. During the night when we had hit the hardest part of the race, we were hungry, tired and cold, this is where Don and I wondered why we do what we do, why run this type of races at all? We couldn't really put it into words, it was the way you felt when you finally did it, chasing something so hard and accomplishing it, it's rebelling against the self-doubts in your mind that tell you that you can't do this or that, it's like Henry Ford said, whether you think you can or can't you are right.

Tuesday, May 12, 2009

"Don't Over think it, Overcome it!". Tjipekapora Herunga

I am off to Namibia for my next race this afternoon, I will be traveling for a couple of days, it will be a bit like the movie Planes, Trains, and Automobiles.

Here is a bit about the race Racing The Planet from the organizers website: "Namibia 2009 gets underway with two hundred and fourteen (214) competitors from 38 countries expected to participate including a record number of past champions who will be vying for top places. Traversing some of the most spectacular dunes and stunning landscapes of the oldest desert in the world – the Namib Desert, Racing The Planet's six-stage, seven days, 250-kilometer self-supported footrace, features a field of 214 from 38 countries. The event kicks off with a steep descent into the Fish River Canyon, the second deepest canyon in the world, an area rich with local wildlife such as Mountain Zebra, Giraffe, Oryx, Steenbok, Springbok, and even leopard. Competitors will make their way through the African bush traversing lunar landscapes and over some of the most demanding and challenging sand dunes in the world to finish at the Skeleton Coast in the charming town of Lüderitz." I am feeling fine except for all the blisters on my feet from running in the wet course at Iron Horse Ultra. I will be sending daily updates from the race whenever possible. I am thrilled to be tenting with some friends at the race so it should be lots of fun as well. I will be gone for close to two weeks and I will miss my kids, of everything the hardest thing will be not seeing or talking to them for so long.

Monday, May 18, 2009
Namibia Day 1
Day one proved to be extremely difficult for almost everybody, except for the stage winner the Spaniard Salvador Calvo, he had a great time. Today we ran Africa's Grand Canyon, 38K in

total, most of the way was rocky, wet or a steep ascend. After making camp the night before we started around 8:15am it took me about 8 hours and 30 minutes to make it to camp 2, I was expecting to be out there for a long time but I never anticipated it was going to take me that long. I am feeling pretty good considering I have just run 100 miles less than a week ago, my blisters are healing. The worst has been being homesick and missing my kids. It takes so long to get to the race place, sleeping at random gates on an airport layover, then it's usually a long bus ride to the final destination and everything about getting there sucks but once I got here it was fantastic. Meeting new people, seeing old friends, sort of like a summer camp for grownups. Namibia is so beautiful, looking down at the canyon today I couldn't help but feel privileged, though it was hard it was worth just to be able to experience such beauty. Tomorrow is not supposed to be as hard, but we could be wrong, I am prepared to have hard days, I am here to finish so no matter how hard I just plan on putting one foot in front of the other until I get it done.

Monday, May 18, 2009
Namibia Day 2
Day two was a bit easier than yesterday and I think We all needed to boost morale. Today we ran 38 kilometers on moderate terrain, descending from the campsite 2 on stony ground by a broken windmill then followed faint tracks not traveled for well over 20 years. Passed an old corral and still

descending with some flat areas and occasional small uphill, finally descending to checkpoint 6 above the Konkiep River, along the riverbed and over a low pass to checkpoint 7 then over the hill via Beacon and onto plains to camp 3 that nested between the hills by a deserted farmhouse overlooking the plains of Africa. I had a hard time running, for some reason my left collarbone was killing me. My pack weights over 9 kilos and even though I have eaten some of my rations, of course, it is still heavy. I came with more weight this time expecting to need more calories and more layers since I am a bit tired from all the races I have been doing. At night I am thankful for my fresh socks, cozy jacket, and extra socks, during the day I pay the price. The mood at camp it's tense tonight. In the morning we heard of a Japanese runner that was lost still at 8:30am he never made it even to the first checkpoint so he was lost for over 24 hours, thankfully they found him few hours ago and he is well. Although Racing the Planet does an amazing job at marking the course people still do get lost, I have been very attentive on watching the course at all times and resist the temptation of listening to my iPod since it's easier to get distracted by it. So many racers are having a hard time. A runner was stranded today, she was crying and had to be rescued by other runners. It wasn't a dangerous drop but fatigue can turned you into a toddler and she couldn't manage to get down. I she decided to drop out of the race after the incident. I am struggling a bit, fatigue taking over but I am positive that I will finish if I only remain smart and focus, after checkpoint 2 out of 3 I couldn't run anymore, the pounding of my backpack on my shoulders sent sharp pain, so I just slowed down, It took me just as long to finish today than yesterday and It was a lot easier but I don`t want to risk hurting my back again. But don`t feel sorry for me, if I were to choose a place where I would want to walk for 8 hours, this will be It, I have missed seeing any wildlife, except for the odd scorpion or snake, the fasters runners today got to see zebras, but this is a majestic place never the less, so as I walked I try to take in as much of the view as possible, after all, I might never have the opportunity to come back. I am making so many friends here, I passed the Danish team today and their team leader Jacob Juul Hastrup ran part of the course with me leaving his teammates behind because they been fighting. It didn't help when I went running by using a roll up sleeping mat as a shoulder pad to help alleviate the collarbone pain, Jacob said he was fighting with one of their team member because he refused to continue because he had a blister. I am happy to say that that team member stoped complaining after I went by because he felt he was way better than me and hated being chicked (pass by a female at a race) especially that female being me. Jacob thanked me that evening at camp, I really don't know if I that was an insult or a compliment. But really, I encourage you to try an event like this, I love the sight of the camp, with all the tents and the fires going and people just relaxing after a long day, It puts a smile on my face. I moved tents, we get assigned a tent at the start of the race but a British family of female explorers wanted to be together so I moved to the Spanish tent called that because at the tent they are all Spaniards expect for me, they appointed me honorary Spaniard. I love the sound of the my language and the smells of their food, we can't share food but being in the tent with 8 Spanish people all eating real food, like cheese and Spanish ham not like my boring dehydrated food It reminds me of growing up in Mexico. Tomorrow is supposed to be an easier day, I will, however, keep in mind that I still have over 600 kilometers in the next couple of months. Not so bad if all the miles will look anything like the ones I have already taken.

Tuesday, May 19, 2009

Namibia Day 3

Well, I am still alive and kicking. I had a better day today since it was only a 35-kilometer stage I decided to bear and grind the shoulder pain and just go for it. I finished on about 5 and a half hours, considerably better than I have done so far, my motivation was to get to camp faster to rest for tomorrows stage which is the feared long day 100-kilometer stage, I have been barely eating since I been coming too late and my tent has the top 10 runners so it's light out and sleeping by 6pm. Today was hot, as usual, we had 3 checkpoints between camps, the course started as a wide valley then quickly turned on to the sharp stony ground, for about 10K then along with the Riverbend. I have to say the best treat was finding out that we camp next to the river, you should have seen us all jumping in the river like little kids, is amazing what little pleasures in life can bring the kids inside. Right now the yellow jersey wearer is Salvador Calvo Redondo from Spain and Stephanie Case from Toronto is the female leader. Stephanie told me she had been struggling with stress fractures and hadn't been able to run for the last 5 months, she literally took her cast off the morning she boarded the plane to come to the race, there is no doubt she would have been the overall winner if it's not because of her recent injuries. Tomorrow is the long stage and there is an option of stopping halfway and sleep for a few hours but right now I might rather push through. I am still struggling with shoulder pain and it's also getting hotter so it makes it harder. I am just going to take it easy and do my best, after all, sometimes that's all we can do

Thursday, May 21, 2009

Namibia Day 4-5 The Long Day

What a long day yesterday with the dreaded 100 kilometer stage. It was even worse than we imagined. After been awakened at 2am then got on a bus to move us to a different location in Namibia we started the race at 8:20am and It was already hot, the course handbook called for a moderate course with 9 checkpoints every 10K or so before arriving at camp Spring Box. The course description was long plains with sandy ascents to hilltops and some intense dunes, fantastic views from hilltops, past the famous Koichab Depression of subterranean fossil water over 1 million years old. The most important thing for me is to finish so from the beginning I took It easy eating

171

and hydrating as much as I could, temperatures reached around 42C in the first few hours so by kilometer 20 people started dropping out, as I came upon checkpoint I was sad to see that Canadian Ultrarunner Sandy McCallum was one of them, overcoming to the extreme heat. I was being paced by Isadoro Aznar and Fernando Guardiola both from Spain and my tent mates, I had given myself 20 hours to finish or even longer if necessary depending on how I felt at the midpoint camp at kilometer 60 where we were given the option of sleeping if we didn't want to run all the way through. By kilometer 30 I had lost one of my pacers, Fernando was not looking well so he slowed down and took longer rest at checkpoints. Isadoro and I press on, him barking orders at me to go through checkpoints quicker if I wanted to continue with him. As we went thought checkpoints we started to pass a lot of people, the heat and the sand in the shoes taking a toll. Imagine blisters being scrubbed by the sand hour after hours. I hadn't anticipated this much sand so I brought regular gaiter to cover my shoes, to protect my feet for rocks and such, but the sand just kept pouring in my shoes but luckily It didn't havoc my feet. So what exactly happens when you are out there for 22 hours, well you get to know yourself and others very well. As people ahead of us started to slow down we started to run with other people, sometimes it will be 5 of us and sometimes just a couple. I started to try to look forward to small things along the way to motivate myself to go steady, like "the next checkpoint I can get the sand out of my shoes", or thinking "the next checkpoint I can finally have my dinner," the hardest part is always the beginning when you have a monumental task ahead, and also the last 3 checkpoints when you have already pass the option of stopping to sleep so you have to keep pressing on but you still have a long way to go. It was around kilometer 70 that I started to wonder why didn't I decided to take crocheting instead to relieve stress. By this time Isadoro and I where around 60th place but he could not maintain that speed any longer so I left him with a group of people that wanted to go slower so he wasn't alone, after that I was free to speed the pace and run hard. It was around 3am so it was nice and cool, I was hydrated and fed and it was no risk of me not finishing at this point. I arrived at camp around 6:17am, a lot longer than I thought it would ever take me, to my surprise, the camp was quiet, I was around the 46th place, shocking considering I keep a pretty conservative pace until the last 30k, I felt great and if a bit sore from the distance and the sand dunes. It's around noon as I write this and camp is a bit more alive, of the 200 plus participants only 108 have come through, the rest have until 6pm today to finish or risking being disqualified. In my tent two of the members have dropped out, by now most tents have casualties. Today I rest while we wait for the rest of the people to come, then tomorrow at 8am we do it all over again, ironically yesterday was rated moderate and tomorrow is supposed to be hard so I am very intimidated but by now my mantra has been to take it slow and one kilometer at a time.

Friday, May 22, 2009

Namibia Day 6

Today we woke up to great news, after having a total of 40 people dropping out on the long stage the race organizer decided to shorten today's race from 28 kilometers to 20. Today's stage was the sand dunes, It was spectacular, the view from the top was worth it having to go through all the pain yesterday just to experience today. We arrived at the campsite by the beach and I teared up when I saw the shoreline. Running a race like this makes you appreciate things, we have to earn our food and sleep every day by running hard, sort of primal. As usual the talk today was around what we are looking forward the most tomorrow after the race is over, food being the top and a nice shower being a close second. I am not ready to go home, not this time. I haven't heard from Brett since I got here and that had not happened before and it's not difficult to imagine why. I keep crying at night and I don't know if it's because I hurt physically or emotionally. But I am ready for whatever is next, I haven't come this far to let a broken heart stop me from realizing my dreams.

Monday, May 25, 2009

Continent 5, Check.

I am done the Namibia race now. It has been a couple of days but I have had limited access to the Internet since I have been crossing the country by bus to get back to the capital of Namibia, Windhoek. The last day of the race went really well.

We all woke up with high spirits since we only had 8 kilometers left to the finish line. The race had staggering start times from slowest to fastest, 3 groups in total. I was in the middle group that had competitors 25 to 110. Of the 220 competitors that started, only 170 finished. At 8am we all cheered the first wave of competitors, some who were in considerably bad shape from the last 6 days. at 9 my wave finally started and it was a mad sprint to the finish line were pizza and beer awaited us, by now after sharing a week of our lives with no other people but ourselves, we had become a sort of a family, and a few of us pretended to try and take each other down on the hopes of getting to the town of Luderitz first and get more slices of pizza. It was a beautiful day, to be running with 80 or so smelly and dirty people along the beach in Namibia. I started to forget all the pain we had all endured the last few days, and that's the reason why I keep coming back. in about 45 minutes I was crossing the finish line and receiving my medal, the whole town had come to the town square to cheer us on. Luderitz is a small German fishing town that began its life as a trading post in 1883, in 1909 diamonds where discovered in the area and had a short surge of prosperity, today, however, diamonds are mostly found elsewhere in Namibia. Exhilaration followed, to be done such a hard race, to endure hunger, tiredness, exhaustion from the running but also from barely sleeping every day. We had the bare minimum with us so we endure sleeping on the cold sand, on the hard sand I could feel every bone on my body, eating tasteless dehydrated food and surviving on gels or bars. I was glad to be done and I was looking forward to some real food and a shower, I grabbed two slices of pizza and quickly finish them, being a German town, we were offered sausages on a bun. The sensation of tastes in my mouth was incredible a symphony of flavors but then I felt someone tugging on my sleeve, there in front of me was a small child, of about 7 years old. He looked at me with big brown eyes and ask me if he could have a small piece of my sandwich. I felt ashamed at that moment, I was arrogant enough to feel that enduring a week deprivation I felt deserving of praise and a medal, this is the life he lives, never knowing what a pleasure It is to enjoy a daily shower, going to bed with a full tummy every night, all of a sudden the medal felt heavy on my shoulders. I realized that I was entitled to nothing, no matter how hard I had worked hard at it or the circumstances, I was privileged to be here and should always remember that with gratitude. Namibia is a big country, 824,000 square kilometers, It offers deserts, beaches, forests but it has the lowest population density in Africa and the second-lowest in the world. This is mainly because of the harsh desert conditions and the resultant scarcity of surface water. Namibia has an average of 300 days of sunshine per year and only rains during the summer months and mostly as heavy thunderstorms when the dry rivers flow for a few days or sometimes even for a few hours. Namibian people are used to enduring hardship, and been here has shaped a bit the way I perceive my life, while I doubt I will give up showering every day, and I am not about to give up comforts, I am rethinking the way I live, I no longer wish to live my life with a sense of entitlement, I don't need a haircut every 6 weeks, I am sure I can do without for a few months, while I might enjoy the odd fancy triple, no foam, skinny fancy coffee, I don't need one every day. I have always heard the phrase that when you give you get so much more in return, I am so grateful for the opportunity I have been giving my time to charities to set my priorities straight. In a couple of weeks I am off to my sixth race in China, and I am feeling really good. Since I paced myself it paid off ,I ended up placing 9th female and 62nd overall, well beyond my wildest dream but I guess that's the allure of a sport like this, everybody truly has a chance to shine if you are willing to though It up and work hard. Ana Sebastian and all the other Spaniards and I went out for some tequilas and wow, all of us geeks know how to party after 250K! I promised Ana that what happens in Namibia, stays in Namibia so my lips are sealed.

Tuesday, June 2, 2009

Continent 6.

It's been about a week since I got home from Namibia and in no time I was back on being Norma the mom not Norma the Ultrarunner. As soon as I got home I was inundated with chores, Dr's appointments and bills. No matter how far I run I seem to return to the same old stuff. On my first day back my niece Marianna was eager to pass the baton, she said that she felt like in a horror movie where the more laundry she did the more it remained to be done. Then there is my car, I need a new one and I kept researching what kind of vehicle I can afford, especially now that I am not working, and I found just the right model for me, it's called a bus pass, and don't even get me started about my leaky basement. I sometimes feel like I am running on a treadmill never really arriving anywhere. I was mopping around the house tired of the endless chores when something caught my eye, there is a life-size drawing of me on my bedroom door, my best friend Nadia's middle son Jake made it for me. His grade 6 class at St Gregory school did a project about heroes and he chose me, I was speechless when he presented me with the drawing, I felt honored to have been nominated and chosen by Jake and his team members. I felt totally undeserving of such honor but what it really matters is that they thought I did. If I were a hero or a superhero, my power would be of resiliency; I could have a Teflon shield that I could activate if I needed something to just rub off. Silly of me to be worrying about stuff like not having a car when in life all we have it's our integrity, my father once said that at the end we are all remembered by our actions, not our wealth, he said this when one of his five kids complained about him welcoming a poor relative to live with us, we were poor ourselves so things just got even tighter. I have never forgotten that and try to follow his example. As soon as I finish my races I can find a new job, given the economy I might not find what I want but there are jobs, I like working and I have never felt that certain jobs are beneath me. I am due to leave for my next race in China next week. As could not be happier that I have 250K to run soon. I have been reading the race roadbook and feel like I need to be pinched, I can't believe I am so fortunate to be once more participating in such an amazing event.

Here is a bit of Culture and history of the Gobi desert taken from Racing The Planet:

CULTURE

The host city and location of the Gobi March are specifically chosen for their rich and ancient culture, and this year's host city and location of Kashgar and Tashkorgan, respectively, are rich in history and traditions which are present today much the same way they were hundreds of years ago. Competitors will experience Ugyur and Tajik culture throughout the Gobi March. The Uygur nationality is mainly distributed in the Uygur Autonomous County (Xinjiang Province). With a population of more than 8.9 million, Ugyur people speak Uygur and have their own writing characters. The Uygur nationality believes in Islam. Their households are characterized by a flat roof with a trap door on it. Within their house, visitors can find a parlor, bedroom, handiwork and storage rooms. The exquisitely decorated niche, carved from plaster, has a rich flavor of the Uygur nationality. The Uygur nationality has something called the "Roza" Festival (vegetarian diet-breaking festival). Your people are known as "the singing and dancing nationality," famous for its "Twelve Muqams" dancing performance, which is a musical epic. The Uygur nationality attaches great importance to clothing – they are always tidily dressed. All the Uygur people wear small four-corner flower hats. The Uygur people have the famous bridal-veil raising ceremony. The Uygur language is a Turkic language spoken in Xinjiang, China. The language traditionally used the Arabic script since the 10th century. The government introduced a Roman script in 1969, but the Arabic script was reintroduced in 1983.The Tajiks: Since ancient times the Tajik people have lived in the Tashkorgan area in the Pamirs, which was both a gateway to China's western frontier and a key communications center between the West and inland China. They speak the Persian branch of the Indo European language family as well as the Uygur language. The written Ugyur language is most commonly used. "Tajik" means "royal crown." The origin of the Tajiks can be traced back to an ancient Persian speaking tribe in the eastern Pamirs. The Tajik nationality has maintained a long-standing friendship with the Han people. In 643, when the Monk Xuan Zang of the Tang Dynasty brought home Buddhist scriptures from India, he stopped over in what is today's Tashkorgan and listened to local Tajik fairy tales. Later he recorded these tales in his 'Notes on the Western Region of the Great Tang Dynasty.' In modern Chinese history, the Tajik people often bore the brunt of imperialist and colonialist invasions of China's western borders and fought courageously to defend the frontier. On September 17, 1954, Tashkorgan Tajik Autonomous County was established.

Sunday, June 14, 2009

Gobi March Day 1

It's a hot day in the Gobi desert. Today's stage was 42.5k of canyons with river crossings, mountain trails, and gravel roads. The area itself is very remote but this is the first Racing the Planet race where I have seen other people not part of the race along the course. Today I felt great the first 20K then I was in a lot of pain everywhere for some reason, I kept telling myself hurting was normal given all the races I had undertaken and that hurting didn't mean being injured. I am not sure why I felt the heat more this time, it could have been that it was snowing in Calgary when I left. After some pain killers at the 30K mark, I felt better and increased my pace, I am becoming an expert on positive thinking, when I am forced to slow down because I am tired or hurting I tell myself I am lucky since I can now enjoy the view in more detail and even take great photos. I arrived at Tiznap Valley after 5 and a half hours and third female to cross the finish line. Another change from previous races is that we are sleeping in local homes instead of tents. we still sleep in our sleeping bags on the floor but we are sheltered from sand storms and the desert coldness. Just by being at homes. We have been very warmly greeted by the local villages, they have gone out of their way to come and cheer us and perform fantastic dances. The villages are humble but clean and since It's communist everybody has to access to running water and electricity. I wonder what the locals think of these crazy, weird-looking and smelly foreigners that are staying at their village. It is nice to see everybody dressed in their Sunday best, quite the contrast since we are all hanging out in our shorts, t-shirts and hotel sleepers, we all carry them since they are light to carry in our packs and we need something when we finally take our runners off. There are a lot of first timers on this race and that makes it a bit unique, I get asked constantly about tips since I am the veteran. Stefan Dani of Toronto is a participant and even though we have never been introduced he told me we once crossed paths in Toronto at a YPO dinner I attended with Brett. Stefan said that he heard me talking about this race decided to sign for the race and told me he will blame me and curse my name every step he will take during the race because he now regretted letting my enthusiasm get to him. When I arrived he was already in, I asked him if he happened to curse my name during the race, he said he forgot, too busy running and taking in the breath taking scenery, that and the fact that he finished 9th overall and will probably win his age group (Stefan is 46). Stefan told me he never dreamed of participating on anything like this and had been experiencing depression the last few years and couldn't not seem to find a way out of the funk and when he heard me at the dinner party talking with such passion he felt the need to come and experiencing it for himself because life had lost meaning and his wife and family were very supportive knowing how hard the last few yards had been. As I listen to him it reminds me of a song that I heard the night before we started this race, a Bon Jovi song that goes like this "Wake up, Wherever you are, This is the life you are supposed to live". Don't waste too much time figuring out why you are where you are, that's just your starting point, go in whatever direction your heart is telling you to go.

Monday, June 15, 2009

Gobi March Day 2

Today's stage was 42 K and it was named Mars on the Gobi referring to the Red Canyon River bed we crossed. It took me a lot longer to finish than yesterday, I dropped to 6th female, I feel fine but had a hard time running my legs felt like bricks. There were not a lot of flat sections and running hills takes a lot of oxygen to fuel the legs so it was a tough day. The scenery still takes my breath away, I am trying very hard to do my best but I also need to stay focus. We still have some tough days ahead, so I am just going to run my race and what every time I finish that will be my right time. I am missing my kids back home, I feel like the last 6 months I have hardly been with them, living out of a suitcase at strange hotels around the world. I know this is an amazing opportunity for me and my kids are well looked after by my mom when I am away but I still miss them when I first leave them for a race.

Tuesday, June 16, 2009

Gobi March Day 3

Today was a tough day, I woke up feeling sick but couldn't figure if it was because I am run down or if it was the virus that it's going around camp. I took some pain killers and decide to push through today's 38K. The first 20K went fast, I was feeling fine and run most of it, we went through Langerville a very nice small town, it was fantastic to see everyone in the village come out to cheer us on, they wanted to shake our hands or offered fruit. The second leg we went through rivers, mud, and farmland, it's hard to believe this is a desert, I run through what I tough looked like rice paddies, but turned out to be wheat. It was after this stage that I hit the wall, I started to feel dizzy and short of breath, I had only 18K to go so I knew I was going to be OK so I just pushed through, slowed the pace significantly and all I could do was walk. In no time runners behind me quickly caught up, Canadian Todd Handcock became my company for the next while, Todd's wife grew up in Calgary and they now live in Hong Kong with their 3 kids, they still have family back in Calgary and they are following the race closely, like many others, this is Todd's first endurance event, you wouldn't know if you saw him, he seems to know well what to do and has finished around the 30th place since the start surprising even himself. It was nice chatting later back at camp with Todd, Eddie Naylor of the UK and Mitchell Stock of the USA all being beginners at endurance events such as Gobi March, it's always nice to hear their comments and observations coming from a fresh perspective. Even I felt like a beginner crying the last 7K totally destroyed, and this is my 6th race in 6 months, I kept thinking how am I going to get thought it?. Katrina Follows of Toronto my tentmate kept me company for the last leg and tried to distract me, Katrina had dropped out of the race yesterday feeling sick herself because of the virus that's going around, she is now staying as a volunteer and it was nice talking to her because she knew exactly how I felt. I am on antibiotics now being diagnosed by the doctor at the race and she said I should be better by tomorrow, just two more hard days to push through and I should be crossing the finish line on Saturday, as I am writing this is been three hours since I finished, people are still crossing the finish line so I am feeling guilty for crying knowing what everybody is going through pain, and at the end that's why we form such a strong bond. Going back to my normal life I realize we are now a society that looks for a quick fix to any discomfort, but coming here I realize that hardship and pain sometimes can be cleansing if it has a higher purpose.

Wednesday, June 17, 2009

Gobi March Day 4

Today was a tough day in the Gobi, the stage was 41.2k and it's called Stairway to Heaven, we climb a total of 1,175 feet of elevation. At the top we were treated to Heaven's gate in a canyon with ladders, It felt more like the ultimate challenge. I feel better after the camp Doctor told me was a virus so I guess is great to know that Namibia didn't leave me trashed, it was the virus that it's going around camp the only bad thing is that I feel better because of the antibiotics but they say to avoid the sun because they will make my sun sensitive, I look like I could glow in the dark right now so sunburned. Today's stage was very tough, as usual, there were several river crossings and we also had to run along the mountain ridge, the path was narrow, single track and the wind was very strong, at one point It picked me up and threw me about a foot over. I kept thinking about the people behind me, like my tent mates that are by now struggling severely because of blisters, as I write this at almost 7pm some haven't crossed the finish line. It took me also longer than I expected but I surprise myself to find out I was the second female across the line and top 40 overall. I spent the evening talking to other racers at camp and it's amazing how many of us are here because of a life changing circumstances that threaten to impact our lives in a negative way. Since I started my seven races I have met amazing people that are refusing to sit down and ask the question that first comes to mind when you here a life-changing diagnosis, "why us" instead we are creating a small army of people that are determined to do whatever It takes to change things for the better. Here I am in Gobi, China with one long hard day ahead of me then I am done, I am feeling blessed for the wonderful experiences I am acquiring, I came here because I was determined to give back but in return, I am receiving so many blessings.

Friday, June 19, 2009

Gobi March Day 5

Yesterday I did the long 80K stage in about 13 hours and 20 minutes, good enough to finish 31st. I felt great and run most of It and the last 30K hard. Camp as usual looks like a war zone with people limping and walking around looking shell shocked.

The first finisher crossed the finish line in about 6 and a half hours and the last finisher finished in about 28 hours. I love camp the day after, people have amazing stories to tell, and if It's your first time doing an event of such, people go home changed. It's amazing how the boundaries of what's possible to expand in a way we never imagined especially when It seem unnatural to push your body so hard, and mentally the struggle is even bigger. We experience pain as an alert mechanism to prevent injury or death, the problem is that it shows up way before there is any damage, sort of like the empty gas tank on a car shows up before you run out of gas. The trick is to know how far is too far. There are many amazing stories of overcoming fears, one, in particular, will linger with me because she happened to be my tent mate and I watched her go through the pain and the doubt. When Hanna walked to camp the first day, people probably bet she was going to drop out just like the way she looks, Hanna Sandlings a UK TV personality so she is extremely beautiful, her skin looks like it has never seen the sun. She was ready to quit after the first day but I wouldn't let her, I know that all she needed was somebody to believe she could do it, I could see she was starting to doubt, my advice to her was to take it one checkpoint at a time, never to think that she had 250K, if she had had enough to get to the next checkpoint and then she could ask herself that question, never quit when you first have the thought, give it sometimes then reassess how you feel. You never want to go home knowing you had one more step left in you. So Hanna is on her way to be a Gobi Race finisher and dear God her sin still looks like it has never seen the sun!. I had a great run, I crossed the finish line 31st overall and second female again, I just looked at the results and I am currently at 3 places 27 minutes behind second overall female giving that is only 9K tomorrow it seems that that will be the final results but this result is way beyond my wildest dream, I thought at most was going to place first on my age group. Ray Zahab did predict the top three, I have to say that I thought he was nuts when he told me that after Namibia, but that's why he is Canada's top ultrarunner and one of the best in the world. Tonight is the last night on camp, then we run only 9K in Kashgar, the mood is light and fun, in our minds we have done it, talks revolve around what we are doing as soon as we get to town I can't wait to have a shower and to change into clean clothes. I came here with a broken heart, on top of the incredible physical toll my body is undergoing. I am glad I had this race planed, I am running this race for my son but I think this time I also ran it as much for me.

Tuesday, June 23, 2009

Gobi March Closing Ceremonies.

Saturday we run the last 10K of the Gobi March in Kashgar City. Kashgar is a remote vibrant city west of the Gobi's Taklamakan portion of the desert. Of all Racing the Planet races, Gobi March is the race that you come in contact with the most culture, the race happens in areas so remote that not many foreigners will find their way to. For the last leg of the race, every competitor was allowed to run, it was nice to see fellow Canadian Leonard Stanmore who had dropped out on day four because of foot infection, and severe foot pain at the start line again for the last 10K. It was amazing running thought town, we must have been a sight to locals, and the local authorities redirected or stopped traffic for us to navigate the city, the smells, the sounds of people going around their business on Saturday morning, then having 110 plus sweaty and dirty runners with backpacks making their way to Kan Mosque. It sure feels amazing having people cheer you along the way. I wanted to run hard the last leg of the race but my legs are so used to the long-distance that they seem to have a mind of their own thinking that we were going yet again for another 40K run. I still managed to run in about an hour, crossing the finish line holding hands with 45-year-old Canadian-Italian and Toronto native Louie Santaguida. It was nice getting my medal, especially since there where some days that I struggle just to finish feeling lousy from the nasty virus. I placed the third female after Diane Hogan-Murphy and Shirley Potter both of Ireland, the overall winner was American Eric LaHaie. The awards ceremony was held at a square across the Mao Statue in Kashgar, I had to give thanks when receiving the award and as usual, I had trouble speaking in front of so many people, it feels weird to be recognized individually for something that so many people helped me achieved. I know that without their support I wouldn't have been there standing receiving an award. I felt a bit sad last night when I left the ceremonies, coming back to a hotel room, too late to call my kids and share the great news I just sat in front of the computer trying to put my thoughts in order, I am glad to be almost done my races, I am glad I am still healthy to run my last continent in less than two weeks, but I am having a hard time finding my place, I now feel this is as much part of my life as it is being at home with my kids, I am not sure I can ever go back to an office job anymore, when I started I thought I was going to be mentally done with living such a stressful and emotional quest I have found that it has made me a happier healthier person. This life now has become my life but I am grieving losing my old life even though I know that here is where I belong.

Friday June 26, 2009

7 77 Run For Sight- 7 Ultraraces, 7 Continents, 7 Months and 1 Heartache

The fundraising party for Run For Sight was a couple of days ago but I really needed a few days to process it all. There is no easy way to tell you what developed at such party so I am just going to tell you what happened. The fundraising party was part of Brett's annual Garden Party and 777 Run For Sight was the recipient of the donations this year. This had been decided at the beginning of 777 Run For Sight quest. I am glad that even though Brett and I broke up he still kept his promise. Brett called me suggesting me not to show up to the fundraiser because he was going to be introducing his new girlfriend at the event and it would be too awkward. I wasn't going to let embarrassment keep me from my own fundraising party so I told him I could handle whatever it was going to happen. My niece Marianna offer to come as my plus one for moral support and to take photos since a local store lent me a fancy gown. No matter how I hard I tried to prepared myself for the terrible moment nothing prepared me for the moment when Brett called me on stage to be presented with the check for $110,000 dollars to my charities and he introduced his girlfriend Sarah McLachan to play her hit song Angel. The crowd went wild and I felt small and too visible. I wanted the superpower of invisibility at that very moment. I stood there holding a gigantic fake check and yes Brett as right, feeling incredibly awkward, while they exchanged loving glances at each other. After a few minutes but it felt years the song was finished I was free to run to the car and hide my embarrassment. I looked for my niece but she was having a great time meeting the other musical guest the Canadian Tenors so when I told her I was leaving she begged me that she wanted to stay and hear Sarah's other hit songs, " Sorry auntie but I love her!" of course I understood, I love Sarah too. Thankfully this was all over. The next day Nadia took me to watch Sex and the City Movie to take my mind off things. She joked that as much as she loved me there was no way she was getting rid of Sarah McLahclan's CDs, I lovingly called her traitor and we settle for the movie telling her I was glad to put as much distance from that awful party and myself and I could finally concentrate on moving on and finishing 777 Run For Sight then the theater when dark and the commercials before the move started, there on the big screen out comes Brett Wilson announcing Dragon's Den's new season with the twist that that some of them will be auditioning for the US version titled Shark's Tank then out of nowhere the SPCA's commercial starts playing and we hear Sarah's song Angel urging us to be the an angels to neglected animals. I have never laugh so hard in my life. There is a God and she has a sense of humor! I woke up today feeling amazing, Brett falling in love with somebody else is not a reflection of me. I have nothing to feel but just pride of how incredibly hard I been working for this goal and to be a role model to my kids. I have raised over $120, 000 dollars for the cnib, Operation Eyesight Universal and Foundation Fighting Blindness and yes it would not be possible without Brett's help and for that I am forever grateful we me. Life has twist and turns, and I am ready for what the future holds, good and bad.

Friday July 3, 2009

Swiss Jura Marathon

I am in Paris and making my way tomorrow Saturday the 4th to St Cergue for the start of the race Sunday morning. I arrived in Paris because this is this is the closes that I could get to Switzerland using airmiles for a free flight. I have never been to Europe so this is a treat. Paris is so alive I am in love with the city!. But I am shocked at how expensive Europe is. My other races have been in remote mostly developing countries so my money lasted a lot longer, I did get to see Johnny Depp on

Champs Elysses on the premiere of his new movie Public Enemy, so I guess it's all worth it broke and all. I have been so nervous about this race, it's the last one and I was having trouble sleeping at home. The race starts Sunday at 8am and it will finish Saturday around 3pm. There are about 63 competitors and 11 of them are female. Most of the participants are Europeans but there is another Canadian and a couple of Americans in the race. Daily distance ranges from 47K to 53K and the daily climbs are between 1410ftand 2020ft. At 350K and 11,000 feet of elevation, it will be a very tough race. It also has a very strict time limit, around 7 hours max time limit. There is one great things about this race, I will not be running with a heavy pack like in Gobi or Namibia, they also feed us at night and the menu looks amazing, I will be able to shower daily and have a massage as well. For the first time I will have somebody to cheer me at the finish line my friend Nicola Fontanesi from Italy was my tent mate in the Gobi March Race. At 6'3 he looks more like a volleyball player than an ultrarunner and we had similar running times so we used each other as pacers at the race. He never wanted to finish behind me, an ego thing for sure and I knew that if I finish not far behind I would be usually top 20. After Brett broke up with me I am not sure I am ready for a relationship but to tell you the truth I am glad he is taking me out to dinner after the race is over so I don't have to sit at my hotel after the race and convince Nadia when she calls me that I am okay for sure. The race itself is low key and we will be sleeping at school gyms or community halls. I hardly feel ready for Swiss Jura, maybe because my short time at home was hardly enough time to recover from my last three races that were back to back, with everything that was going on in my personal life and my kids' end of the year activities kept me busy as well. There are times however that I am amazed of things that happen around me, I was approached at Notre Dame by an older lady, she came straight at me and without hesitation gave me a gold ring, she spoke in French, of course, I panicked and told her I didn't speak French she then spoke in broken English, she told me she wanted to give me the ring because I was lucky and pretty, the ring is a wedding band, I didn't know what to say, well, define lucky, there are many times that I feel extremely lucky but this is a wedding band, after all, being divorced for the last 9 years I am sure that I am not that lucky at relationships, but she just kissed both of my cheeks and left, I kept it, she did say lucky so I am taking it with me to the race along with my the lucky charms that my kids made for me. Author Tim Rice did say, "We all dream a lot - some are lucky, some are not. But if you think it, want it; dream it, then it's real. You are what you feel."

Sunday, July 5, 2009
Swiss Jura day 1
Today's stage was 47 kilometers long and 1677 feet of elevation. At 6:45 we got on the busses to be transported to Geneva for the start of the race. At 8am we stated along the waterfront towards St. Cergue. Swiss Jura is not an ultra-race

194

like the ones I am used to. Swiss Jura is run fast. Today we had 7:30 hours to finish 47K with elevation, I have been worry about timing out and today my worries didn't seem to be unrealistic. I ran the first 22K hard, or at least I was in pace with the top 20. I knew I couldn't maintain their speed when I saw them running hard the uphill. Rule number one in ultraraces for anybody especially if you are not elite, walk the hills, I couldn't believe when I saw them attacking the hills like Lance Armstrong at the Tour. The next 20K were really hard, I found having to tell myself the same things I tell people on the races about not giving up, its only pain and don't think is 350K just think next checkpoint. I was in so much pain. Everything is for sure catching up, I feel tired and my legs had just about enough. Usually, this is not a problem since they are generous on their times but Swiss Jura has a very strict time limit and they don't welcome power walkers, walking poles are banned from the race. The course is sure beautiful, we mostly run on dirt roads and some neighborhoods in the surrounding areas. It was so hot at the beginning I sunburned right though my shirt then about halfway it poured, I was absolutely soaked, fortunately, I had only a couple of hours to go. There is a high possibility that I will be timing out, I arrived with only 30 minutes to spare, not much of a buffer if you ask me. Now the worst-case scenario will be that if I time out, I then get moved to the shorter distance, 175K so usually a half marathon a day. I know I should be excited about the possibility of running less and enjoying more since I will not be disqualified, I still get continent number 7, but I really want to run the longer distance. I could have signed for the shorter distance from the beginning but when I was planning the races, I wanted to be the most difficult challenge my body could and my mind could ever imagine. I lay here in my sleeping bag feeling sad with the possibility of not being able to accomplish this. I had many emotions during my run today, doubt has been consuming me more than ever, maybe because I didn't anticipate the ripple effect of such quest. At one point the image of Brett and Sara McLachlan at the party when I saw them together for the first time kept playing on my head over and over again, I mean Jesus, she is beautiful and an incredibly talented artist. Even my friends were calling looking for advice on what kind of exercise routine and diet I thought she followed since she looks amazing. "OMG did you see her!"   I ran harder and screamed on top of my lungs, "But can Sarah trail run like me!!!!!! My old life keeps going and I feel that I don't quite belong there anymore. I care for the people in my life and I am afraid to go home and find out that my kid's friends are more important than me or that my best friend might have another best friend since I am not around as much anymore. I have lost as much as I have gained since starting my races but in life, there are no guarantees and I wanted to take chances accepting the consequences. One thing I know for sure is that running makes me incredibly happy and don't want to live my life without passion. I am happy for Brett and Sarah, they feel about each other the way I feel about my kids and running so we have the life we want and deserve. If I was writing this story I might not write it the way is happening but I am determined to let destiny take its course, I am living a much fuller richer life now, and I want my kids to live their life with passion and purpose. Hebbel said it best "Nothing great in the world has ever been accomplished without passion."

Monday, July 6, 2009

Swiss Jura Day 2

What a day today. The stage was 45 kilometers long with the same altitude as yesterday 1679 meters of elevation as the highest point. Last night was a bit hard since everybody seemed to be finding things so easy. I felt lost since I felt I didn't belong here either. I had a great chat with 51-year-old Rob Jansen, he was born in the Netherlands and move to Canada about 30 years ago, I guess you can call him Dutchman Running Wild. Rob will be the kind of guy you will love to hate because he is so talented if it's not because he is so nice. Last night Rob was sitting with his brother and other Dutch friends, all been finished for a while when I came in and they asked me my finish time for today's stage. I told them I came with only 30 minutes to spare, one of them call me an eco runner, I had no idea so he explained that the eco runners are the slow runners that are always stopping to take pictures and lingering at checkpoints like it's a cocktail party eating and drinking. Then it hit me, he just called me a jogger, my ego was sure bruised especially since I had been running as fast as I could not taking photos and barely stopping at checkpoints. In the morning things became a bit clearer for me, the worst thing I could do was to be beaten mentally so then and there I decided to fights hard until the end and to be smarter and not to try and keep up with everybody, just to run my race. My race is between my body and my mind. I started at a conservative 8K per hour knowing that I needed at least 7, I ran slow and even some of the hills at a much conservative pace, yesterday I was doing 11K per hour to only bonk at 30K. I felt great but I was still worried about timing out, about 32K into I was passed by absolutely everybody, then it became more real that I would be timing out if I didn't find the strength to run hard. Have to thank my kids for putting music on my iPod and thanks to the Foo Fighters, as well. When the song The Pretender came on and the lyrics spoke loud to me, "What if I say you are not like the others, what if I say I will never surrender, you are the pretender". I was not the pretender I am a runner, not a jogger, I ran hard for the last 10K the faster I run the faster I wanted to go, I made a decision, to be who I am and not to be afraid whatever the outcome that is what who I am supposed to be. For the first time in my life, I allowed myself to say, I am an athlete, I felt every bit as I fought hard to not be disqualified on the 350K distance. Something changed in the last hour. I made the decision to be happy with who I am to be proud, to focus on the wins but not on the losses, to see them as part of the journey. Things are changing at the race, people are hurting, while I came smiling and in better shape, than yesterday most people found it harder today. There is no way to predict who will finish or who will not today I did it, tomorrow is another day and I will welcome it for the wonderful opportunity of becoming the person I was born to be.

Tuesday, July 7, 2009

Swiss Jura Day 3

Well, day three is over and I am still on the race, sort of. Today's stage was 56k long, total ascend +1650 and total descend was - 1920. I am going to be brief on my post since I have to post on my Blackberry, we have been sleeping at local gyms so there is no internet. I had an outstanding day today even if the outcome was less than desirable. I felt great if a bit slower but I managed to keep up with a lot of people. The view was as usual spectacular. I was doing great and was running with 3 other women who had previously pass me for more than an hour but in the end we all time out including three other males. We are all allowed to miss a cutout time once, but that is it, if I miss another cut off time then I have to move to the shorter distance. I feel a bit like Rocky Balboa in his movie. Rocky' where he is down for 9 counts and saved by the bell. The other three women running and I we had to decide to either stay on the 350K or move to the 175K. Maria Madueno of Tijuana, Mexico decided to switch to the shorter distance feeling there is no way she will meet any of the future times of the 350K. Maria is a 3:10 marathoner with 10 years of ultrarunning experience and a former Olympian in cycling. The rest of us that are given another chance will be going for the longer distance. The stages are getting harder and I am getting slower so it will be very tough to accomplish this with 4 days to go, but it's not impossible. I don't want to go home and wonder if I could have done it if I try and I still fail then I will know for sure. I will tell you tomorrow of the stars are aligned, and like my best friend from Calgary Nadia said once when I had a hard time on a race, run strong and when your legs can't carry you any longer, run with mine. Well, Nadia, I hope you are ready for tomorrow.

Wednesday, July 8, 2009

Swiss Jura Day 4

Well, you can't blame me for trying. I desperately tried to make it to the end but I was still a few minutes too late. I feel great about it, It is rare since anybody that knows me can tell you I am not good a losing. Feel good for two reasons, I gave it all I got and I was still running strong. As usual, we got up at 4am, breakfast at 5, pack your belongings and start at 7am. I awoke around 1am to thunderstorms, we were sleeping at a tennis complex and the sound of rain on the tin roof woke me up, it rained solidly until the just before the start of the race, not a good sign if you are hoping to better your previous time, I remember thinking if that's not a sign that it's all over I don't know what it is. It was worth it if only to see competitor Joerg Schreiber from Germany running on his speedo, nothing rare if you were in Iron Man but not here in the mountains and he also tucked his wallet and mp3 player on down his front. Today's stage was 47K long with +2020 total ascend and -1770 total descend. I ran very well the first 14K, not far from second and third female, it looked very promising, the second checkpoint was a bit harder to get to on time because of the climbing and the incredibly slippery conditions. My lungs burned trying to get enough oxygen like an asthmatic at a smoky bar. I missed the checkpoint by just 10 minutes. I was disappointed but I am still glad that I am still healthy to finish the seventh continent if for a shorter distance. I wanted to try hard, I wanted to not feel regret when I got home. My fundraising has been extremely successful, not entirely by me, Mr. Brett Wilson's famous garden party did a record fundraising of 110,000 dollars for 777 Run For Sight and the donations keep pouring in as I type this. Yes, his celebrity status and the fact that his beautiful and talented girlfriend, singer and songwriter Sarah McLachlan was there at the party where a major factor of why people were so generous but there other factors, the fact that an ordinary individual like me can accomplish extraordinary things. I am glad we successfully passed our fundraising goal, cnib, Foundation Fighting Blindness and Operation Eyesight do amazing work and deserve every penny. I now move to the 175K distance, I am still feeling healthy so I am expected to finish the race and accomplish my record on time. At this moment I haven't really had time to think about what it all means, at this point, I am still taking it one day at a time. As usual, we gather around the dinner table talking about how our day was like we are one big family, we become close even though we are complete strangers because we rely on each other so much. All of a sudden the world seems a lot smaller now that I have a much larger family.

Friday, July 10, 2009
Swiss Jura Day 5
Today's stage was 53K for the long stage and 28K on the half distance. I was fine going to bed but it was hard to see my former group leave this morning while I waited on the later start. To the untrained eye, the emotion I felt would have been called envy, disappointment, but to me, it was called desire. The desire to improve and be better next time. I have enjoyed this race tremendously, I have never ran better on a race before even if I am falling short on my results and it's because everybody else around me is better and that inspires me to try to improve. Swiss Jura race women and man have the same time limits but an average male can run faster than a woman of the same fitness level, so every year about half of the women move to the shorter distance and only about 1/3 of man do but instead of feeling it's unfair it motivates me to want to be one of the few female finishers. Today was 28K long and very little climbing about 400m or about 9K for the 175K distance, I felt fantastic and ran it all at a reasonable pace to let my body recover while still making great time. I crossed the finish line, 6 female, in about 3 hours and 45 minutes, I feel guilty to tell you that I had such a great day and enjoyed every minute I was there. We

usually start 3 hours after the early group, we drive to the halfway point then run the last two checkpoints, this is the first time that I got to see the lead runners on the chase, overall leader of the 350K is Nemeth Cesna of Hungary, this is his third year defending his title, the race directors call him the Swiss Watch because he logs identical times every year, he comes to Swiss Jura to win for the prize money, he said that allows him to take his family to a vacation every year. My new friend and fellow Mexican, Maria Madueno is doing great but told me she is still in pain from the burns she suffered a few days before coming, it has been raining hard every day that makes it hard since the dressings stick to the burns but she is a trouper hardly complaining, although according to her family she is the original Mexican Running Wild but they gave me permission to share this name with her. Yesterday I told you that we were like one big family and today I regret that statement since things got a bit strange. As usual, we arrived at the next Community hall, where we are spending the night, it rained hard and I was full of mud and was looking forward to a nice shower, when I walked in I found the shower was co-ed, full of naked people, man and women. just one shower room for us all and close quarters too. I was raised Catholic, even looking at your own body naked was frowned upon! I saw my friend Lydia Gomez of Spain showering already with all the guys so pretended I was European too and not bother at all, remember the German athlete running on his speedo yesterday? I thought I had seen enough of his body!. I am slowly panicking, two more days and this is it, 777 Run for Sight will be a reality, it has changed me forever and it will also impact many people's lives because the fundraising was so successful, I am full of hope that if I can accomplish something that seems impossible just a few months ago then is not difficult to imagine a cure for my son Karl either. after all, all this crazy quest started because a mom, me, just wanted to show her kids that while things that seem unfair will happen, together we can overcome anything. I miss my kids so much. I started running two years ago when I was facing a breakup, uncertainty in the future and the hardships of raising two kids alone, one with a disability and its exactly where I am at this moment yet I feel at peace. Instead of feeling overwhelmed when a problem arises no I feel like screaming on top of my lungs *Ha, is that all you got!*. Nothing has changed in the exterior but everything has changed because of the interior changes I have undergone.

Saturday, July 1, 2009

777 Run For Sight- Mission accomplished!

Today July 11th about 12:58pm Switzerland time I crossed the finish line of my last race in the 777 Run For Sight. Last stage was 27K long, with the same altitude that the previous days but instead of taking four hours I finish in under three, I felt like Forrest Gump on his movie where he is been chased by the bullies and he literally runs from his leg braces, all of a sudden the heaviness of my legs lifted allowing me to run and run. I was worry that because I was running the shorter distance it was going to be anticlimactic, but through the 3 hours of my last day running, the last few months played on my head like a movie, sleep deprivation in Brazil, the pain in Namibia, the laughter in the tent in the Gobi, the amazing moments I have the experience, it was sure to grand to ignore. I arrived from Geneva to Basel 7 days later forever changed, I am still the same mom who worries about her sons but instead of feeling despair, I am now full of hope.

Here are some stats of the last 7 months

Total distance run officially- 1272 Kilometres

Weight before the race 110.8 lbs- after 104.9 lbs

Number of toenails lost- 7

Number of running shoes used- 14

number of Honey stinger bars eaten- 74

Number of gels- 103

distance traveled- 48,425

Number of hours spent running- 283

I have dreamt about this moment for so long and its finally here. It feels so weird to be experiencing this alone. Except for a few phone interviews for local Calgary papers I will just go back to the hotel like nothing extraordinary just happened. Honestly this is exactly what I need right now. After a couple of days In Italy with Nicola I will be then be off to Valencia Spain to see my other sister Lourdes, I haven't seen since she move to Spain with her family in 1993 so it's the perfect way to celebrate this amazing accomplishment. The overwhelming response to 777 Run For Sight shows to me that like me many people in the world are looking for a more meaningful life. And of course, you might be wondering what's next. Some of the people that I met were mountain climbers that have switched to ultrarunning and they are encouraging to give mountaineering a try. Who knows, why not climb all seven continents!. Of course, my family was a bit hesitant when I told them of my plans, after all when my mom showed concern when I started running ultras I told her not to worry, that it wasn't like I was climbing Mount Everest or something like that. In the end, they understood that I was going ahead but as usual I was checking my ego at the door, I have really nothing to prove. In the end, somehow instead of feeling like is the end of a story, I am left feeling like this is the beginning of something wonderful.

To be continued...

Thursday, August 20, 2009

Transrockies Run

My best friend Nadia and I are off to Colorado for the TransRockies Run. It's going to be so much fun. Last year we ran Boston to celebrate my 40th day and it was a blast. This time is Nadia's turn to celebrate her 40th. There are other reasons to get away as well, Nadia is going through a separation and we have a lot of catching up to do. I haven't been there for her, she couldn't have timed her separation any worse, just before my first race in Brazil I told her, haha, as if there is a good time to divorce!. You should see my house now, it has become the headquarters of single mothers, between Nadia, Lisa Kauffman and myself we have 7 boys between the ages of 14 and 11, my house resembles Monday Night WWW Raw. Lisa, Calgary's original supermodel, moved back from Brazil with her two sons, Christiano and Caetano after her divorce, we met a few months ago but it's like we been friends forever. TransRockies Run is 113 miles, starts Aug 23rd to 28th from Buena Vista to Beaver Creek, Co. it's a team event, Nadia choose the name for the team, Crash and Burn, my choice was Cinderella's Stepsister's since prince charming isn't exactly knocking our doors but Nadia sees herself more as Cinderella than an ugly stepsister. Some friends are coming to the race as well, Leslie Gerein and her husband Keith. Katrina Follows her husband Rob, and Lenny from Toronto all whom were my tent mates at Gobi March this year, coincidentally they are also the three people that have summited all 7 highest peaks on 7 continents and are the ones that got me thinking when we were hanging out in the tent in the Gobi that this is something I could do and have been preparing to climb ever since. It's funny how things seem impossible until you meet somebody who has done it, then it becomes a possibility. This is surely the best way to celebrate the end of the summer. I am looking forward to the race, I have been overwhelmed with the preparations for the climb. I go for training in the last two weeks in September and if everything goes well, I start climbing late November. I met with Jamie Clarke Calgary's elite climber who is heading to Everest in the spring, I am asking him to be my adviser, since I don't have a lot of experience climbing, I need somebody who is not biased to judge if I am ready for Everest in the spring if everything else goes well. He is a bit hesitant to make it his call, " what if I say to go ahead and you die?" " I will hate that" of course I told him that I can't see myself dying, why survive all the things I have survive so far, the kidnapping in Mexico City when I was 17 for example just to die? Mexico is notorious for young girls disappearing and never seeing again, taken in broad daylight, I am one of the lucky ones that escaped. Or surviving a murder attempt in Japan at age 23 years old. Of course, there is always a risk, even though I don't intend on dying, I am 41 years old and have had a full life but my kids need their mother so I will take my preparations very seriously. I feel calm and compose and can picture myself accomplishing it, sort of Richard Dreyfuss on Close Encounters of the Third Kind, where people thought he was crazy but things seemed so real to him. I will continue to put my kids first though especially when things are a bit more difficult for Karl at the moment since his friends are taking their learner's permit and are starting to ask girls out and Karl pretends he is too busy to care. I am not afraid of climbing Everest, I am very afraid of watching my beautiful son Karl not realizing his dreams. My inspiration lately is coming from Miley Cyrus new song " The Climb". Nadia laughed and said " What are you 12?!" when I called her recommending Miley's new song "The Climb".

"Keep on moving, keep climbing
Keep the faith, baby

It's all about, it's all about the climb

Keep the faith, keep your faith"

Sunday, August 30, 2009

Transrockies Run! What a Party!

I am back from the Transrockies Run. It was my first time on the race and I can tell you it will not be the last time. This race was like Spring Break for runners. Nadia and I arrived in Buena Vista, a cool small town in Colorado and the start of the race. I developed a low-grade fever on the previous days and found myself being incredibly tired. I decided to run anyway since looking at the rooster, the race had big names such as Nikki Kimball, Hal Kroener, Dean Karnazes, Anita Ortiz, there was no chance we could place at all, also Nadia promises she just wanted to have fun. Dean remembered me from Sahara and we had a blast catching up. His father is recuperating from a heart attack and is thankfully doing well now. From the beginning I struggled, I had trouble breathing, day 1 was 20 miles with 2721 feet of climbing. It was Nadia's first ultra-event but it didn't show, she ran strong and climbed fast, waiting for me at checkpoints because we needed to cross them as a team. I forgot my sleeping bag so it went from bad to worse since the nights can be very cold. By day two things had changed, Nadia went from thinking "I wonder if I can finish this race to" I can win it!", even though the field had big names, as usual after a few days is anybody's game, as teams bickered and broke up and injuries made runners quit (Dean went home on day 4 with a broken rib) in few short days the top teams where unknown people. Nadia kept asking me if I wanted to quit after watching me deteriorate but I didn't want to quit, everybody thought she was so sweet since she was concerned, however, we knew the real reason was that she wanted to trade me for a healthy team member instead, I told her that since she had shamed me into coming to the race with her when I told her I didn't feel up to a few months ago then she was now stuck with me. I was taking her down with me as punishment, having both of our names attached to my slow running time. I couldn't run fast at all but it would be incredibly rude for me to stop just because of that, after a few days everybody was suffering from something, especially when we arrived in Leadville, the town is 10,000 feet above sea level. A lot of us suffered from altitude sickness. I didn't run on day 5 and choose to hike the entire distance instead, I told Nadia just to run Stage 5 on her own and wait for me at the finish line, we were penalized for that but I knew Nadia was dying to see how fast she could run it. Her ego had suffered enough as she waited for me at every checkpoint. I had a great time with the teams in the back, after all, it was Colorado, the view was spectacular. I love joining ultra-events and surround myself with amazing talent, but I have found myself on the back more than once and I love the spirit of anybody who decides to take life to the fullest level. That day I hiked with the Japanese female team, one of the team members was Sumie Inagaki the 48hrs Ultramarathon record holder, her friend was slow but she came to spend time with her regardless, also on the back was the Old Goats Team, two 70 + year old guys who had a fantastic time enjoying themselves. It was only the last day of the race that I felt great and I decided to run hard, I knew Nadia wanted to place top 3 for at least a stage so we went for it, we came short and crossed 4th but had a blast chasing the other teams. Even though I was very sick, the race was so much fun, I mostly stayed at my tent but it was great watching my best friend have the time of her life, she became the race's it girl. Every night she would come back to the tent after hanging out with everybody at the campfire and we would chat until late laughing and giggling like little girls at a summer camp. We developed code names for almost everybody, especially the guys at the camp, Plan B was a guy who ran shirtless almost every day and casually hinted he was single, Sleeping Bag was a guy who offered his sleeping bag to me when he overheard I was missing mine, one catch, he offered the bag with him on it, before long we figure he was married so he became *married* sleeping bag, Fastimes at Ridgemont was a guy who kept asking me to stop by to check his trailer everyday forgetting he had asked me the same thing the day before. The race was fun but the top teams pulled fantastic times but don't be fooled by all the fun, Transrockies is it's still a serious race. Ultradistance runners have a reputation of being top athletes and party animals at the same time. Nadia plans on coming back next year and try for a top team. An ultra is a race where I get to watch somebody who has never thought could do it accomplish something incredible, I got more pleasure watching Nadia smile wide like a kid every day than any medal I have ever received. This is something I learned from leaving in Japan, Buddha's teaching said "Thousands of candles can be lit from a single candle, and the life of the candle will not be shortened. Happiness never decreases by being shared."

Saturday, September 12, 2009

"The Sun Shines Not On Us But Within Us." John Muir

I have been busy training for Mt. Aconcagua, I am scheduled to leave Nov 29th, I am so excited and nervous to be leaving soon. I am off to Columbia Icefields to train for ice and snow climbing this Friday and hoping to Summit Mt Athabasca Monday at 3am. My body is starting to get used to new training, while I still get tired is not the overwhelming exhaustion I was feeling a few weeks ago. Even the mental strength required for my next quest was overwhelming, in a very short time I went from being the best mother to the worse, I have been getting a lot of heat for planning my Everest quest, is no use for me to say much after all this is something that I didn't understand myself a few months ago, now, however, I have been learning a lot about what it takes to make it. A few months ago I talked to a sports psychologist friend, Hap, he wanted to know more about what goes to my brain when I face so many challenges yet I make no excuses and try even harder to overcome then instead of giving up, that after all is what he is hired to do. The question was is it Nature or Nurture? and I think is a bit of both, when I find myself with an obstacle I dig deep and find a way either over it or around it. The truth is that the resistance I find now is nothing new. When I was 19 I left home to Japan, I was thrilled with the opportunity, we had no money and this was a great opportunity for me to pay for my university and help my family at the same time. My sister has a baby girl and things where though for us, the town being Catholic didn't take well that my sister was an unwed teen mother, so when the opportunity presented itself I took it with all my heart. Where there any risks?, you bet, and at the end it did not exactly turned out to be what I was promised but after a year in japan I found a way forward. I worked hard and saved all my money while I worked and went home with enough money to put a down payment on a house in a nice neighborhood and to finally go to University. When I came home, however, my family started to be harassed, the whole town speculated about how a 20-year-old could have bought a house and after a month I left Mexico and never returned. Japan became my new home. I worked hard for the next few years to learn Japanese and pass the exams to go to University there, by now two of my siblings were living with me in Tokyo and going to school themselves, by the time word had spread around the world that Japan was experiencing a bubble, I was already fluent and working very successfully but everything came to an end one evening I stopped at a club to meet with friends, when I arrived they weren't there but I recognized some people that waved me to their table, that is the last thing I remember before waking up the next day face down on a pool of my own blood, with blunt force trauma to the head, my front teeth where smash and I couldn't recognize the face on the mirror. On the way to the hospital, I kept asking the same questions over and over, why? this was early 90's Doctors didn't know about rape drugs being used on drinks so they didn't believe me when I said I had just one drink. I was 23 years old. There have been many years after that incident, I hardly ever think about it anymore, fortunately, the positive memories are the everlasting ones, that baby girl that I help raise is my nice Marianna and now lives with me in Canada, she is 23 years old and studying English. My brother in Japan just received his MBA and it is expecting his first child, looking around, all my siblings and their kids are doing great, what those guys in Japan set out to do break me and my family, they really didn't accomplish it. Every time I hear words that tell me, how do you think you are? I say, I am the girl that survived the unthinkable and its now ready for the rest of her life. While I will never understand why I suffered so much abuse or feel OK to see my son struggle, at least I can somehow make sense that maybe what I went though was preparing me to face my current life with dignity and to stop questioning life every time it threw a challenge my way and instead help me launch into action to change it for the better. And next time someone asks me again, "who do you think you are?" I can say, *who am I not to be what I set out to be.*

Tuesday, September 22, 2009

Ice and Snow Training Weekend.

I am back from Columbia Icefields where I spent the weekend training for crevasses rescue and glacier climbing safety. The 3 days I spent learning the basics like equipment, and safety than putting it into action Monday at Mt. Athabasca was the most inspired three days I've had in a long time. I loved everything I experienced, the guide had very specific instructions, place your feet exactly on my steps so you don't slip and drag us all to the cliff down below. I developed the concentration, not unlike the bomb squad. So why exactly did I love it so much? I am learning the difference between what's hard but possible and what's just plain crazy. I have found a new level of athleticism that is on a league of its own. I am definitely growing as a person, I think adversity naturally makes you grow if you concentrate on the positives of adversity. I am learning to be less judgmental. Like watching kids ski jump, I used to think *what kind of parents allow their kids to do that?*, what I wasn't taking into consideration was that before they are allowed to jump they are trained on how to succeed, my opinion was based on ignorance, not knowledge. I am ready for Aconcagua, I leave Nov 28th, I am excited and busy setting it up. I am giving a presentation at St. James School where my kids attend and I am having them follow me on my journey, I am going to have as many schools in Calgary as I can interest participate on the progress and ask questions. I am hoping to teach them the value of goal setting and hard work. Emphasis on hard work, I just lost my Everest sponsor so everything is up in the air. Just like learning to walk, I am all of a sudden having trouble standing up on my own, since I am no longer with my well know-well connected ex-boyfriend it seems like my value had gone down. One by one I see the doors closing, gently but closing. As much as it hurt, I realized that if they weren't interested in my quest is because I have failed to show my worth. Looking in detail my life seems to be working like somebody's idea of a nightmare. I am single and for the first time I am thinking that maybe I will be forever, after the course I came back to the hotel to bad TV and my thoughts went to last weekend meeting my ex-boyfriend Greg's Brazilian girlfriend Flora at my kids swim meet, it seems that Gisele Bundchen is the girl next door in Brazil, Flora really is amazing, she came to meet my kids since my ex talks about how amazing they are, but instead of crying myself to sleep, I smiled after that though. I have learned that happiness is a feeling, not a checklist. I am so happy that my happiness is not determined by other people's unhappiness. I am still optimistic that everything will work out in the end, what I need to do is, as usual, put my head down and work hard, I still believe that I am in the right path even though it's the one less traveled one. This is one more thing that I hope to teach my kids that passion runs deep, sometimes all we have is the belief in ourselves. It is not the number of times one falls but how many times we are willing to stand up.

Updated note: Greg and Flora married and have two beautiful children together. Flora and I remain great friends.

Thursday, September 24, 2009

Welcome Aboard.

What an amazing couple of days. I received a lot of mail of support, it was overwhelming.

Last night I had a great chat with MLA Dave Rodney, he is a big supporter of my quest and even spoke on my behalf at the Legislature Assembly of Alberta, he has summited Everest twice, he has been wanted to talk to me as soon as he heard I was planning on climbing Everest, I thought he wanted to persuade me not to do it but instead, once more he offered his support. We talk about what it takes to make it and how going there for the wrong reasons can be dangerous, instead he said the fact that I am such a good mother will keep me safe, imagine that. Other developments are that Helly Hansen and Clif Bars are going to be my sponsors, I was thrilled when they call me to tell me the news, I am still looking for summit sponsors but this is a great start. I spent all afternoon putting the presentation together for my kid's school, I have a lot of pictures, what it struck me was my smile in them, I am truly loving what I am doing, I kept thinking how did a little girl who was born in Mexico, poor, is here in these pictures, smiling and believing that she has what it takes to make it to the top of the world.

Sunday, October 25, 2009

Bathroom Stall Poetry. "Whatever Love We Think Deserve Is The Love We Receive" Written in a Bathroom Stall At The Chinook Mall in Calgary.

Is about a month before I head for Argentina, I have been really busy preparing, both physically and mentally. I know my trainer Ray Zahab is the best in the world but let me tell you, his workouts are tough, he makes no apologies for it, I told him I was exhausted after he asked me how I was feeling and he said. " good, you should". The kick-off for Aconcagua will be at my kid's school, the teachers been asking me to talk to the kids since registration to sports especially cross country has been dwindling. Things are falling into places, I stopped feeling angry and forced myself to understand better. It's always been easy to feel the " ifs" as in " if I had the money" " if I had a partner" but that isn't the case. I have been asking for something that I haven't proven that I am ready for and I should work hard on making sure I am, and that's what I have been doing recently, training hard. I call it surrendering, it's really different from giving up. Once I understood this, the anger went away, if I work hard everything is still possible, dreams don't have expiry dates. Unfortunately training it's not as easy as is with running, I can't just simply take to the mountains as I easy as I can step out of my house and run, even my long runs at times I was able to put my kids to bed and run all night on my treadmill so I wouldn't leave them alone for 12 hours. The endurance part I can do, I practically live at the gym but the skills are a different story, the second-best is to read as much as

I can on the subject and head to the mountains whenever I get a chance. My favorite magazine right now is Gripped, it has an amazing article about staying motivated, it says that we need two types of goals, end goals, and process goals. End goals are external things such as accomplishing a race, a climb or quitting smoking, process goals are the things you learn in the process of your external achievements, they are internal such as the ability to increase your lactic threshold or experiencing less anxiety from not smoking. The order of the goals is very important too, making process goals more important will keep you motivated even when things get tough because you see them as a valuable part of the end goal. I have been doing just that without knowing it, I have been looking forward to the training because I think it will make me a better runner too, hills have never been my strength and seeing how much better I am at them makes me want to train harder and harder. To increase my motivation I also picked the other end goal, running Atacama Race in March and aim for the top 3 females. My favorite climber right now is Sean Isaac from Canmore, I am learning that mountaineering is a sport that attracts incredibly athletes but humble in nature, the best way for me to be accepted is to keep quiet and let my work speak for me. it's very important to be able to do the climbs only if I earn the respect of everybody that I share the mountains with. Sometimes the most talented people are the ones we never hear from, they get no satisfaction from glory, just from the act itself. I am also finishing my university course (international Business) and looking for a job as well. I need to start working in January and I have narrowed the search to 3 jobs. It has to be casual so I won't stress if I need to take my kids to the doctor or go to a parent-teacher interview, it also has to be shift work since I need to take my kids to their swimming practices right after school. It was a bit tough to get my head around the choices, housekeeping for the Fairmont Hotel, Barista for Starbucks or a grocery store clerk. It was not a problem until I realized I need to name references, I kept thinking please don't call my ex-boss!?. My last job was as a Marketing Director, I mean isn't it supposed to be backward? housekeeping then director? but I need the money and I should never be embarrassed to work, no matter what the job is. My kids are growing up, they will be able to do things on their own and then I will be able to work full time at an office, by then I should have also my Bachelor of Management from Athabasca University. Of course, as my goals increased, so did the level of difficulty to accomplish them, yet I have never been happier, the goals keep getting harder and harder but since they are still things that are important to me I am happy. I guess that's when you know if the path you are on is the right one, I look around and I like what I see, when I look into the mirror I see somebody working hard to reach a goal, and in the process, I am teaching my kids the value of believing in yourself. "The mountains have rules. they are harsh rules, but they are there, and if you keep to them you are safe. A mountain is not like men. A mountain is sincere. The weapons to conquer it exist inside you, inside your soul." Walter Bonatti."

Friday, November 13, 2009

" You Can Live three Weeks Without Food, Three Days Without Water, But Not a Moment Without Hope". Lewis Mumford

Two weeks before I head to Aconcagua, my gear is almost ready, I have been in Mountain Equipment Co-Op buying my gear and I spent more time trying day packs than I ever did try wedding dresses when I was planning my wedding! Although the last few weeks been though since my niece Marianna broke her ankle, I feel that if I write a book the title of my book should be Murphy's Law. It has been challenging to keep my training schedule and keep my house functioning. Luckily I have as usual try to use the challenges as motivation to keep my focus. Wednesday I broke down crying, my niece was in pain, teachers were calling me to come to school right away because one of my kids had assignments missing, I had a short window to accomplish it all so it looked like I was going to have to push training to until late that evening when everybody went to bed, I was already tired from my first workout early morning and now I wasn't going to bed early. I was so mad at myself for breaking down crying that in the evening I added 10 extra kilos to make my pack 40lbs in total and used a 15% incline on my treadmill to hike for a couple of hours. it felt so good afterward, life keeps telling me, this is a far you are possibly going and I just keep saying, *I don't think so, you think that was hard, how about I make it even harder!"*. I did a couple of talks on behalf of Foundation Fighting Blindness and Operation Eyesight, I loved the energy, I get nervous because I always think I have no business been there, especially when I have broken down crying numerous times in the last few weeks. but when I am there it just feels natural, not motivational speaker natural but as a regular person who is facing daily challenges but chooses to see the positive kind of a way, my message is always that as a mother of a son who is losing his sight, I am learning that it is us the ones that are not, that see limits. I am inspired by Karl every single day. He teaches me to not dwell on the pass and to not worry about the future, it's the now that matters. Karl doesn't worry about perfection either, waiting for the perfect time, or perfect weather is just an excuse to delay making a decision. He also teaches me that if you aren't willing to make a fool of yourself you are cheating yourself on learning something new. He tried for the school Badminton team and even though I knew the outcome I asked how he did when he came home. " I didn't make the team' Karl told me without a hint of sadness, " you never know" he added. Then we couldn't stop laughing when he told me he made it farther in the tryouts than some of his friends. My other son Hans interjected "Imagine your blind friend beating you at Badminton!" I loved that about us, we face things head on, we don't hide, even if we fall short we proudly go for things, we either win or fail spectacularly nothing in between!. I have been approached by a daytime US talk show to possibly appear, such is the exciting times, but I can't think of why I should be interviewed. it's my son Karl who, with his grace is guiding us all, like the captain of a rowing team, I am rowing the boat but it's him with his directions that is making sure we get to finish line. But like any amazing person, he doesn't think what he is doing is such a big deal. the cnib is training him on their ambassador club to be a community leader, Karl doesn't understand why. He asked me why does everybody think is amazing that he doesn't think is a big deal what he is going through since it just simply isn't. I am sure there are far worse things in life, he simply said. His teachers also told me how much of a positive influence he is in the classroom, his willingness to participate in class rubs off, at 15 years of age most kids disengage in class since it's not cool to be into school, Karl for some reason was born with his own manual, what's the point of going to school if it's not to learn, even if working your hardest ends on just a C or worse. Every single day there is not a moment I don't count my blessings, my kids are teaching me to have fun, to play fair, to always give your best and to never be afraid to get your hands dirty.

Saturday, November 28, 2009

Adios! On My Way to Aconcagua

I am almost ready to board the plane and I have been going crazy to make sure bills are paid, freezers have enough food, Christmas concerts, band concerts, swim meets and school rides are arranged because my mom is looking after my kids and she doesn't drive. Things were crazy, okay, they were downright out of control for a couple of days, my basement flooded again and it sends me on a crazy bizarre journey of calling a realtor to sell my house and move to Vancouver to be closer to my sister Muñeca, it turns out my house is hard to sell, busy street, can't be subdivided, unless I want to drop the price significantly, which in it means I can't move to Vancouver either, if they ever make a movie about me, they will cast Mr. Bean to play me. Things are fine, my kids are happy to see me go, I am a bit suspicious about this, and my niece is mobile once again after having surgery to repair her birthday party injury, so I can now go and do what have been dreaming about for the last three months, to climb Aconcagua, I feel confident and ready. I am scheduled to start climbing until Dec 2 once we have acclimatized properly for a few days before the climb on the town of Penitentes, there are two local guides and five of us climbing, two Australians and two South Africans.

Tuesday, December 8, 2009

Base Camp, Plaza Argentina

Just a quick update. I am in base camp Aconcagua, plaza Argentina. We climbed to camp 1 yesterday to bring gear before coming back to base camp as part of acclimatizing, climb high, sleep low. I had a terrible day, I barely made it, I was the only one of the team members that didn't hire a porter and I was carrying 18K of gear. I have trained to carry heavier gear but we climb to 5 000 meters, my quads were burning and my lungs were screaming for air. Today we rest before we continue to camp 1, then do the same, bring gear to camp 2, then 3 before the summit. I am struggling a lot, on a scale of 1 to 10, yesterday was a 10, I had a very hard day and I am not sure I am physically able to do it. Patrick and Jacqui a couple of South Africa have paid for a porter for me, it´s incredible, I have never met them before, yet, out of kindness, they have paid $150 dollars just because they felt bad for me. Tomorrow is the other day, I am positive that since I climb without gear I will do better. A lot of people felt bad for me, I was the last one to make it back to camp last night, almost an hour and a half after the last team, but like I told them, a bad day in a mountain is sure better than a great day at the office.

Saturday, December 12, 2009

Aconcagua, It Was Just Not Meant to Be.

Just got back to base camp after making it to camp 2 yesterday. I have a lot of emotions that are building up. I suffered from severe dehydration and Matias decided that the best decision was for me to turn around. I felt fine, just weak and tired but since the team was heading to camp two again. I respect his decision, from the beginnings I told him that I was going to follow his orders. There were a couple of things that I did wrong, first carrying all my gear instead of hiring a porter proved to be a mistake, second, I needed to learn to speak up, emotions are running high in the group, there was a screaming match between our guide Tomas and some of the climbers because of not enough toilet paper, broken tents and at the end I ended up climbing to camp 2 with only half a liter. At one point I felt I was climbing with the Kardashian sisters. I am incredibly sad, it's hard to say but I still think I could have made it to the top. I guess now it's time to go back home, regroup and see what I need to change then give it another go.

Monday, December 14, 2009

Aconcagua- This One is For the Brokenhearted

I am back finally in Mendoza. If you just want to know where my head is, failure to the summit only means I will come back to Aconcagua and attempt again. Now after a 9-hour mule ride back to civilization over treacherous terrain, I had a lot to think about. The last day at base camp was like nursing a broken heart, I spent most of my day tucked in my sleeping bag before people around camp staged an intervention. Alpine Accents team was just heading out to camp one and they asked me to have dinner with them, little by little my mood lifted, had so much fun hanging out with the people that live at Camp Argentina, for three months of the year, Veronica, Pelao, Mauricio and other Argentineans leave their families for the summer holidays to work at base camp, they are a lot like a family, nothing like a great company and great food to mend a broken heart. Yesterday, Juan Horacio, an Argentinian Arriero pick me up with a pair of mules to ride back to Penitentes, there are 3 ways to get out of base camp Aconcagua, a three-day trek but you need camping gear to spend the night at designated camping areas, by helicopter, the last resort and only used in emergencies, or by mule. Fear depends on your options, we watched the mules balance our gear when we hiked to base camp over narrow terrain and even saw a couple of mules take a tumble, now here I was for the next 9 hours riding back to Penitentes with Juan.

Everything was OK, except for the moment when I looked back one more time and saw it, Aconcagua behind me, a perfect day to summit, it looked so beautiful, I cried as hard as Jen Aniston must have cried when she saw her then-husband Brad Pitt and his new girlfriend Angelina Jolie play house on the cover of W Magazine. For the next 9 hours, Juan and I got to know each other well, I also got to see my trek backward, great memories keep coming, the last 10 days had been hard but also been incredibly fun. Juan was one of the Arrieros that carried our gear when we hiked in, he incidentally found my video camera on the road and returned it. On the way, other Arrieros called him *suegro* or Father- in- Law, Juan then told me he is the proud father of seven daughters and has one more the way, all by different women, he told me with a smile, something became apparent to me, Arrieros must love women and fathering kids. It was a perfect way to end my trip, the adventure, and the memories will stay with me. The practical jokes we played on each other, It was funny until the joke was on me. Tony my tent mate faked a love note to me from Carlos one of the guides, fooling me was easy, the ego is a terrible thing. The worse part was when Tony convince me that thanking Carlos was the right thing to do even if I didn't feel the same way, imagine my surprise when Carlos had no idea what I was talking about, the best part was the payback when we convivence Tony that Carlos was mad of his joke because he had a fiancée and was worried she would wrongly hear the rumor and might dump him. Carlos played the part rather beautifully when Tony approached him to apologize and Carlos made him believed they needed to take it " outside". As usual, the people I met become the most important part of my journey, is like finding out you are adopted and your real family has invited you to a family reunion, you all of a sudden surrounded by people you have never met in your life but share a lot of things in common. Made new friends as usual friends, Marianne, a 66-year-old Canadian woman was going strong, nothing like getting your butt kicked by someone older than you to get your ego in check. Aidan and Tim, two best friends from Washington, were also scheduled to summit soon and of course the rest of my climbing team, I wish them a safe summit. Of course, I am coming back to Aconcagua, I can't hardly wait to start planning my return, next time though I would love to return with a friend, not as part of a team. Until now to be my friend all I needed was for you to either can make me laugh or let me cry, now however there is a new requirement, must love climbing, I am taking applications for new friends. It's an amazing world of madness that I have entered, mountaineering will not definitely be your first love but it will be your first grown-up love, it will your Harley Davidson riding boyfriend. I am not sure that I am coming back a better person or changed at all, I will be home happier and more I know for sure than I am in the right path. I have seen the summit, and however hard it has been to even get as close I got, it's definitely worth it.

Sunday, December 27, 2009

My Great concern is not Whether You Have Failed, But Whether You are Content With your Failure." Abraham Lincoln

Thanks so much for all the kind words. It was hard coming home after not making it to the summit of Aconcagua but setbacks like this are just nature's way of making sure of keeping us humble and honest. Success is a double-edged sword, just look at Tiger Woods in the news this week, when things are too easy and we stop challenging ourselves we tend to lose perspective of our priorities. The trick is to actually realize that there is an opportunity to learn and to grow and allow it to happen if we just stop dwelling on the negative. I like coming home and spending time alone and listen to the internal voice. I am always thankful for the opportunity to see clearly the path ahead of me, with all the challenges and the frustrations I am still passionate about what my life is all about and what it represents. Is through adventures that I express myself because of what's life but a great adventure. I was a bit embarrassed when I had to ride out of base camp, but then I realized that I should only be embarrassed the day I let my ego get on the way and I don't recognize when it's time to turn around safely.

Thankfully for me, the only frustration was because it feel I have what I takes to make it all the way. I felt fine but the guide was overwhelmed trying to keep everybody happy at camp 2 and at the end I ended up being the weakest link. Overall the experience was a fantastic opportunity to see how my body reacted to altitude, the rest can be accomplished with discipline and training. Passion and desire can't be taught and I have that in spades.

Tuesday, March 2, 2010

"For Those Who Believe, No Proof is Necessary. For Those Who Don't Believe, no Proof is Possible." Stuart Chase

Well I am back running and even though I haven't quit mountaineering If anything my commitment has strengthened. I am scheduled to run Atacama Crossing Monday 7th to the 13th. You are probably aware of the situation in Chile, the earthquake meant that very few flights are entering the country. My trip was canceled and I have to come clean, I had been delaying booking my flight because I am permanently waiting on checks to arrive, I am still not working and I depend on sponsors to get to the races and cover the expenses(OK, and people like my best friend Nadia who gives me money for groceries because she says she believes in me), there is no room ever in my bank account to cover the expenses until the money arrives. I am sure I am not alone here, that's the reason most people choose to work instead of following their passion. This has caused some concerns from my family and I have to agree that maybe I would feel the same if I wasn't in my shoes, there is one factor that determines why I can't work full time or even part-time unless is flexible, Karl's condition is getting more complicated, as you all know he has BBS and he is struggling as school as well now, he is working very hard yet he is failing at school. The day he got his report card was a bad day for him, he couldn't understand why he is still not passing," I sit and the front, pay attention, participate and work hard, I don't understand why I am still failing" he told me. I told Karl that we were going to fight this together, that I was proud of him and that yes that we needed to work even harder but it was either that or giving up and that's not what I want for him. He is doing so much better now, I guess he just needed to feel understood, that he is not alone. Sometimes shame isolates us, we all feel alone only because we are afraid to show how vulnerable we are. Fortunately, I wear my emotions on my sleeve, I am Latin, we are not good at hiding our emotions, for better or for worse and if you are my best friend sometimes is for the worse. I am off to Chile tomorrow and it's been a mad scramble to get there. I will have to flight to Salta Argentina, it will take me 42hrs to get there then I have to take a 14hr bus ride to San Pedro de Atacama before you think I am highly motivated to my cause this time it was people around me that made it happen, I went to bed several times thinking that there was no way to make it happen just to find my email box full of people that wanted to help. Even childcare proved to be a problem since my mom couldn't fly from Mexico this time but then my best friend

Nadia and my sister Muñeca, rally up to cover the days that I will be gone, it was like watching them build a quilt, taking blocks of days back and forth until all days where covered. I also heard from people I have never met helping me find the best possible fare and option to get to the race, it was overwhelming how people came together so fast. I feel incredibly fortunate to be surrounded by such amazing people in my life. If you ever been to my house you will know that I have no money but I think of myself as a very successful person, I see my life meaningful, the friendships I have and the bonds that I have with the people close to me are invaluable. Yes, this is ultimately what I need to do for my son but it also turned out to be the best decision I have made, I watched my investments shrink by the bad economy but wealth in the quality of people around me has increased substantially. I am dating Charlie Engle he has also been an amazing support on many areas, such mentoring me on fundraising, he is very passionate about having an impact on such issues as clean water for everybody to child obesity, and let's face it he makes me feel normal, having run very successfully the races that I am running he is a source of knowledge. I know is not thanksgiving but I am so thankful for everybody for helping me. "Be thankful for what you have; you'll end up having more. If you concentrate on what you don't have, you will never, ever have enough."
Oprah Winfrey

Thursday, March 4, 2010

Norma Goes to Chile....Hopefully.

Norma Blogs 2010 Atacama Crossing.

My name is Charlie Engle and I will be writing blog entries on behalf of Norma Bastidas about her journey across the Atacama Desert in Chile. I am doing this for many reasons. First, her passion is infectious and I wanted to help out. Second, I am her boyfriend and I believe in her and what she stands for. And finally, I am a runner too. Norma is nothing if not passionate and adventurous..........and maybe a little obsessive. When she sets her mind to a task, you can bet that she will get it done. As her boyfriend, I have learned very quickly not to argue with her when she gets that determined look on her face. I can either help her or get out of the way. This time I chose to help. It's the safest choice. The latest example of just what Norma "does" is the Atacama Crossing, a 7-day stage running race across one of the driest and harshest places on earth, the Atacama Desert. She must carry all her food and gear for the entire time while running about a marathon per day. No hot meals, no showers, no beds. But there will be plenty of hardship to go around. I have done a few of these races myself and I can say that they are very tough. It requires great determination to get through it. I have no doubt that Norma will thrive. She is like a magnet for other people, drawing on her energy and positive outlook. Normally one would expect that running 250K through the desert spread over 7 days would be the hardest part of a race. In this case, that may not be true. Just getting to the start has been an enormous challenge. And she is not there yet. Norma's plans were all set a few weeks ago. Her plane tickets were reserved and she just needed to pay for them. Money is tight so she was waiting for a check to come in. Then an 8.8 magnitude earthquake slammed Chile and everything changed, especially for the people of Chile. Most flights were canceled and the ones that were still going were completely filled overnight as people scrambled to get to Chile. The race organization, Racing the Planet, let everyone know that the race would go on as planned. To cancel it would just bring more economic hardship to the locals that were being hired by the race. Fundraising would take place to help out the needy. But the fact was that Norma was now stuck in no woman's land with no way to get to Chile. She would just have to accept that fact and start planning for the next event. Okay, maybe that's what most people would do. But Norma is not most people. She and I spent two days discussing options. Was it possible to go through Brazil or Peru or Argentina? Could she find a helicopter or private plane? Could we shoot her out of a giant cannon? Don't laugh, she would do it!. At one point it seemed that she had finally reached the logical conclusion that this event was simply not going to happen for her. We even started to plan for her to run a substitute expedition from north of Banff all the way to her front door in Calgary, about 250K. It was Monday night and that was the plan when she said goodnight to me. I felt guilty as I admitted to myself that I was a little relieved that she was not going. The earthquake, multiple planes, and busses with no traveling companion just worried me. My phone rang early

Tuesday morning. Norma says "I'm going". I say, "going where?" She says, "to the race of course". I said, "Who is this?" (Ok I didn't really say that but I wanted to). Instead, I said something eloquent like, "wow, great. Next, she proceeded to tell me how things had changed. It seems that the whole world has decided to help her get to Chile. She has offers of plane tickets, bus rides, travel agencies, donkeys and rocket propulsion jet packs (I made that last one up). Offers were pouring in and Norma was fired up. And it only took a moment for me to get fired up too. I quickly set aside my selfish worries and asked her what I could do to help. Really I couldn't do much except listen to her and offer an occasional opinion which she usually just politely ignored. She was not going to let her supporters down. She was going to find a way to get to Chile. Norma lives for her kids. Nothing is more important to her than their health and happiness. She likes to tell them how important it is to honor one's commitments. She found a flight to Salta, Argentina but it would take more than 40 hours to get there. She found a ride from Salta to San Pedro de Atacama but it would take 14 hours by car. And then there was the matter of money. Nothing was cheap because everything was being booked in desperation. It was a seller's market for sure. But she haggled and pleaded when necessary and she was able to scrape together the needed funds. She was on her way to Chile. Against all odds, she made it happen. It was amazing to watch. As I am writing this, Norma just called from Caracas, Venezuela. It is Thursday night, March 4th and the race starts on Monday. We spoke for a few minutes. She sounded tired but okay. She was stuck in the airport for 7 hours before her next flight. It looks like her luggage has been "misplaced". I asked her if she had shoes and she said that she is wearing running shoes but not the ones she intended to wear in the race. It sounds as if her challenges will continue. She may be borrowing clothes and food along the way. I think she mentioned hunting down a goat if she has to. If challenges make us stronger, then Norma should be a powerlifter by the time she reaches Chile. Oh yea, and then she gets to run 250K.I will be updating every day if possible depending on the information I can get. Norma wanted me to thank all of her friends and family members for their incredible support.

Charlie

Saturday, March 6, 2010

Just Plain Tired.

It's all fun and games until the airline loses your luggage. Then before you know it, the only shirt you have to wear is borrowed, ugly and two sizes too big. For Norma, lost luggage is an almost comical addition to an already challenging trip. More character building I guess although I think she has enough character already. She would rather have her bags. The worst part is the loss of food. She will find clothes and shoes but food for a race like this is not so easy. There is no REI down the street to go and resupply. She will have to make do with whatever she can find locally. Racers normally use energy bars, protein powders, and freeze-dried food. Not much chance of finding those items at the local Atacama Desert store. In fact, the odds are exactly zero. But she will make due. She will probably just run down some wild desert chickens and cook them over an open fire. Then squeeze some juice from a prickly cactus. If she would just pretend to be helpless for a bit, she would have tons of offers of help. After all, most of the racers are guys. But that won't happen. She will do for herself and find a way to get through it on her own. No matter what, she will make it to the start line ready to run. I did get to speak to her very late last night. She had arrived at her hotel in Salta and was going to get some sleep. Understandably she was tired but seemed in good spirits. She had just gotten word that there was an outside chance that her bags might arrive in Calama, a city about 3 hours away from the race start. If this happens, then she will have to catch a bus and go retrieve the bags herself. This would mean another 6 hours of travel but after almost 60 hours already, why not? It would still be best to have her own gear and food. If I had to guess though, I would not count on the bags arriving. It is just the way it seems to work. I once lost 3 bags in Africa and they showed up at my house in North Carolina 2 months later. Fingers crossed though. She slept on the floor of a couple of airports during her trip and was happy to have a shower and a bed, if only for a few hours. Early in the morning, she would be leaving with several other racers for San Pedro de Atacama, the headquarters for the race. The drive would be 14 hours. Apparently, nothing is close to anything else in the desert, or at least that's how it feels when you are out there. A cameraman named Mario has joined Norma and will be documenting her journey to and through the desert. If the first few days are any indication then this documentary she will be part of will be highly entertaining.

The race starts Monday.

Charlie Engle

Sunday, March 7, 2010

Beg Borrow and Hope for the Best.

San Pedro de Atacama.

I spoke to Norma briefly this morning before all the racers left for Camp 1. Later in the day, she sent me an email and some of it is copied below. She is always the optimist. Charlie Engle

We travel for two hours from San Pedro here and on the bus ride it was when I allowed myself to think about the last week. I managed to find everything except a head torch that I purchased for $10, the sleeping bag came from a porter from Kuma hotel where I stayed, he went home and got if for me, from 9:30pm last night to 1pm today people went out of their way to help me and that's amazing if anything this has taught me is that people are kind and generous, we hear so much on the news about the small % of bad people and we forget that the majority are kind and friendly, especially in races like this, it attracts positive people. I am worried about my shoes, they are track shoes so they fit me just right and as you know feet swell so I will get blisters for sure and they are thin so I will feel the rocks and the heat more easily. a lot of people that have run the race before are shaking their heads over the fact that I am still continuing considering everything is borrowed gear, even the food and bars and gels are things I have never tried before so it should be interesting. I am not letting anything bother me, the only question I asked myself was to either do it or not and I already knew the answer and it was a yes, no need to drive myself crazy with details. there are no ideal scenarios and I will just deal with the issues as they present. I am finding myself in a different situation where I am even thinking not sure I can finish it if my shoes ripped and become destroyed that might be the end. I am not afraid of that happening I would just be very sad, but I want to teach my kids to continue and give their best even when things aren't looking up, after all, this is when believing about something that you are committed and passionate is always not only when things are falling into place.

Monday, March 8, 2010

Let the Pain Begin-Stage 1

Monday, March 8, 2010

The race begins!! Norma made it to the start line and actually did very well today. She finished Stage 1 in a little under 6 hours. Considering the conditions and the crazy circumstances of just getting to Chile over the past week, she did amazingly well. I have been in a similar situation myself and so much energy is expended before the race that it feels like running in quicksand when the race actually starts.

Here is part of a short e-mail that Norma sent to me after today's stage:

"Babe!, I sure kept thinking of you a lot today and your advice. It was very hot, I was ok for the first two stages then from checkpoint 2 to 3 it was so hot I just couldn't run anymore. I wish I was doing better, I want to make you and everyone back home proud but I also know the worst that can happen is to not finish so I am looking after myself, I remembered what you told me not to go too hard in the beginning. I think I am running as well I can possibly do, my shoes are too thin and I felt every rock, and I had sand in my shoes the entire way, I know my feet will be a nightmare but I am ok at pushing through pain. as long as I am safe I can push through the pain. not a lot to say about the race, just keeping my head down and getting it done. I loved looking at the ring you gave me for luck, it made me feel better. I am feeling ok not worry about not finishing anymore, as long as I keep doing what I am doing it will work out."

I think that she sounds very strong and resolved to fight hard this week. She is currently the fifth woman in the rankings and I know that she will try to catch a couple of them. Okay, more to come tomorrow.

Charlie Engle

Tuesday, March 9, 2010

Stage 2 Norma Busts a Move.

Hi This is Charlie again. Make no mistake, this race and this blog are about Norma, not about me. But I am getting a solid dose of my own medicine today. I am traveling to Seattle today and I feel completely out of touch with Norma and the race. I know she is out there in the desert running. It's not that I can do anything for her anyway, but I do truly feel helpless. I am not enjoying being an observer. I am anxious to get to my hotel and hopefully find that Norma has finished Stage 2 and has written to me. I am worried about her feet. She actually has pretty nice feet for someone that runs the way she does. It would be a shame to have them blistered and bloodied but I am afraid that's what might happen. It won't stop her of course. When I ran the Atacama Crossing a few years ago, I remember two things very clearly. It was hot and dry. Or maybe it was dry and hot. And there was altitude too. Okay, that's three things I remember. And the sand was really pervasive. And the salt marsh was unpredictable. So I remembered five things. Whatever. The point is that the Atacama is a feast for the senses but some of the items on the menu really suck. And speaking of sucking, I can remember a section of the salt marsh where I broke through the crust and the salty muck actually pulled both shoes off of my feet. I had to stop and practically dive in to save my shoes. Losing my only pair of shoes was not an option. So, of course, today all I can think of is Norma dealing with the same issues. It's a weird feeling because I am not worried about her ability or her toughness. She has nothing left to prove in those areas. Instead, I am just anticipating her suffering and I want to be there to tell her it will all be fine. I want to absorb some of the pain for her. Although if I was there, it is more likely that she would just be assuring me that she is fine and I shouldn't worry.

6:30 PM in my hotel room. Okay, so I just received a note from Norma and she seems great. She had an amazing day and ran very well. Here is part of her note to me (minus the mushy stuff)

"I did really good today, I thought of Karl how hard he has it, moving forward and it was enough for me to go hard. My pack is still over 10 kilos and I burned the bottom of my feet since my shoes are too thin. it hurt a lot but I can take pain and discomfort so I just went for it. I climbed in ranking but not sure where I am, I notice because I finished among the guys who are better than me, also I was the third to arrive in my tent and yesterday I was the last, there are 7 of us and all guys except for me, cool guys, I have met a couple of them on races before. Today was a hard day 42K long and a lot of people have passed out from the heat, the camp looked like a war zone, at areas it has reached 45C, we also run out of the water the first leg and ran on sand dunes on the second leg, a great opportunity for blisters to get full of sand. it's after 8 hrs. since we started and the majority hasn't reach camp." I looked at the standings and Norma has moved up about 12 places from yesterday in the overall and she moved up to 4th among the women. More importantly, it seems that she may be getting stronger. That is really the key to these multi-day races. Don't start too fast and really be ready for the 50-mile day. That is where the race is won and lost.

Charlie Engle

Wednesday, March 10, 2010

Norma Struggles Through High Heat and Sore Feet.

Today was a tough day for Norma I think. I did not hear from her today but as I look at the rankings, she dropped a few spots which tell me that she struggled today. She is so competitive that I am sure she would not choose to let anyone move ahead of her. From what I can tell on the Racing The Planet website, many people struggled today. Temperatures were very hot and it looks like a couple of aid stations may have run low on water. Mary G Adams, the race series owner, and race director does an amazing job of orchestrating these events. The logistics are just baffling but she gets it done every time. But days like today are just part of the experience. We go to the deserts to suffer and to struggle in hopes that we gain knowledge. I think a lot of racers learned something about themselves today. I am hoping that Norma remembers that she is not racing the others. Instead, my hope is that she takes a deep breath and remembers that there are many people out there that are just pulling for her to do her best. I know that she feels some pressure to perform well and that can be difficult when things go wrong. My experience is that every race has its highs and lows and neither of them should dictate the lasting imprint from the experience. All of these multi-day races are about adapting to the changing circumstances. I guess the same could be said for most aspects of life. Business, relationships, running, and family is pretty much the same. Our success is usually dependent on our ability to adapt to the changing circumstances. In Norma's case, it appears that the desert made the rules today but if I know Norma she will get up and go after it again tomorrow. I love her for her spirit and the fact that she is never afraid to put it all on the line.

Charlie Engle

Thursday, March 11, 2010

Norma Fights Through Day 4.

I am sitting on an airplane heading from Seattle to Jacksonville, Florida. It's a long flight and I don't like being "disconnected". Earlier today, I was watching the Racing the Planet website and there was Norma's name in the scroll. I had to catch my breath because by the time I could really read it they were showing the names of competitors that had withdrawn from the race. I patiently waited for the scroll to start over. As I am watching the monitor, my brain is spinning because I don't want to see her name in the dreaded "DNF" (did not finish) column. Okay, there she is again. It says Norma Bastidas comments that "today's stage is like being a three-year-old playing in the mud." Phew!! Okay, not only is she okay but she is cracking jokes. I am relieved for sure. These races become really interesting after the first few days. A lot of people start dropping out. Day 4 is usually very tough because the body is very beaten up by now. On top of that, racers have been sharing a tent with 7 other people, mostly strangers. Sleep is usually pretty restless. Most racers try to pack very lightly which means not bringing the thick sleeping pad or the cushy sleeping bag. In Norma's case, she had nothing at all for comfort since her baggage was lost. Everything she is wearing and eating is borrowed. Well, technically only the clothing and equipment is borrowed. She will return those items after the race. The food? She gets to keep that. The other reason that Day 4 is tough is that it is the day before the dreaded "long day". Day 5 is the 50-mile day. I have always said that Day 5 is the crux of the race. You can gain a lot or lose a tremendous amount of time. But for now, Day 4 is the focus. I will check later from Jacksonville and see if I can get an update. I never heard from Norma yesterday which tells me either that she had a tough day or they had technical problems.....or both.

11:00 PM

I just finished a speaking gig in Jacksonville Florida for Challenged Athletes Foundation and the Gate River 15K. That was fun but the best news was that I had an email from Norma waiting for me when I finished. I am so happy. Here is what she had to say.

"Hey, babe. I am still working hard and keeping my strength. I had a hard night last night but after drilling my toenail to relieve the pressure my toes were fantastic! I ran relatively well, I was ok but had a bit of tummy issue and couldn't eat after checkpoint 2 halfway, but I could hydrate so I was ok I just lost a bit of steam. Today was 42K long and tough, the salt flats where hard to run on my thin shoes but walking was fine. I lost my other toenail today but it didn't hurt as much since there was no sand to fill my shoes to make them tighter. I almost broke my ankle coming after the sand dunes and into the river when I stepped on what I thought was sand and it was rock and I slipped all the way down but managed to catch myself before the fall. I had to Spiderwoman my way up the rock face, I am happy for all the rock climbing lessons I took. Other than that I had a good day finishing 47th. I am feeling great good spirits but I am not taking things for granted, out here things can go terribly wrong fast so I will be careful and not do anything foolish."

I love that she says that she will not do anything foolish in the same paragraph that includes the statement "I drilled my toenail to relieve the pressure". Is it any wonder that I love this woman? Tomorrow is the long day, 50 miles. I will keep track and post some results when I have them.

And finally this from Norma,

"Please remind my kids to look after the cats"

Funny.

Friday, March 12, 2010

50 Miles And No News Yet

No news is........a bummer. I have been checking the race website and it appears that about 75 racers have finished the 50-mile day. But there is no finisher's list posted yet so I can't be certain that Norma is finished yet. Based on the previous 4 stages, it makes sense that she should be done. But I want to see her name on the list. Today was the long day, about 50 miles.

For me, this stage was always the one I really was aiming at all along. It is the day that a runner can really make up a lot of time or lose a tremendous amount of time. The heat and the sand and the four previous days have really taken a toll on most runners but one really strange thing can happen on this day. The body has actually adjusted to the stress if the runner hasn't redlined it too often. In essence, a runner can run himself into condition during the race assuming he came into with decent fitness. It is all relative of course but I feel that I usually had my best days on stage 4 and 5. I hope that the same thing has happened to Norma. I am going to keep checking but I am hoping that I can confirm her finish tomorrow morning. The only thing left after that will be a short run, about 10K, late tomorrow afternoon. It is mostly ceremonial and gives the runners a chance to enjoy their accomplishments. And it is an amazing experience. I can't wait to hear the stories in Norma's own words.

Saturday, March 13, 2010

It's All Over Except for the Sunburn

Charlie again, 1:00 PM- I have had a perfect day so far. I woke up early in yet another strange room and bedroom. I have been in Jacksonville, Florida for 3 days in support of my friends at Challenged Athletes Foundation. I especially had a blast with 6-year-old Timmy, a below the knee amputee that just blew me away with his positive attitude. If he is handicapped, then we should all be so lucky. I ran the Gate River 15k with my good friend Chris Roman and about 18,000 other runners. Okay, all that was fine but I was totally preoccupied wondering about Norma and how she was doing. And then the best part of the day happened, I got an e-mail from Norma!!! My phone "dinged" and was overjoyed to see her name on my phone. I was really frustrated by the lack of information that is available from these races. Although I have to say that the Racing the Planet folks did a good job considering they were in the middle of a giant desert. Today it was worth the wait for information. Here is what she had to say: "I made it, it was a tough go physically but not mentally, I lost 3 other toenails and the sharp terrain cut through my shoes, it got better once I decided to slow down. it took me about 15hrs to finish, too long. There were a couple of parts where I could run and I started to get on rhythm and then sharp hard terrain came and I lost all the time I had just won again and a lot of people overtook me . This happened several times and I was so frustrated but then I realized that's what my son Karl feels all the time, having to be tutored just to catch up to everybody all the time. so I shut the FU and put my head down and continue the race without complaining. Mario also asked me on camera if I was disappointed since I could have done so much better but I don't want to focus on what I didn't accomplish but instead, I realized how amazing is the fact that I am here finishing the race given the fact that it didn't look like it was going to happen. The amazing support of everybody that came to my rescue. also, the team Red Hot Chili runners, the 4 boys that came on the bus with me from Argentina, 4 friends from London told me last night while on the course, we were all struggling, that they are going to donate the funds of next year's annual fundraising to a charity of my choice, it's incredible that I managed to inspire them. The boys are your biggest fans now, after playing Running the Sahara documentary on the bus, and I told them that if we don't have anything on that date next year, we might come to London to join them at their fundraising party. Well. we start at 12 noon and suppose to run 10K, then I will run to chat with you. I am looking forward to hearing your voice soon. Love Norma

8:00 PM- Norma sent me one more short e-mail to say that she is FINISHED and very happy and tired. She is already trying to deal with the problem of getting home but having problems arranging for a ride back to Salta. She didn't get to enjoy the finish for very long before having to deal with reality. But she asked me to tell everyone that she is fine and she could feel all of the amazing positive energy everyone was sending her way. Norma will take back her blog in a few days. Thanks to everyone for tuning in. See you down the road.
Charlie Engle

Saturday, March 20, 2010
"Its's Always Darkest Before It Turns Absolutely Pitch Black" Paul Newman

I am back in Calgary after my amazing adventure. I don't think that I have ever worked as hard for a race before, sure they are difficult races but the stress never left even after crossing the finish line. Every single time something else kept coming up I simply tried to breathe and told myself that I don't *have* to do what I am doing, even if I am doing it for my son Karl, I *want* to. As soon as I said that every problem seem a lot smaller. Sure they were times when I thought, "you have to be kidding me!" overall, the experience was amazing. I had a camera following me around this time and many people asked me if that made it easier or harder. The truth is that after a while, it didn't matter, the camera was there to record the truth and that's what I intended on doing, pretend it wasn't there. Mario and I got along well, that was great since he got to see me crying, he was very respectful, but I knew he needed to do his job and they are after all doing me a favor. Here is a list of the things that made my trip challenging and how it unfolded:

Fri Feb 26th- My designated childcare person, and other single mother that I had looked after her son for months in exchange, canceled 6 days before my scheduled flight because she met someone.

Sat 27th, the earthquake hits Chile and my flights get canceled. Direct flights prices went from $700 to $3,000 in a matter of hrs.

Sun 28th- direct flights go up to $6,000 (no, you don't get to keep the plane for a week, I asked)

Mon Mar 1st- The search for cheaper alternative flights begin (the coffee brew nonstop that day)

Tue Mar 2nd, 1:50pm- Booked a flight to Salta Argentina. 4pm My sister, Muñeca and my best friend Nadia volunteer to look after my kids. 11pm pack my gear and go to bed.

Wed Mar 3rd, 4pm start my 41hrs trip to Salta, Argentina.

Fri Mar 5th arrive in Argentina with no luggage, my only possession, my laptop, my school books, and the clothes I was wearing.

Sat 7am leave by car to San Pedro de Atacama, 13 1/2 hrs. drive. two flat tires, endless checkpoints later we arrive in San Pedro at 9:30pm

Sat 6th, 9:30pm the hunt for gear begin, Miguel a Kunza hotel porter goes home to lend me his sleeping bag.

Sun 7th, 1pm, gear is complete, just in time for gear check, I get my bib and I am allowed to run the race. 2pm. we leave to camp one.

Mon 8th Atacama Race starts.

Sat 13th 1 pm, Atacama race finishes. 4pm my luggage finally arrives at the hotel. 6pm the hunt for a ride home begins after confirming buses are full. 10:30pm a private car agrees to take me if I find one more passenger with both of us paying 2 1/2 times the price. 11pm I convince Kevin my Australian tentmate that Salta is a great city to tour, I carefully avoid telling him the ride is 13hrs with no restaurants in between so yet again we will be surviving on chips, and he has to lend me some money since I can't afford the trip back now, a great offer if you ask me.

Sun 14th 9m, Kevin and I wait at the lobby for the car to take us to Argentina. 10:30am after calling several times to confirm and telling us they are just running late the office secretary tells me they are not coming, lost in translation she tells me; did I tell you Spanish is my first language? 2pm after hrs. of trying to convince them the company agrees to take us to Argentina

Mon 15th, 1:15am arrive in Salta Argentina. 1:30am to 4am chat with Charlie on Skype he lends me money to pay Kevin back, he arranges to have money at a Western Union in Salta. 8:30am, go to Western Union close to the hotel to pick up money, they refuse to give me the money since the transfer is not addressed by my full name, my middle name is missing, I run around in Salta for the next hr. trying to find the other branch that will overlook this. 9:45am Charlie runs to his local branch to add Angelica, my middle name, to the transfer. 10am get the funds!. 10:30am arrive at the hotel, pick up my luggage, leave an envelope in the front desk for Kevin who is still sleeping and go to the Airport. 10:45am check-in and begin my 35hr trip home

Tues 16th at 12:35pm arrive in Calgary.

I would be lying if I told you that I wasn't expecting things to go wrong, everything told me that maybe this was not the best time to go to a race. Maybe because I've been raising kids alone for so long I been operating on stubbornness mostly and sometimes that has drawbacks. There were times when I didn't want to go, I get tired sometimes of working so hard all the time and I am human after all, I had an opportunity to bow gracefully of a race, on the pretense that I had tried everything but while I could lie to everybody and make excuses I couldn't lie to my kids and tell them that I wasn't going because I had tried everything and came up short, had I really?. That's how I found myself in the Atacama running 150 miles across the desert on borrowed gear, I didn't always have fun, and more than once I cried but it is a reality, two weeks in San Pedro de Atacama Chile was hardly punishment. I am scheduled to speak at the cnib luncheon May 7th, it's a time for me to reflect on the time when I found myself alone with my two kids after the diagnosis made anybody close to me very difficult to cope with and they had to pull away. 4 years later I am surrounded by amazing people that are offering their support, to let me know my kids and I are not alone. I think is also a wonderful opportunity to offer hope to anybody that is going through a hard time, that if we stay positive, things will get better. If until now, the love of a mother has been an incredible source of strength that has brought fantastic things, now that I have the support and love of amazing people around me like my best friend Nadia, my boyfriend Charlie, my family, I can only imagine what kind of change we can create in the world.

Wednesday, April 28, 2010

"Time is a Companion That Goes With Us on a Journey. It Reminds Us to Cherish Each Moment Because it Will Never Come Again. What We Leave Behind is Not as Important as How We Have Lived". Captain Jean-Luc Picard

I should be on my way to Mt McKinley in a few weeks. In my mind I am already there, I can see the mountain, feel the air in my skin, smell the wilderness around me and hear the stillness of my own breathing. I have wanted to be back climbing since Aconcagua. It is been calling me back. This is the first time in my life that I am experiencing selfishness, I have always lived fully yet never forgotten my responsibilities. Now I want to do things because they make me happy and I expect everybody to understand. Sure they are still things that are positive. Happy is the new black. Things have been kind of crazy around me, dating Charlie has both advantages and disadvantages, if you watch his movie Running the Sahara you will soon realize we are really the same person in theory but we couldn't have more different personalities. Been apart and traveling so much leaves a strain and Charlie is not the kind that is happy just watching from afar. And then there is the documentary, to my incredible luck I was asked to be part of a documentary where they follow some women, all mothers and all doing things to help others in our communities. The documentary will air on a new channel, OWN, that is developed by none other than Oprah. It is an opportunity of a lifetime and I couldn't pass it. It, however, left me feeling overexposed. The more the put a camera on my face the more I wanted close the door and be alone with my family, I guess to counter the feeling. In an age of reality shows, most of which I have never watched, it left me to wonder how can they do it and not lose their soul a little every day. I have done acting, but acting is living a fake life like is real and a documentary is living a real life like is fake. They sometimes try to morph my life into what is not, I am far from perfect and I am okay with it. I am incredibly grateful to be part of it though and the producers could be nicer to me and my family and will be ready to watch it on TV when it airs, it also allowed my son Karl to be a somebody for the few days they were in town, I loved watching him smile and be so confident. Karl told me it was so nice to feel special when the cameras came to film him at his school. But what I am about to do is very serious and it needs all my energy and focus, so I am glad I can go back to my normal life after the cameras are gone. The best part of it is the part where I go out for a run or training, on my own, nobody watching, just me and nature. My preparation for Denali, Mt McKinley's former name, is down to trying to stay fit but not overdoing it either, I have no injuries but I am ran down from not giving my body a break., I am scheduled to leave May 17th and until then I will just keep my head down and try and stay focus.

Thursday, June 3, 2010

"People Always Seemed to Know Half of History, and to Get it Confused With the Other Half." Jane Haddam

It used to be so much easier to post about my adventures. Nothing has really changed so it should still be the same. I start an adventure, work around the things that seem to be obstacles to what I want, go hard and try to accomplish successfully what I set out to do. In essence, nothing has changed yet everything seems to be. I just got back from Mt. McKinley after a successful summit. Except for split toes, yes that's a thing, I got back healthy and happy about my performance. From the moment I announced my intentions on climbing, I had to fight the wave of criticism, I tried to just put my head down and not pay attention but it just seems to be coming from everywhere. Even Charlie chimed in and told me I was not ready for Denali and shouldn't attempt it. Many times I lay in bed wondering why everybody all of a sudden seemed to be reacting negatively to my goals. Why is it that as a woman I can't be anything more than a mother or a girlfriend? As if that because I have kids and I am in a serous relationship that should be my end goal and wanting more for myself that doesn't include my kids or my boyfriend is view as selfish. My intentions was never to foolishly risk my life if anything understanding the risk made me pay more attention and never take the mountain for granted. I talked to many people about climbing and discover that it can be done safely. So in spite of the wave of controversy I left for Mt McKinley May 18th. Patrick Delaney an accomplished mountain guide and a friend was my companion in the journey. we arrived in Talkeetna around midnight and by the next day at 3:30pm we were on our way to base camp at 7200 ft. Things never slowed down after that, we didn't stay at base camp and we continued to camp 7800 ft carrying about 200 lb. between both of us. The next day we almost made it to camp 11,000ft, we build a shelter and camp at 10,600 ft, the weight clearly slowing us down. Let me tell you, slowing didn't really mean slowing, through it all Patrick and I maintained a relatively high pace. It was not until we carried gear to camp 14,000 that I had to have a talk with Patrick, we never climbed together before only trained together and yes I don't know much about mountaineering but I do know pace and heart rate, I knew that at the rate we were both going it wasn't sustainable at altitude. So after that Patrick slowed down, we were tracking to summit second faster than any other team that season and he wanted to beat them but that team had a casualty so I my concern was about safety. One of the advantages of being a female in the world of endurance is that we are more patient most of the time, it didn't bother me to see groups ahead of us, I didn't have anything to prove to them. The hardest days were the last 3, we had to carry gear from camp 14,000 to high camp 17,000 and then summit, Patrick's style is fast and light so we only carried a light tent, a couple of days of food and our sleeping bags to high camp. We climbed and slept with what we had on. On day 9 since we started the our push to the summit at 5:30am. I was tired almost immediately as we started, the only thought that kept me going that day was the desire to be done and come home. By the time we made it to the summit, around 1:30pm, I was cold and exhausted. I didn't, unfortunately, find nirvana, all I wanted was to finally go home. On the way down we came across two climbers on distress. One was suffering from frostbite on his right hand and was screaming from the pain, the other climber was just as confused and was yelling at his partner because he didn't want to turn around so close to the summit. Patrick quickly got them on their feet and we helped them down the mountain. It was a tricky situation to help these men incredibly shaky and awkward on their feet, I understand why they say most accidents happen on the way down, it takes a lot more coordination and exhausting impairs your judgment easily. It was hard to be roped together and one of them slipped a couple of times but we managed to hold on to him until we finally got to solid ground. At the end it took us 14 hours to get back to high camp. The next morning, we went hard all the way down to try to meet the last plane to Talkeetna, we skipped breakfast and with only a liter of water, we headed down from high camp to base camp, a loss of over 10,000 of elevation. We stopped briefly on camp 14,000 and 11,000 to get the rest of the gear that we had cached and gave away the rest of our food that we didn't need, pop tarts were a huge success especially with the Koreans who never had them before. I learned at 6633 Ultra at the Arctic Circle that PopTarts don's freeze so they make excellent cold weather snacks. Things were going great but I was in pain from trying to maintain some sort of control using my feet to break our downhill speed on the slippery hills carrying a sled and ultimately I split my toes in half but it was of no use complaining since we needed to get down no matter what. Just before we arrived at base camp, only about 5K away, we came across Hans a German climber going back to base cam alone since his team had ditched him because he was so slow, he was falling into a crevasse and only his sled had stop him from going down the hole, after rescuing him Hans asked if he would travel with us. It took us two hours to arrive at base camp going slow making sure, not one of us ended up at a bottom of a crevasse. we missed the last plane but thanks to Patrick we both ended up nominated for an award thanks to rescuing climbers in trouble. What an amazing adventure it was! I felt very fatigued but understandable considering we didn't have many rest days. The only problem we encountered was when I left a bag of waste in one of the camps. I was determined to follow the " no trace left behind" rule always climbing with bags to dispose of our waste they were tied to the outside of my climbing bag and I dropped them by mistake, the bags are marked with our climbing permit so no need for DNA, it was double-bagged and ready to be disposed of at base camp as instructed. In the end, I picked a $250.00 fine, ouch, but I agree with the "no trace left" rule. So I guess you can see why this time around it's hard to write about my adventure. What it used to be a trait to be admired, persistence and undeniable commitment to my family became, egotistical, delusional. I haven't changed but being part of an Oprah documentary has created a lot of friction with people around me including my boyfriend Charlie that he things I am only interested in fame as if I haven't been like this, stubborn as hell, all my life. I don't have the energy to tell you that Charlie was also charged with fraud while I was climbing Mt. McKinley, I was excited to get cell coverage when we got to high camp and when I called Charlie he told me what happened. I was shocked and concerned because I had no idea he was under investigation for fraud but then he yelled at me for being selfish and not there for him when he needed me. I am very professional and finished the climb successfully but I cried myself to sleep that night. At the end, as long as I am home happy with my kids I know that I am on the right path. My outer circle might change but as long as my inner circle remains the same, I accept the consequences. I hope that my kids learn to never be afraid, to be true to themselves, to follow their passions with all their hearts and to know that they have a mother who would do anything in the world for them.

Thursday, July 1, 2010

"Out Of Suffering Have Emerged The Strongest Souls; The Most Massive Characters Are Seared With Scars". Kahlil Gibran

I refuse to spend a single second feeling angry about my relationship, I am done crying. My kids I leave for Africa tomorrow. I am taking them to see their dad to Tunisia, so it seemed a perfect opportunity to go to Tanzania as well. Nadia and I will be trekking Kilimanjaro via Umbwe route, here is a short description of Umbwe. "The Umbwe Route is generally regarded to be one of the hardest routes when you climb Mount Kilimanjaro but has spectacular scenery including a number of caves that can be viewed on route. The Umbwe Route is the hardest route on the mountain. The route is certainly raw and unkempt and very steep until it reaches Barranco at 3,984m, from which point it intersects the Machame Route. Only two days are spent reaching the same point that is reached after three days on the Machame Route and for this reason, headache and mild nausea are relatively commonly on the Umbwe Route, even below 4,000m." Make no mistake since Nadia was able to come, it will feel more like tweens on a sleepover listening to Justin Bieber than a hard climb. Considering how crazy life is at the moment I am surprised to be feeling well, I have had some great runs. I sold my house and even though the original intention was to move to North Carolina with Charlie but since I broke up the engagement I decided to move to Vancouver to be with my sister since she was recently diagnosed with Lupus. Muñeca is doing OK, she is working hard on trying to figure out how her life is going to change. My kids are a bit stressed since dad is not crazy about us moving to Vancouver even though he doesn't even live in Canada he still like to be in control, yes I know the common story of the men in my life. I know my kids are angry with me but in time they will understand that is okay to make choices that are unpopular, in time everything falls into place. We must always persist when pursuing a goal. I wish everybody had the strength to not quit and find an easy way out, there were many times that I had my choices question and I almost did settle, fortunately, I am my own worst enemy or my best adversary and I am unable to do something that at the end doesn't feel right for me. What I do know is, acting out of fear, pain or ego is not something that will lead to a fulfilling life. I use those emotions to channel the courage necessary to get things done. I happen to think that obstacles are just opportunities waiting to be discovered.

Monday, July 12, 2010

"The wild dogs cry out in the night, As they grow restless, longing for some solitary company. I know that I must do what's right, As sure as Kilimanjaro rises like Olympus above the Serengeti I seek to cure what's deep..."TOTO

Today we just walked around downtown Moshi and got some snacks for the climb. People in Tanzania are very friendly, walking in town you would think it was the 90's, they are selling cassette tapes and the for the movies playing in theaters are for old movies. It's very cool having Nadia here, I love having the company, usually, I arrive at a town and meet people, it's always great but this makes it so much more enjoyable. I was a bit tired and not very excited this time, it just seems like I am constantly leaving my kids and I feel so selfish sometimes, they are in Tunisia with their father so my boys did roll their eyes at me and told me they are old enough to be alone for a few hours a day until dad gets home from work and that I wasn't leaving them behind as much as letting them spend alone time with their father. There where endless planes, airport security checks and trying to sleep at yet another airport gate, trying to find room on the floor beside a sea of strangers. I think this is the first time that I wasn't excited when I boarded the plane, then just before landing in Tanzania, there it was, Kilimanjaro! So amazingly beautiful, the plane circled around a bit, and I could feel all my hesitation fading. Kilimanjaro is such a beautiful mountain, it stands so tall, the clouds resting below its peak. I noticed that I was already smiling hard, this is the life that I have forged for myself, every step I have taken, stubbornly it's taking me here, how grateful I am to be me. It's back home that we sometimes feel like our problems seem bigger than they really are, it's because we have surrounded ourselves with comfort and material things that we give status and materialistic things so much value. I am not feeling guilty anymore, how can anybody judge me for trying to feed my soul? I will go home having more to give to my loved ones, I think we have become a society that we try to see stress and unhappiness as a badge of honor.. People here in Tanzania have it all figured out, I am always grateful to travel because it reminds me that the media is lying to us, we don't need all those material things to be happy, just the basics and nature and family, anything else is just stuff that you need to dust or clean. I didn't see, gyms, just a soccer ball, a street and a bunch of friends as a form of exercise and later you can always gather your family and watch a good family picture like Ghostbusters at the local theater. I definitely feel ready for the climb, how can I not be grateful and happy for the opportunity to surround myself with so much beauty, I decided to live my life collecting memories, not possessions, and I hope my family follows suit, and the only way they will do it is by example, it doesn't matter what I say, it is how I live my life that will teach my loved ones what I think life is all about. Charlie and I are still in contact and has apologize and I am supporting him as a friend. I have decided to put out problems on hold and be there for him at as he prepares to go on trial.

Saturday, July 24, 2010

Kilimanjaro.

I have been back in Tunisia for a few days and I am still trying to find the words to describe my trip. Africa is an amazing continent, is so unexpectedly beautiful. in our world, we constantly try to find happiness by upgrading our lives, cars, jobs or fashion. in Calgary, every time I go out I am bombarded with things that I don't have that I ought to. In Tanzania I felt different. I am not going to romanticize it, people in Tanzania, work extremely hard for their money. Nadia wanted to know why people that are so poor can be so content. Having been born in Mexico in poverty I could answer her question. Is all relative, she was comparing her life to theirs, compared to her, they don't have much but she is comparing apples to oranges, we all compare, I don't remember growing up been aware of our limitations, it was only after I left and started to make money that I understood how much we lacked but I also know that we didn't need it, it just made life more convenient that's all. Growing up poor in Mexico, we used to things never working out, when they did we were so happy and when they didn't we didn't complain about it for long, after all, that was more likely. In developed countries we expect and can demand that things work out, after all, that's why we have democracy and pay higher taxes. It's weird that what once used to be my life, sleeping in cramp places, food that is not the best is what I now call adventure. I am still learning to stand up and demand more without feeling guilty, on the other hand, I doesn't take much to feel happy anymore. I guess you could say that growing up like Karl teaches you a lot about feeling grateful. I watch him struggle in Africa, trying to learn and adjust to his new surroundings, he still asks to be independent, I would like to bubble wrap his environment but I am aware that I shouldn't do it, he needs to learn to deal with adversity on his own. I sign him to play water polo at the resort we are staying in Hammamet, the other players had no idea that he has limited vision, he did OK for the majority but there were times when he passed the ball to the opposite team, why? they asked for it, they will yell pass and he simply did. His team members were not very understanding. Karl never complained even though I am sure it might be incredibly hard. My other son Hans struggles emotionally more than Karl and that is because he is used to doing well, things usually work out so when it doesn't he doesn't handle it well. As a mother of two very different children, I am constantly reminding Karl that is OK to demand more and Hans to be more grateful. I learned a lot in Kilimanjaro, I feel very confident about choosing the toughest route. Climbing 1000mt or 3000 ft a day is perfectly fine, I wasn't taking into consideration that I am very tired. The route that we choose was incredibly beautiful and isolated, we never run into anybody else until we merged with the normal Machame route. Nadia and I were treated to an amazing experience, we had a crew of 9 guys all to ourselves, we thought it was a bit over the top but the government in Tanzania is now demanding that locals are hired, it was mandatory, it makes sense, tourism is one of the main sources of revenue. We hiked for about 5 hours per day, by the time we arrived at the camp, our crew already had our tents set up, on day one we lost one member of our crew, he had an incredibly hard time keeping up, we later learned he was suffering from Malaria, unfortunately, it affects a lot of people in Africa. Climbing Kilimanjaro was incredibly rewarding, the trail was incredible then we had outstanding meals. Nadia and I giggle like schoolgirls, my best friend has always been strong and a fantastic climber, most of the time Nadia and Azizi our guide would go ahead of me, I enjoy being alone it's usually my time to think or to simply unwind. The last day we skipped one camp and went ahead to the next to prepare for the summit. We arrived around 6pm had our supper and call it the night around 9:30pm, summit attempts are done at 1am. Nadia and I supposed to be ready at 12:30am for tea. Azizi overslept so we ended up being one of the last to attempt the summit. By now I was feeling incredibly tired and I wasn't sure that skipping camp 3 had been such a good idea. Just as we were getting ready to leave, I got a bit too close to Nadia as she was picking her pack and her poles sticking out of them and ended up with a black eye, Nadia felt terrible, I was angry at myself once more, at the last minute I decided against bringing crazy glue, I failed to see the point of bringing it, lucky for me I managed to stop the bleeding. I have definitely been doing it for too long when all I can think that I am much rather crazy glue an injury that to cancel a climb. The next few hours, I had a hard go, I managed to catch up to the rest of the slow group, it must have been quite a sight, there we were walking so slow, I am sure that we resembled extras at a zombie movie, like a scene of the Night of the Living Dead. Nadia did amazing, she felt great and climb very well. When I saw her at the top, I broke down crying, partly because I was glad it was almost over and also because for the first time I had done an adventure with a friend. Nadia and I have been friends for over 10 years and we have supported each other through tough times as well as celebrated together the good ones. The way down was a piece of cake, there is a route specifically for descending, it's incredibly easy. We had decided early to descend all the way to the gate and make the trip officially 4 days from start to finish, but Nadia and I decided to spend one more night in the mountain, it seems crazy since making it all the way it meant we had to arrive into Moshi ahead of schedule and pay for accommodations and meals, in the mountain, except for the tip it was paid. It turned out to be the best decision, once again we were treated to a beautiful camp and on other night sleeping under the stars. The next morning, after an early breakfast we ran the last few miles and arrived at the gate just 58 minutes later. Even though I have a hard time in altitude, this is what I want to do for the rest of my life. The shifting that is happening is a positive one, running is a solo event but climbing is a team effort and I love it. The farther I travel and the higher I climb the more I discover how important my loved ones are. "The most important thing in life is to learn how to give out love, and to let it come in." Morrie Schwartz

Monday, September 6, 2010

"What We Call the Beginning is Often the End. And to Make an End is to Make a Beginning. The End is Where We Start From." T. S. Eliot.

In Vancouver finally. It is a bit weird to try and fit a lifetime on an 8"x16" storage space, trying to decide on what to keep and what to give away. I have never been emotionally attached to material things, but it was hard to walk away from the sentimental value of the objects that have surrounded me for the last 12 years. The last few months have been incredibly busy, I guess you can tell that my move to Vancouver was somehow me trying to escape something. My house was not healthy anymore, I had spent so much time and money trying to keep the stability that my kids needed but the cost kept increasing, both emotionally and financially, in the end, I just didn't want it anymore. The first step was a clear one, sell my house, the other steps were not as easy to figure out. I thought I was going to be marrying and moving to North Carolina, Charlie had asked me to marry him, but when you have kids, falling in love and getting married is not as easy as the first time around. The last months have been a maze of suggestions and decisions to be accounted for. Doing things right by my kids is what made me happier, I do want things for myself, but I also know that is only a few more years that my kids need then the rest of my life belongs to me. Things aren't exactly easy for Charlie right now, and since he means so much to me the last few months have been of deep soul searching and I longed to go back to the core of my being, the one thing that made wake up every morning and figure out if I was the best version of myself. I decided to just go hard with what I do best and that is to live my life the best way I know, honest and openly. I am a lot happier, I am gone back to dreaming again on the things that give me joy. I dream of climbing the highest peak, I feel alive and focus. That's how I know when I am on the right path, things where chaotic around me, nobody really seemed sure of my decision yet, at night when things quiet down, I once never doubted, I stood firm yet I had no desire to explained more than it was necessary. I hated being called selfish for being assertive about what I want and decide was right for me but at the end I have to stop wanting to be liked. If I am hated for standing my ground then so be it. I moved to Vancouver so I could get back to the things that require my full attention. I need to get back to work, soon, but I also have to make sure that my kids are not spending too much time alone at an age where is critical that I am involved, I am also experiencing some challenges with both of my kids, one is losing focus and wanted to quit swimming, while what type of sport is not exactly important to me, teaching Hans the valuable lesson of following through is a lesson I want him to master. All the talent in the world is wasted if you don't have the discipline and the desire to work hard. Karl, on the other hand, quit exercising because it became too hard for him, the last few years I did what any other single parent will do, I spent countless of hours working at something that was putting food on the table, while my kids were home alone, even long after the paychecks stop coming I kept thinking that it was right around the corner, I just needed to work a bit harder. So while I am stopping my adventures as a possible source of income, I am now pursuing them just as hard as a passion. It's been a crazy ride and one that I will continue to do as an amateur. So my decision to move came after analyzing all the obstacles and coming with the best possible solution. My sister lives here so supervising kids will be easier if I have family close, also when I go back to work, having somebody hand me a homecooked meal once in a while will mean everything. The next few years will be crazy and difficult but I feel that I am nearing the finish line, you know, by now your lungs burn, your legs hurt and all you want is to quit. But this is the exact moment where been focus is most important. I believe that if I work hard, I will set my kids on a path that will take them to the life they were born to be. I used to think that that was not possible anymore, just because I was single and struggling financially now I realized that it is not true, is passion, hard work and unconditional love that will give them the tools they need to succeed in life. And by success I only mean happiness. As for me, I do believe that if I stay true and do things for the right reason the universe will take care of me too.

Friday, October 8, 2010
The Perfect Storm.

There are moments in life when words seem to fill the space that surrounds you. I am on my way back from what it probably was one of the most difficult weeks. Charlie was found guilty and I am shattered. While words fill the space in between my mind and my body none can come close to describing my feelings. I can't begin to explain, but one question keeps coming up, how can it be? He began to be investigated because one IRA agent saw Running The Sahara and wondered how could Charlie afforded such lifestyle? How can somebody persist for 500hrs and hire an undercover agent to record Charlie and why will Charlie brag about lying about a loan application to a woman he just met? And she happened to be an undercover agent btw. Then I saw her and she was fit and pretty and I understood why and my heart broke again. I felt terrible to be making this about me, he has kids and they are understandably devastated. I don't know what to think when I see big banks being bailed out in billions and an individual being punished for a few hundred thousand. So here I am on my way home to my kids trying to piece this affection and love I felt for Charlie into something meaningful. They do say everything happens for a reason right? This is not about me, is about Charlie's kids, his two sons, I am grieving for them. I know Charlie is a good man, flawed yes but good man that made a stupid mistake. But knowing him and his history we will overcome this after is all over and come out stronger and better than ever.

Sunday, December 5, 2010

Adventuring in times of recession

"It Always Seems impossible Until It's Done". Nelson Mandela

Unless you are Bill Gates I am sure that you are feeling the belt-tightening right now. For me, it had definitely slowed down and some of the initial plans have changed just because it is so hard to find sponsors or to even fund the adventures myself, but when the adventure is in your blood, nothing can stop you. I am still dreaming of adventures, they might not be the ones that I originally planned, some of them are out of my reach, at least for the time been or maybe forever but adventure still runs in my blood. So what to do to create an adventure? simple, just start. Adventure is doing something that both excites you and scares you. Go for a personal best, try a new sport. I am back training hard, I have postponed climbing because it is too expensive but I also want to be ready, so when the time comes to climb again I will be in top shape to pack my bags and head out. To tame the beast I looked hard at things that I could do that would be more approachable, I signed to do Ironman in Texas, My ex-husband is there, so I have a place to stay and he can help me with air miles. I am also looking for races that are close to me, the nice thing about having moved to British Columbia is that there are a lot of races that I haven't done yet. There are also races that not as popular therefore registration is lower than the usual high profile races. Arrowhead 135 mile race is less than $200 for registration. Yes, I have to run with a sled in Minnesota in the middle of Winter but that is just part of the adventure. As well you can find groups such as the Fat Ass Club that for a small fee will let you participate in races that are fuss-free and fun. This type of race is not for beginners, there are no markings or checkpoints. So much like it was at the beginning before ultra-races became the thing to do for ambitious runners who needed more after the marathon. I am taking advantage of this slow time to work on the things I neglected when I was so busy, like spending more time with family, and I could take family and friends to runs with me once in a while because I wasn't on such a tight training schedule. Right now is also a great time to take the times to improve on other things, I am working on running faster, something that I been struggling. Having had so many races last year, there was no time to train properly, I basically survived. I am now looking at a fewer race but hoping for a faster time. Yes, there is a recession, that however shouldn't stop you from waking up excited every day, all I have to do is remember that beginning of my running almost 5 years ago, the car camping, eating jelly beans bought in bulk to save, searching Craig's list for much-needed items that I couldn't afford new. I was fortunate to have experienced some amazing races and climbs using nothing but the best but in the end, all I want is to be out there. It is amazing how little it takes when you make up your mind, for Halloween my sister Muñeca, her friend Leticia and I ran the Halloween Howl 10K race on a costume and it was a blast! yes, I love ultras but it is all about the excitement of running no matter what the distance. To save money some races are also offering the option to charge a smaller fee if you don't require a t-shirt. So even if there aren't many races on my calendar, I am back training as hard I as did last year preparing for an adventure. It is all about giving your best and knowing it. Things are not going to change, I always expected to go back to my normal life once I found I had run out of options, I would have just admitted to myself that it had been one helluva ride and move on, no chance of that, this is who I am, curious by nature. Adventure is out there still, good times make us lazy, just watch a kid and everything and every day is an adventure. I have a couple of 50K's coming up, the first next Sunday in North Vancouver's Lynn Valley Park, Fat Ass Club is putting it on so are no-frills for sure just trails and a bunch of people that have something in common, love to run. Even as a broke single mother of two I still find the motivation and desire to find a way to find a race. I hear very often elaborate excuses of WHY they can't do it and I meet sadly very few who spend time thinking on the HOW to do it. It all comes down to one thing, things are very tough right now for everybody and the ones out there working hard on doing it are the ones that want it the most, as for me, all I remind myself is that I don't *have* to do it, but that I *want* to do it. Adventure is the act of doing something that a few dares to do. So what if your next race is only the local 5K? I can't tell you that I enjoyed watching my sister crossed the finish line more than I did qualifying for Boston, she has been in a lot of pain since she was diagnosed with Lupus so I was in awe watching her finish the 10K knowing how painful is for her to run. I am thankful for that, last year, I couldn't have taken the time to encourage her to do it. Just *remember to go hard with what you got.*

"Adventure is not outside man, it is within." George Eliot.

Wednesday, January 19, 2011

The Formula.

I have tried to post for so long just to lose my courage. Just like my good friend and fellow adventurer Bill told me, "your postings really sucks lately, you are evasive, it was better when you spoke honestly". So here we go. If you are looking for adventure or running you should stop reading right now. I am not sure how much I want to share yet so it is PG-13 or N-17, I have always been brutally honest to my friends, none of this is news but to strangers is not exactly small talk. Things keep coming up and as usual, I just deal with them as they come the best I can when I find myself on a situation where I think I am over my head, either in an expedition or a relationship I ask myself questions honestly and try to figure out, to a lot of people this seems cold and calculating especially if it's about something personal but this works for me, there is nothing worse than spinning your wheels and getting nowhere. Let's look at my current situation, for example, I am in Vancouver still jumping hoops to get a job as a personal trainer, hell, I don't even get a call back to volunteer at one of the gyms, I am not special enough, Vancouver is full of great athletes and my resume is not opening doors yet, I broke my right hand when I went to see Charlie because his family was worried about him, one evening he was so miserable that he is going to jail that he started to be mad at me for no reason, as if I had anything to do with him going to prison, I even lent him money for child support as he is away but in his mind I was still to blame. I was so mad at myself for being there that I punched the wall hard once and broke my right hand. I was so angry for allowing people to convince me to fix a situation that was not mine to fix, I was there only as a friend and paid a terrible price. Had to wait until I came back to Canada to get it looked after since I didn't have US insurance and by the time the Doctor saw me it had been badly set and they broke my hand and reset it twice until it finally healed okay. I am missing Arrowhead ultra as a result and most likely Badwater ultra since haven't really run enough races to qualify, last year I was MIA in the ultra-world because I was climbing instead. I lost my sponsors so climbing is off until further notice. I haven't talked about it to anybody because of shame. But I am great really. Every time I find myself in a situation that promises to turn into something too stressful, I use a formula to dig my way out of it.

So here is the process:

First, realize that it could be worse. A long time ago I promise to myself than I could handle anything except something happening to my kids, so instantly no matter what happens I feel grateful that is not that.

Second -I am honest to myself so I avoid the blame game, nothing good comes of that, then why is important only so you can hopefully stop it from happening again, after that throw it away or you go around in a useless circle of self-pity. The world is full of people like Marlon Brando's character Terry Mallow on the movie "On The Waterfront " screaming "I could have been a contender"

Third-Find the good things that this opportunity is bringing, no matter what it is if there is something hanging on for dear life. If there is nothing then go to step four.

Fourth- Make something amazing out of whatever challenge you overcame, don't let it be in vain, things don't happen for a reason, is up to you to give them meaning. Just imagine the incredible courage that it took for the mother who lost a child to a drunk driver and then created Mother's Against Drunk Drivers. So for me, Vancouver has proven taught but it has also given so many opportunities for my kids, my youngest son Hans is like a twin with my nephew Taylor, they are very busy with sports and it makes me happy to know he is not hanging out at the 7-11. Karl's grades just exploded, thanks to the accommodations the school is making he is back to where he was before he was diagnosed, all A's and B's, he is feeling so confident that he even decided he wants to go to Emily Carr University to study Visual Arts, you should have seen my sister Muñeca's face when Karl told her, "visual arts?!!" I am still smiling about it until now everybody has focused on what Karl was able to do, not on what he is capable of accomplishing if given the right tools. So by now you probably forgot that I can't find a job right? I not only stop the pity party, but I also threw a party for the newfound opportunities, whatever you feed your brain is what you will get, anger in, stress and depression out, happiness in, laughter love and excitement out, simple. If you are reading this and thinking of excuses for why you really can't overcome this, whatever it is, a bad job, a bad relationship, go back and try the steps again, if you still can't find it is for one reason and one only. You don't want the change, and it's OK, is perfectly fine, is OK as long as you don't drive yourself crazy over this. Own it or it will own you. One of my sisters use to drive herself crazy over her weight, she use to call me crying all the time, she cried because she missed her treats, so I reminded her that she was certainly not movie star shape but healthy so it was OK, but she cried and cried because she wanted to rock a bikini, then she used to also call me when she had a cookie, I finally couldn't take it anymore, I told her to eat or not eat the cookies I didn't care, to just made up her mind about what was more important to her then to stick to it. In the end, she stuck to it until she reached a comfortable weight, not bikini but short dress weight, then made sure to enjoy her cookies responsible, easier to maintain than to lose the weight. Of course, I always get easy for you to say, and no, is never easy for anybody and since when is it a competition? and what do you get then, *yes your life do really suck, you win, now go and live miserable life guilt free*? is in it the whole point to, ALWAYS find the way out? For me, life has shown me many opportunities when the skill to quickly survive and excel at a challenge proved a lifesaver, the first time I was rape I was 12, I was left to care for a relative and took advantage of me, and you want to know what it's worse, that relative was blind, so later I had to learn to overcome what blindness signified to me but for my sons and for them I will do anything. So no, it is never easy for anybody but I have seen what giving up looks like, I wasn't the only one in my extended family of course and it pains me to see the others who ended up with terrible lives as a result. So there you go Bill, I hope you are right when you told me that by sharing I will allow others to find their peace. There is something about keeping secrets that destroys you. For me everything changed when Oprah talked about it on her show, I felt relieved that somebody else had gone through it too, not only did she survived it but thrived, make no mistake, I will never say that it made me who I am, I am who I am *in spite* of it, I will never give credit to the people that hurt me, this should never happen to a child ever or any human being for that matter. So how did I overcome this? I kept focusing on things such as sparing my other little cousins of the same fate. It took me an awfully long time to find the courage to tell, once I did they couldn't keep my mouth shut. There seem to be thousands of years between that child and who I am now, that been the lowest point of my life then, recently I felt the same pain only stronger when Karl was diagnosed with Cone Rod Dystrophy and I was waiting on results for my other son Hans to see if the growth on his bone was benign or cancerous, thankfully turned out to be benign, I learned that whatever pain I felt was nothing compared to the one I felt then, so never again will I complain about me, but I wish for my kids a long and uneventful life. I am ready again, I will be going to the drawing table soon to find something that I CAN do, enough with what I can't, I am sure that if I dream hard enough I will find an amazing adventure waiting to be had.

"When it is dark enough, you can see the stars". ~Ralph Waldo Emerson

Tuesday, March 1, 2011

Coyote 2 Moons part 1.

I close my eyes and think, when I open them I am afraid to think again. So many things going through my head. I didn't think this was important to share, even I get tired of me, but if I don't write I will not go to sleep and I am tired. I am still trying to figure out if I should go to Coyote 2 Moons or not. I have been working hard to find a balance, it is not easy after all the last few years have been all about extremes. I am trying to be responsible and be home more for my kids, and it's working, grades are going up and the house is livable even if I die a little every day looking at the world continue, mountains to be conquered, races to be run, but I truly believe that things can happen I just have to be patient, the most important thing right now is to make sure my kids' dreams and hopes come true, just like any other parent on an endless schedule driving to and from sports lessons and homework. My kids are happy, I count the days until my next race or continuously daydream about my next adventure, I am so grateful for that, not sure what I would do if I didn't have dreams to keep my mind healthy. Today I found out I failed part of my final to become a certified personal trainer, the truth is that with so much going on is no surprise, taking classes, training, kids and constantly traveling to see Charlie was difficult for me to concentrate on my classes and had to postpone quite a few to accommodate my trips to the USA since I broke my hand and the programs had to be written by hand I had to write them with my left hand and were not my best job, but I had to submit them or fail and at the end the result was the same. Sometimes I feel like my life is one giant game of chutes and ladders. After the call, I sat on the car thinking, "What happened?"" I even had my wedding dress picked a few months ago" I know that true life is for better or for worse but I have seen plenty of for worse, I am so ready for the better part. Is no use trying to quit, I have tried before and I just delay things, I quit acting before when I found myself stressed and unable to manage the pressure of such industry, I have tried to reinvent myself many times over, to take college classes, to try to be taken seriously but I should never worry about what other people think and I should have followed my passion. Here I am now, working as an actor again, I think is ironic that I didn't think that I was pretty enough to be in the industry, and now I found myself knocking on doors and having the very same door that I closed before opening, now that my hair is going grey and the wrinkles stay even after I have stopped smiling, how wrong was I. But I guess maybe I needed to take a long detour, so I could be ready for my life. The wonderful thing about being older is that I completely refuse to quit, I want this life badly enough that I am willing to wait for as long as necessary, more than the acting, adventure is where I feel at home, so yes, I am not sure how I will manage but I will make it to Coyote 2 Moons 100-mile ultra and Ironman, TX even if I couldn't learn to swim because I broke my hand, I will doggie paddle Ironman Texas if I have to. I am not quitting my passions anymore, life owes me that, I am a good mother and I deserve to do the things that are positive and make me happy. I am doing it for me but also it is for my kids' own good, the reason why they are dreaming big is that they feel safe at home, safe to dream big and nobody will laugh at their dreams no matter how unattainable they might seem.

"So many of our dreams at first seem impossible, then they seem improbable, and then, when we summon the will, they soon become inevitable". Christopher Reeve

Tuesday, March 15, 2011

Dream Big.

In a few days, I will be running Coyote 2Moons (C2M) and I am unreasonably nervous, I couldn't put it into words, the dreading feeling until I had a conversation with Jack who is generously helping me with the logistics and letting me crash at his hotel room floor " if you find space" apparently I am not the only ultrarunner wanting to save money. He was asking me about my reluctance and I realized I felt like a plane crash survivor, I was feeling guilty for going to this race as Charlie is in jail right now. Yes, I had nothing to do with it yet I feel terribly guilty. I have wanted to just lay low and work at a Starbucks for a while but it seems I am not good at it. The great thing about taking some time off to sort things out was that it was a wonderful time to take care of the things that were neglected, having moved to Vancouver proved to be right, as hard and time-consuming as it turned out to be, my kids could not be happier or healthier, I get to see my sister Muñeca every day and scheduling things with her help is so much easier than I wonder how did I ever do without her. Like now, I just get to leave and she takes over until my ex-husband comes to town for the kids for spring break. Once I made up my mind I could feel the excitement building up, in a few days I will be with some awesome people that I have never met on an amazing adventure, the joys, the pain I will savor it all. I want my life back, all of it, I am going to stand tall and admit that I want more from life and I am not afraid to go for it. I am fortunate to be given the opportunity to live this life, a life of adventure that I have learned to love and refusing it will be ungrateful to the universe that had so generously offered to me in the first place. I can see my life clearly, I will probably not die wealthy I love my family too much to watch my bank account get bigger and as they struggle, there is always a family member that could use my help. I find it weird that some people just write a check to a charity get a tax receipt and don't really take the time to see if there is a niece who can't afford school tuition or a sibling who lost a job, I might not have a big bank account when I die but I will die as someone who cared for those around her. For C2M surviving will be the main plan, I haven't run 100 miles without stopping since Iron Horse Ultra in 2009 so it will be smart to stay conservative and see what happens. Howard is in my start group and I will be shadowing him all the way, Howard finished shy of 30hrs last year and he said it was hard. I am starting to stay awake at night dreaming of what else I want to accomplish, it feels so good to have dreams and goals again. So my question to you is" if I gave you permission to dream big what will it be?"

"Let go of the past and go for the future. Go confidently in the direction of your dreams. Live the life you imagined."- Henry David Thoreau

Wednesday, March 30, 2011

Coyote 2 Moons Race Report.

Well, this one is for the books. This year's C2M race is one to remember for anybody that participated. Saturday night at midnight the race director canceled the race due to unsafe conditions when a blizzard and high winds hit the race course. The race director had the daunting task of getting everybody down the ridge safely. Organizers and volunteers were so busy trying to keep the shivering runners scattered in 3 different aid stations warm and it was unsafe to go out and see if there was somebody still in the course that I found myself lost and desperately trying to find shelter since I was so far behind everybody else as last runner and because of the white out conditions on the top ridge I couldn't see the mark course anymore but I digress, let me tell you what happened from the beginning. Pre-race activities included an evening of bowling and if you wore the best costume could earn you bonus points, the picnic had us all singing, fail to join in the fun and you earn boner points, it was amazing watching such serious runners like Karl Meltzer so relaxed bowling in a costume just days before that race. Make no mistake; the race is competitive and very challenging. The race package included great quality items such a Patagonia jacket but the majority of the items on the loot bag were useless items such a stir stick from a cheap hotel bar, last year's calendars, or irrelevant pamphlets from places that aren't even in the area. I started on the M3 group; we start from slowest to fastest with the intention that everybody finishes in a 4hr window. My start time was Friday at midnight, two previous groups first as early as 6pm, while Howard drove to the start and tried to nap for a few hours, I ended up trying to relax back at the room watching my favorite novel Eva Luna. Jack and John kept my company pretending to be interested in the storyline when they knew and I knew the only reason why they let me choose the channel was that Latin soap actress is easy on the eye. Finally, at 11:30 we decided to go to the start line at Thatcher School field, It had been raining already, I was dreading it for many reasons, I was hugely undertrained and the weather forecast was calling for a storm Sunday morning so while I stood there in the rain with 10 other runners waiting for our start I was already questioning my decision. We set off and I could feel my excitement increasing and I started forgetting about the rain. I stayed behind with Mark and Ty who insisted on calling me Ramona because they didn't think Norma was exotic enough for me. It was hard to see with all the fog but it helped that the road was wide enough to run chorus line like and all three head torches complimented each other. I found the course challenging in the way that is hardly ever flat, either straight up or down, but not very technical, at least not the first 50 miles. It was fun running together and howling at the moon, a C2M tradition I am told. The 10.9-mile trail to Sisar Canyon was almost without incident, 100 yards from the air station a creek had spilled over the road and form a pond right in the middle, I slipped and fell getting wet when I arrived at the CP yelling " my bike, where is my bike" they looked at me wondering what I was I saying, "I didn't realize it was a triathlon, I did the swim part now I need my bike." Next was Topa Aid station on mile 17.2, I started falling behind, the chilly night and wet clothes were a horrible combination, again it was a steep climb, when I arrived I was mildly hypothermic, I was really disappointed that I could potentially drop out so early, thankfully volunteers were kind, they took my clothes and dried them on the bonfire and they sat me on a warm car wrapped in a blanket, in about an hr. I was ready to head out again, with drier clothes and volunteer Matt's socks (thank you!). By the time I was on my way to Rose Valley aid station I could see how far behind I had fallen, I was about two hours behind the group I had been running with, but was glad to hear that Canadian Jenn Segger who had started at 3am was smoking the course, Jann is all class, I had the pleasure of going for some Mexican dinner with her and Bruce another Canadian runner the night before and had a blast with them. By the time I reach Topa Aid station and 32.4 miles later the very fast 100 runners such as Karl Meltzer had reached Topa for the first time and were already on their way to Rose Valley aid station, I had started 10 hrs. earlier and in no time he was going to pass me. As they went by I looked disappointed said, " what? I am not going to win it?" One of them yelled as he was passing by," Remember to hydrate and you just might!". Even though it was a bit warmer I was still feeling a bit cold, and by now I had trouble keeping food or drink, out of nowhere the fastest registered female runner who was wearing a hat with a propeller tap me on the shoulder, another C2M tradition, the fastest runner pass the had to the slowest, I had just been passed by the fastest female making me officially the slowest female on the course so I had to wear the hat, great, *the only thing worse now* I though is that if *I got to Ridge Junction Aid station and I found out that my high school reunion was been held there AND my high school crush was still hot and recently single.* By the time I arrived I was shivering again, I sat there wondering if this time I was going to drop out, I sat there watching the 100K runners who had started Sat morning starting to come through. Again the volunteers went out of their way to warm me up and send me on my way, a few quesadillas later I stood there shivering ready to go when Luis Escobar pronounced "let's make a vapor barrier out of a garbage bag!" so after 40 minutes wearing a garbage bag and the propeller hat I set out again, "living the dream" I thought. The most amazing thing was that not a single one of us thought " wait a minute, this is a bad idea, maybe she should just go home" The truth is that while I had been previously been embarrassed because I was so slow, after almost dropping now I was determined to finish. It was back to Rose Valley Aid Station, by now it was raining again, I must have been a sight when I started descending to the next aid station, wearing a garbage bag and a propeller hat" I know" I said when they smiled when I came around " hard to believe I am still single" by the time I left the aid station the weather started turning for the worse, I was nervous, I had lost my map when I fell on the creek so I was now relying on course markings on the course and anybody that had participated on C2M, course markings are very few. As the weather turned and night came and I made it to the top of the ridge, it was storming and I had trouble raising my head to see where I was going. I was a worry since I couldn't see the course and was worry about missing the turn, after an hour I decided to turn back to Ridge Junction Aid station that I was sure it was the exact opposite direction. For about 4 hours I struggle with the wind and the cold, by now I was desperate to find shelter, I decided to turn back to lower ground because the wind was picking up and I realized I could blow me off the mountain, I also started to hallucinate because of the lack of sleep and dehydration, I saw army men on winter fatigues laying on the ground ready for action, the bushes turned into beasts and fought each other, bus stations, kids jumping rope, the hallucinations were incredibly detail, also fatigue and the cold was making me sleepy so I sang hard to force my brain to wake up, sadly the first song that came to mind was The Wheels on the Bus. What to do? I needed to make a decision, I was still safe but I couldn't possibly wait for anybody to come and find me, I didn't know that they had already canceled the race. At this point I considered calling for help, I always carry my spot satellite for emergencies and I had my cell phone but I didn't want to endanger the lives of rescuers unless it was absolutely necessary and at this point, things were still under control, plus I had absolutely no idea where I was so it was going to take longer for them to find me that for me to find shelter. it would be an incredible irony that I have been in inhospitable places for races but it will be in California where I would be saved. The one thing I decided to do was to find a road, Rose Valley Aid Station was by a main road, I knew they had dismantled the aid station because we were not scheduled to go back that way but I notice a couple of men that were camping, they had stood there watching us go through the gate with amusement, I was hoping that they were still there but also there was a bathroom that I could use for shelter. As I started to run downhill the snow turned into heavy rain at lower altitude I knew that if the guys were not there I was in serious trouble, I had trouble running earlier but by now I was running hard, like the saying goes, I was running for my life, amazing after running over 50 miles I had no problem running fast, if I could only do that at races I thought!. Fortunately, when I got to Rose Valley Gate about 45 min later, I could see two tiny tents, it was almost 1am so they were asleep for sure. For a few seconds, I thought about how ridiculous it must look, been awakened by a strange woman wearing a garbage bag and propeller hat and a racing bib. I yelled for help waking them up. I told them that I needed help, fortunately, Brian and Tony turned out to be Navy officers, they recognized that they needed to act fast, as soon as a stop running I got cold quickly, in a matter of minutes I was slurring my words, they took the matter as seriously as an official mission. I was out of my clothing again (to clarify I always wear under armor sports underwear that looks like biking shorts in case I need to change on a race, but do listen to your mother and always wear clean undies) Brian later told me that when I started shaking and my eye rolled back he knew it was serious. They are both trained for medical emergencies so I could not have stumbled upon better help. After a change to dry clothing, hot chocolate, and some food I was feeling better, fatigued but I was still hallucinating so the boys chaperoned me to the race headquarters to notify the RD that I was safe and sound and then later drove me back to my hotel, I am telling you chivalry is not dead, Brian and Tony's wives are very lucky women indeed. I arrived in my room close to 2am and my roommates arrived about 30 min later, one by one, Harold, John, and Jack were all taking turns with the stories, Harold was showing signs of hypothermia as well, apparently, I talked lengthily but made little sense but then again you are Mexican they told me. The next morning we woke up to the damage, fallen trees everywhere, most of the C2M crew vehicles had to be left at the ridge, the roads disappeared on the mudslides and they called a group to volunteer to bring one of the volunteer crew members that had been stuck on one of the checkpoints all night. Overall, there were no serious injuries, amazing considering that there were about 100 participants and some of them where caught by the storm wearing nothing but shorts and a singlet. There was talk of this been the last of C2M's edition since last year weather created havoc as well. Would I stop running trail races after this incident?. Not a chance, trail races especially ultras always carry a degree of danger, is part of the allure, if I was somebody that didn't want that kind of risk I would sign for a local 5K race. Besides from the incredible discomfort, the fact that I managed to remain calm tells me is where I belong. Sure there were times while I was running wild to try and find the help that I thought, "damn, I need to quit doing this to myself" but I knew that that was not possible anymore, at dinner last night, sharing a bottle of wine with Harold and Jack the talked turned to races that we had done and I could feel my heart rate go up with excitement at the talk of some races that I haven't done but are on my bucket list, they don't call it a passion for nothing.

"Security is mostly a superstition. It does not exist in nature, nor do the children of men as a whole experience it. Avoiding danger is no safer in the long run than outright exposure. Life is either a daring adventure or nothing." Helen Keller.

Thursday, March 31, 2011

Coyote 2 Moon- Corrections

I keep getting in trouble when I whine about a race I don't finish. I want to clarify somethings about my race report, I hope it didn't come through as a whiner, I just wanted to tell you *my* experience. Never did I intend to make anybody that organized or volunteered at C2M responsible for what happened. On the contrary, I received plenty of emails from Chris the RD to be prepared for, and I am quoting him, CaCa weather. There were a couple of things that Chris called me on, and eventually even cost me to be penalized on the final results.

It is not Coyote 2 Moons but Coyote 2 Moon. It is not a race but an event, although I disagree with that, I am sure if you are in the back you will think of it as an event if you are in the front you will think is a race. The loot bag was *not* full of irrelevant paraphernalia, although I am still waiting on his response on the meaning on the stir stick from Best Western, two 2009 agendas and pamphlets such as Elvis Presley's impersonator show in Vegas. And the most important clarifications was that they *were* aware of my absence, I think that Chris and everybody involved did an amazing job of getting everybody down from the ridge safely. When I finally was able to find help my main concern was to notify that I was safe, and when I approached a volunteer at an aid station later he told me he had no knowledge that there was any talk of asking about any stranded runner, so there my understanding that they had not realized yet that I was not at any of the 3 operating aid stations on top of the ridge, I was not surprised or anything, given the sudden nature of the weather and the number of people that needed to be looked after. I am sure that everybody is wondering how can I even get lost, I made many mistakes and I was aware of the risks, nothing too dangerous, but I have always respect nature, I knew I was safe, I can run for a long time so keeping warm was not a problem but is the outdoors after all and I never take it lightly, the best thing is to think ahead of what the problems might be, in my case, when I worried is when the wind became too strong and I was worried that if it picked me up and send me flying they will not have found my that easy and if I get hurt and became unable to move that could be trouble. Rule number one, always know when to turn around. I also shared with Chris that I felt fully responsible, I knew I was ill-prepared, I was already struggling at the beginning, some people might think that I had no place there but think that I do, I wanted to be there, I will probably never have a life that is optimum for that kind of adventure, by choice, my lifestyle is 100% based on my priorities, I could do more but that would mean that I spend less time doing the things that my kids need from me, is their time now, not mine, in a few more years they will be gone and then I can pursue my passions fully. But as hard as it will be I still want to participate such events, I have the feeling that my life will always have this kind of obstacles, I lived for my family, but I much rather be there for them and push through a race or a climb than give up on that kind of lifestyle. I am also aware of my limitations so I am careful about not finding myself in a situation where I have to cut my arm to free myself. The bottom line, I highly recommend C2M. Coyote 2 Moon is for anybody that is looking for a challenge, elite or not will feel at home.C2M, is a lot of fun but the course is challenging enough for anybody even at the elite level, so don't skip it if you are serious about other well know races like Western States. The volunteers are nicest and most dedicated people I have ever met on an event, I mean, one of them gave me his socks so I could continue, they wanted me to continue as much as I did, they didn't have to care but they did. I left the original post, everybody experiences things differently, I want you to read both sides of the story, also it reflects the chaos on my brain that usually happens after something like that, and trust me, this is not the last time you will find me in a chaotic state again, Ironman here I come!

Tuesday, April 5, 2011

Kindness Is the Language Which The Deaf Can Hear And The Blind Can See. ~Mark Twain

I have been thinking lots about why I pursue time-consuming and difficult paths since really nobody is watching all the time, why not just skip a workout or eat junk? We have the life that we deserve, happiness and kindness attracts that, more happiness and kindness. I am working as an actor is a difficult jobs because it has a viewed as superficial but how can it be when it feels so enriching when I am working on set. There are many reasons why pursuing happiness is worth it here are some that relate to me. I am 43 and turning 44 this year, my skin is healthy and hardly feel the need to wear makeup. I was diagnosed with Post Traumatic Stress Disorder in my teens and twenties had lots of health problems that couldn't be diagnosed, vertigo, lumps on my breast that had to be biopsied. I spend years trying to figure out why until finally one smart Doctor told me that it was my lifestyle that unless I changed it was only going to get worse. It has been 20 years since the last time I had to say in bed because of stress or depression or had to self-medicate with alcohol or cigarettes. I still have some symptoms of PTSD but they are manageable. have deep and meaningful relationships with people close to me, my kids, family, and friends. Kindness brings internal and external peace while I adore participating in events that are exiting, I crave order and peace in my personal relationships, things get chaotic from time to time and they are dealt with when they raised but there is no need to bring any more chaos into my personal life. It is not necessary to make big changes right away, for me, it has been a long road to find myself here, it started with minor changes than major ones like quitting smoking at age 24 and then drinking heavily. I never did it for health or vanity, it was simply because I was tired of treating myself badly, is in funny we are great at nurturing others but terrible at nurturing ourselves? self-compassion is a very difficult thing but is the best gift you can give yourself and to the ones close to you. So what is it?. With me started with one word " enough" as in I am enough and I had enough, I am very glad I been journaling since the age of 12 is great to see the progression and also when I was ready I was able to see that sometimes I wasn't kind to myself, maybe I believed that I deserved it but it took one brave day to say enough, of course, it was just the beginning, I took many steps back but just as many forward and that is what I needed, to just take the first step to accepting who I was. So kindness starts with you, you can't give what you don't have. Here is the actual entry of in my journal July 19, 2002 (coincidentally is the year of my divorce)

"It's almost midnight, the clock is turning to the 19th day and today is the start, the beginning and it all starts with a single word, enough.

I had enough of living my life complaining about what I don't have or what it should have been.

I had enough of waiting for the perfect man, job, or my kids been at the right age to be fully happy and fulfilled.

It's enough with just what the universe has granted me

I am enough.

From this moment I promise to never compromise my life anymore.

I will respect me.

I will believe in me.

I will not compromise in the things that are my core beliefs.

I will work had to accomplish the things I believe I can.

I will not seek an easy way out.

I will honor my beliefs.

I will do what it takes.

Because I am worthy of a great life and all I need is the courage to take control of my life again".

Of course, there were days that I cried after that entry but I went back over and over to it and I still do when I find myself at crossroads, I go back to remind myself of the things that matter to me and also to avoid making the same mistakes. Why am I sharing? I know there are some people out there that are having a hard time right now that need a friend, I want to extend my hand and say the same things I told myself almost 10 years ago, you are worth it, just have the courage to make the changes necessary to have the life that is meant for you, kindness starts with you.

Sunday, April 17, 2011

"Seize Every Opportunity Along The Way, For How Sad It Would Be If The Road You Chose Became The Road Not Taken." Robert Braul

It was a great morning waking up to an email from the race organizers from the TransAlps Ultra welcoming me to the race. The story of how I got invited is interesting, Bernd whom I never met has been asking me to be his partner for the race since the race has to be ran by teams for two., I declined but he kept emailing me with reasons why I should consider his offer. Better judgment told me not to go, I am not the best at teams, especially the ones required to stay close through the course. Mountaineering is different because there really isn't a safe way to do it alone. Races like TransRockies and TransAlps where you must cross every checkpoint together or risk being disqualified, there is just no escape. I love the solitude of running long distance races, I enjoy going for a run with my best friend Nadia talking and laughing once in a while but is a completely different matter to be out a race especially if its someone I don't know. I been a single parent for so long that races are the solitude I need because as a single parent your kids are constantly going, "mom, mom, mom," so when Nadia and I were at TransRockies I was going crazy with all the chatter, but thankfully I know where to push her buttons so after a few hours together, I told her something that I knew would get her upset, something that was true and that she needed to hear but knew she didn't want to and then she would speed off and wait for me just before the checkpoint and I would have a few glorious hours to myself, she never knew why I did it. I cancel on Bernd several times, he likes is too talkative so my instinct told me immediately to say no, but something kept telling me that I should consider going, here is an opportunity of a lifetime and I should be taking advantage of it, his sponsors are paying, second, I get more fan mail from Germany than anywhere else, actually, I only get a request for signed pictures from Germany, the first time I showed my sister Muñeca the email, I was asking her if she thought it was a joke. Why will anybody want a signed picture of me? My sister looked at it and said that it looked legit so I send the picture away, then other requests started to arrive. Then I got word that I had made the cover of a German Trail Running magazine, apparently in Germany, I was the David Hasselhoff's singing career of runners, that was all I needed to decide that I should go to TransAlps since the opportunities to find sponsors would be easier than in Canada. I started focusing on running again I am also working on being more of a team player. I am well aware of my shortcomings, just as I am well aware of the consequences. Every act has a consequence, your life is a direct reflection of your priorities. I strongly believe in taking full ownership of my life, it strengthens the commitment to the choices I have made and it helps me decide, some choices are hard to make, we all have choices, when we struggle is when we are making the ones we are forced to make, they are not the ones we want to make. They are some people that know me well and can tell you that I might be the most unsympathetic person in the world, Nadia gave me for my birthday a "whining" sand clock, not for me but for her, it saved our relationship, she got one minute of release and for me a time when I could just say, OK, time is up. I work harder on two things, either changing the situation or accepting it, there is no middle ground, the world has never made any progress but just having countless of hours of just talking about a problem, now you know why politics is difficult, you have a lot of smart people terrific at identifying a problem but not great at the action. The problem is not the wasted time, the problem I see is the choices you make while you feel you have no choice.

"I might as well just give up and eat myself to death, I am never going to lose weight". Sometimes acceptance is just patience, contrary to what some people believe, I don't enjoy been single but I dislike the choices I have to make in order for me to be in a relationship, it took me a while to figure out that, yes, it is me. It was not until I met Charlie that I realized that. Somebody that I believed was right for me didn't work out at all after we broke up I did almost what an alcoholic does and made amends, contacted some of my past relationships to apologize," Sorry remember when I told you that it was really you? sorry, I guess it turned out, it was really me." And it's okay, I will now try and do better because I know better. I am well aware that as long as I am committed to the choices that I make, the amount of time I spend training, raising my kids alone, and the involvement with my charities, I have to suck it up and not complain if I spend Saturday nights folding laundry while my kids are out with friends. Of course, this is not an easy thing to do, with every choice there is a consequence, I disliked making the call to the charities telling them that I was aborting all future climbs because my ex-boyfriend needed me and spending the money in helping him instead. I disliked calling Charlie and telling him that I couldn't do it anymore ,what's more difficult, it brought criticisms no matter what direction I took, staying or leaving him so as usual I had to rely on my judgment to make the decision and made myself ready to face the consequence. Sometimes the choice is made for me, I get cc'd on every conversation Karl school aid with the visual aids specialist for the school district, like the one below. "Can you get a speech to text software for Karl's computer? His typing skills are very poor and we believe his eyesight may have deteriorated since school started- he couldn't use it at school so much but he would be able to use it at home for essay writing. It is necessary to 'train' the software to your own voice so he should have some help getting this accomplished?". I take full ownership of the fact that I have focus more in fundraising for charities that cater to my son that in lucrative sports sponsors because I want to talk about why I am doing a certain adventure more than the equipment I am using. I stand by the outcome while fully understanding that, I didn't have to be involved on the charities, they were never going to blame me if Karl goes blind but I had to answer the question did I do everything I could? Every day. I know that my financial struggles right now are directly related to my choices, part time work to take my kids to their appointments, quitting to pursue fundraising for charities that helped my son adjust to his new life and help Charlie financially when he went to jail even though I knew there was a great chance he was never going to pay me back. I stand by those choices because I made them for the right reasons and so I have to also accept the consequences. You can't have one without the other.

Sunday, May 8, 2011
"Gratitude is When Memory is Stored in the Heart and Not in the Mind". Lionel Hampton

It is so hard to write right now, I am for the first time having a hard time explaining my feelings. Extraordinary Moms aired today. There are so many thoughts racing on my head. I never anticipated that we were going to be in a documentary with the likes of Christina Amanpour, Hilary Clinton and Rossie O'Donnell. Been associated with Oprah Winfrey is enough to want to pinch yourself, been attached to all these amazing women featured it made me feel like "Why me?". I have always known that there is no such a thing as an act without consequences, sooner or later you will have to face them. I try to live my life the way I believe is right for my family. I refuse to believe that there is not going to be a cure for my son Karl, I need that if I am to kiss my son every day, to be doing what I do is no different than any mother would do for their child. What Extraordinary Moms did and allow me to reach a wider audience to hopefully inspire more people to dream harder. To convince more people about what I have already known, *nothing is impossible.* One incredibly surprise was to learn that when the news arrived in my hometown, it was received with ecstasy and they want me to come to Sinaloa to speak to local schools, it seems that somebody from the Governor's office read my comments about me wanting to inspire kids to stay in school, to not choose a life of crime when I heard that it was probably the most emotional moment for me, this is incredible in many levels, after all, I was one of those kids, I am forever grateful for the insight of knowing that shortcuts eventually end in tragedy, that through hard work and the stubbornness to not quit it was where I would find a way out poverty. The negative side of such exposure is having to face my past in a way that I never wanted to face anymore. All this attention of where I came from is opening doors I shut long before and never wanted to open. I am struggling again to work and it's affecting me at home since I am struggling just to survive. I am unable to go back to my old life because I can't hide behind the invisible shield I had created for myself and this means that until I find a flexible well paid job, I take whatever I can get to supplement my income, and sometimes that might even mean cleaning homes, I have never felt that I am above anything but it was hard to go back and start from the bottom after reaching management level, I particularly remember bringing my youngest son Hans to one of the homes I had to clean because he was sick and didn't go to school, it turned out the house was one of his classmates, a girl in his class, I could see he was embarrassed, he sat in the front porch and I gently teased him that if I found a note that read " I love Hans" tucked in her room I was sure to let him know, that made him smile but I am also aware that I am also teaching him something positive, he will forever respect anybody no matter what their status is. My own embarrassment lasted even less, whatever felt the first day I cleaned strangers home is nothing compared to the pain I feel when I hear my son ask me what's for dinner *while* he is looking at the plate, mash potatoes, perogies, pasta, ravioli they all look the same mass to his eyes. Or when he asks me which bottle among all the ones in the bathroom is the hand soap because I kept buying different brands of soap depending on what was on sale and he needs to memorize the bottles. I can get pass my ego, the thought of failing my kids is the pain sharpest I have ever felt in my life. I am thankful for being able to experience it fully, for the sharp awareness, that is what fuels the desire to wake up every day with a purpose beyond wanting a better car or living at a better neighborhood. So is maddening when somebody suggests that if I work on polishing my speech I could even have a career as a public speaker, this is about dedicating my life to making sure I leave a better world for my kids. If I improve naturally in the process I am ok, but I refuse to stand in front of the mirror to practice, I want my heart to always speak first. A friend even suggested that Karl might be getting too old to have his mother advocating for him, imagine that person telling Dick Hoyt that his son Rick might be getting a bit too big to be carried around on a stroller, there is no more powerful bond than a parent-child bond and no matter how old my kids are I will always be their mother and if I feel the need to speak up for him I will God damn do it. So I don't expect the road to get any easier, I am here for my kids, make no mistake, when the last article is written about my adventures I will still be waking up early to make sure that I am doing everything I can for them. That's OK with me, I can't imagine a better life than the one I already have.

Sunday, May 22, 2011

"Seize every opportunity along the way, for how sad it would be if the road you chose became the road not taken."

~Robert Braul

I am so glad I survived Ironman. I had so many doubts about coming to Texas to do my first Ironman, when I registered for it I just sold my house had some extra cash and I was sure I was going to be able to train for it properly, then life happened. Every race has been less than ideal this year, I decided that since the last two years I was busy doing all the races and climbs to help the charities I had to put my kids' needs on the side so now they come first, life is all about balance, while my kids don't expect me to drop everything for them all the time they are times that they do, now is one of those times, recently I have slept little worrying about my kids, Karl's eye condition and Hans strong personality, I get to see their teacher more often than the gym nowadays, Karl's teachers worry that he is falling behind, while he stands strong saying that they are overreacting that he is doing just fine, Hans teacher has long conversations with me about him been uninterested in class, of course, we both know he discovered that girls don't really have the cooties. So the best thing to do is to let go and work with what I have, running is still my priority so most of the time was spent running, the other available time was spent cycling or swimming, it was very rare to have a week when I had a chance on doing all three sports with consistency. I arrived in Houston with my kids, the reason why I choose Ironman Texas was because it gives my kids something they adore, the rare opportunity when both parents are at the same time together, something that my kids cherish and my ex and I tolerate. I strongly believe on maintaining a relationship with the father of my kids something that has caused me a share of arguments on my relationships. I was very worried about not making the time limit, on the flight I was telling Hans about this but he gave me a pep talk, it is fantastic, Hans was telling me that I could do it, that at least I had to show up and try my hardest, by him voicing those words they would be forever imprinted on his brain, those words had a deep meaning now. I was feeling very confident now until we pass through immigration, as usual, the officers wanted to know the reason for our trip, Ironman, I replied, he looked at me and without smile said," You don't look like an Ironman" I wanted to say a lot of things, that I run ultras and all that but the truth was that I had never done Ironman so that was true, Hans, however, had something to say "you don't know my mom" that's all he said, Karl had a big grin too. I just realized how deeply our bond is and that they are proud of me just like I am of them. Ironman was going to be hard but knowing my kids had deep belief in me was worth trying. Go through your pictures right now, the ones that will remain when you are gone they will tell your story, how many are of you holding a drink or sitting on the couch? I can tell you that I have very few of those. The welcome dinner was different than the usual than ultraraces, you could sense of pride in the room, you belonged to an elite private club. I sat with some strangers, three of us were about to do Ironman for the first time, the rest were veterans, of course, the veterans wanted to give us advise, the really fit veterans always said, "you will be OK, you have 16hrs to finish, plenty of time" the not so fit ones, the ones that sneaked by more than once had a different view, to them even attempting Ironman you had to prove that you were worthy of claiming such title. Talking to one of them in particular, a middle-aged man on my table, it felt more like an interrogation than a conversation, "So, of course, you did at least done a half", *nope* "wow, you must have an incredible coach then if you feel confident that you can finish" "a group to train with? *Again, no*, then he lost it with me "why would you think you will have a chance?!" by now he was clearly annoyed, middle-age men who brought a date to the dinner clearly to impress her, judging by his clothes and physique he had more money than athletic abilities, I wish I possessed the confidence of an average white middle age men. I told him that I had ran many running race in hopes of putting the conversation to rest not caring to chat with him anymore, Mr. CEO was determined to not let it go, I could tell that people around him had to prove themselves to him. "Well, how many of your races last for 12hrs!" "You are right, not many, most of them are over 24hrs, I can't believe that I will be home tonight after ONLY 12 hrs. what a treat!" and then I left the table not interested on sitting next to him anymore, and also because it made me look cooler to the rest of the table. Of course, I was very intimidated by Ironman but I was not about to let him know of that. Race day came, Saturday 5am about 2600 competitors stood at

Woodlands Lake for the 2.4-mile swim, because of the water temperature reached the high temperatures they call for a no wetsuit swim but you had the option to use a wetsuit and not be considered for placing of Kona slots since there was not a fat chance of that happening and I needed all the help in the water I decided to go on the wetsuit corral with about 500 others. I was dreading the swim, I was close to tears when the lady standing close to me notice my nervousness and held my hands and said a prayer, then at 7am, 10 minutes after the pro start we were off, I stayed behind to avoid been trampled since I knew I was going to be on the back, I alternating from poorly executed freestyle I had seen on YouTube and breaststroke that resembled more a doggie paddle. I tried swimming the distance at my community pool, but things are different. I tried my best but it seems to go on forever, as we were coming into the finals stretch I could hear people screaming "go, go, go!" I thought they were cheering but they were basically telling us to go harder because we were about to time out. This was going to be a very familiar scenario through the race. I was so glad to be out of the water 2hrs and 14 minutes later, but now the next part was going to be just as tough, I had not done a ride longer than 60 miles. Although they called for thundershowers it was just overcast and no rain, it was still warm but the sun was hiding behind the clouds and I was so thankful, I had a hard time from the begin, my arms ache from the swim and my neck too from cranking my head to see where I was going. I was already 25 minutes more out of transition that I had originally anticipated so I just suck it out and try to go hard, I kept playing two mantras on my head to overcome the fatigue, " you don't know my mom" and 'I am Ironman" I wanted more than anything to tell my kids that I did it, they believe I could, obviously the distance wasn't going to be an issue but ability was, at the 60 mile turn around and first cut out, I made it with 5 minutes to spare, I did calculations on the speed I was keeping and knew it was going to be tight, I went hard again, every time a looked at the 10 mile markers I had to smile, this was the farthest I had ever gone, I pedaled hard again leaving behind all the excuses that I wanted to give to not come to the race, also behind were the tears that I shed out of frustration the last few months. I reached transition in 8hrs and 14 minutes with 10 minutes to spare, I was the last one to make it, everybody behind me had either drop out or timed out. I have never worked so hard to be allowed to run a marathon, finally, things were fine, I knew there was no way I was going to time out anymore, for the first time I relaxed. It was almost 6pm but it was still very hot and humid, the course was a 3 loop course with aid stations every mile or so. It seems the whole town was out, it was like being in Boston, the music the people cheering, music everywhere. I want to thank people that make signs for their friends, a runner name Brent had his friends and family go to a lot of trouble to make some amazing ones, "112-mile bike ride because 110 would be wimpy". " Congratulations, you made it to Ironman, bad news you are now broke". I was happy to make for some of the lost time, it felt good enough to run, lots of people were walking by now, the heat seemed unbearable, the air stations were offering iced sponges and had hoses out to spray us. Ironman is often said that the run is the hardest, your quads are thrashed and the body has been pushed to the max and you still have 26 miles to go, is while on the run where I saw lots of people collapse, stumble and drop in front of me, the sounds of sirens were constant through my run. 15hrs 26 minutes total I crossed the finish line and it was the best feeling especially because about 4 miles before I crossed the finish line, I spotted the annoying men from the dinner table, I was running relatively well by then but by God I picked up my form and you would have thought I was Chrissie Wellington, I tapped him on his arm as I ran by him and gave him a thumbs up. But honestly, having my kids watch me finish was the best feeling. I can't tell my kids that they can do anything, I have to show them. I loved everything about Ironman, the thrilled the fast pace, the aura, I don't think that I will be doing another full unless I train harder, but I can see me doing half's for fun, I like doing too many other things than to focus on just one sport. I have been wondering many times when I am just to overwhelmed with everything that it's time to hang the racing flats, why compete, why not just train that way there is no pressure but races give me the peace I seek, no matter how hard my life gets out there it doesn't matter, we are all equal, no status, no race, no background, of course, were you place is many times determined by one or all of the factors but at the starting line we are all the same, after crossing the finish line we all win at some level. To me knowing that I am shaping my kids' lives in a positive way its most valuable than a gold medal.

Sunday, June 12, 2011

MEN WANTED...For Hazardous Journey. Small Wages, Bitter Cold, Long Months of Complete Darkness, Constant Danger. Safe Return Doubtful. Honor and Recognition in Case of Success...(Ernest Shackleton's 1914 Ad)

Things are settling down after the madness of the Oprah Winfrey Network, slowing down in terms of exposure, "back to normal" thankfully means I am back to training and working hard. I am grateful for it, there are some things that I can't seem to stop thinking though, I was happy with the results of the documentary, it was positive and great exposure for the charities. One thing that I didn't predict was that some members of my family would end up being disappointed in me. When the news reached my home town I did an interview, the final result was fantastic, not entirely accurate, I haven't summited all the peaks for example but overall the tone was right. When the reporter asked me about my childhood in Mexico I made the comment that it was humble, we didn't have a lot, something that was true, that didn't go well with some members of my family. My mom's family are well off, she was brought up on a comfortable environment but she married a very poor man, while her family had money, we didn't, no biggie, in my mind I had all the basic necessities. A lot of it was handed me downs some from my mom's wealthier sisters kids but to a child that never matters, except for the fact that I have more male cousins than female so when the boxes arrived my better-looking sisters got the girl's clothing leaving me with boys clothes, I was dressed as a boy until about 12. But some families don't like to talk about it, is shameful, I wonder what my mom would say if it became known that my father was a raging alcoholic? Oops. This is the life that shaped me, I loved my dad but that didn't change the fact that I also feared him, that the years he was sober, two before he died of a massive heart attack, where the best of my life. But families like to keep things like that secret, don't air your dirty laundry, is nobody's business. I am going to tell you the problem with that. I am more proud of my mom and my siblings for doing it in spite of everything, they taught me to move on, to stop wishing for things to be different and just deal with what you have. It is very weird to be embarrassed for not having much, there is no shame on that, I would be more embarrassed if I had been raised with money but was not a decent person. I know that by sometimes being very direct I hurt people that are close to me, but I realized that the people who benefit the most of my postings are the most vulnerable, sometimes I am like a Wedding Magazine, you need me for a short period of time, and sometimes is a deeper relationship. I once met a woman who suffers from depression who could quote entire passages from my postings. So why? the problem with secrets is the shame, there is no secret that I have been sexually assaulted several times, more then I care to name, while that is traumatic enough, the most damage was done on how it was handled it. Some people genuinely thought that they were protecting by telling me to never talk about it anymore. We all know that once you open up about abuse your life and decisions get questioned, the most humiliating moment were after the attack, friends refusing to take me to the police because some of them were in Japan illegally, but when I did go to reported, the police paraded my dress in the room and told me that no wonder I had been dragged and raped. For the record the dress made me look very pretty but it was far from trashy, but who the fuck cares! that should never be an issue. In Singapore for example, when an intruder broke into my hotel room the police scolded me for not wearing pajamas to bed, they knew because I ended up running out of my room to find help, sadly a woman is not safe at home either. On most occasions, the attacker could have been found and prosecuted but none of them were, partly because I behave like a victim, once I was shamed when I spoke up, I never pursue it farther as soon as they start blaming me for it I just stopped talking and many times I even claimed I had lied to preserve whatever sliver of dignity I was allowed to keep. And this is where the problem lies, I have so far been safe, and I think it comes with making the decision that never again will I be let victimized, I don't have to be afraid to go out, or to wear makeup, that is also a behavior of a victim, is never your fault, of course, I practice common sense but there was a period of my life that going to the store in daylight made me hyperventilate, I should never be attacked ever again, and if anything remotely like that happens again, I will stand up for myself no matter what, I think that that is making me less of a target, is well researched that a woman that shows confidence has fewer chances of being picked. You matter, we all do, I have been playing with the idea of writing a book for a while, I have been approached several times, but to me, it has to be meaningful, not about telling people all the things I have accomplished, but it should be about convincing the reader that no matter the circumstances happiness is possible. That is why it is so important to do everything in my power to make sure my kids have the life they desire, I want them to feel that they matter, that nobody has the right to take their dreams away or hurt them in any possible way, physical or emotional. Why do it by ultrarunning or climbing? Adventure is a true sign of emotional health, it serves no purpose other than to feel alive, we don't dare to dream when our basic necessities have not been met yet. To somebody who is in a tough place getting out of bed is a struggle, forget convincing that person to run a marathon, but I want to show them that getting out of bed is not only possible, making it all the way up Everest is also possible and fun. So go ahead, you matter, dream hard, don't let anybody tell you differently.

Sunday, September 18, 2011

TransAlps Race Report.

I just got back from TransAlps race and mental note, "always trust your instinct Norma". I arrived in Kempen Germany a few days before the race; I was to meet my teammate Bernd for the first time in his hometown before heading to the race about 7 hrs. away. I lot of people warned me against running such a grueling race with a stranger, even one of the race organizers wanted to make sure I understood that it was risky since on such events even the best of friends have disagreements. Even though I had a couple of minor problems with him before the race I decided that since we had talked about expectations, I wasn't fast, that he could do better if he wanted to place. My teammate Bernd said, "You have endurance, that's all that matters." So how bad could it be? Ha!, famous last words. I loved Germany, people are friendly and everybody welcomed me warmly, we did a couple of interviews, my teammate was known in his small town for having won a local triathlon for his age group a few years back as well as winning local races. Problems really began once we started on the road to the race, I seemed whiny to him when I complained of long drives with just water and no food, I have been knowing to be very cranky if don't eat well, I really dislike junk, but I would have settle for gas station food if I had to. Bernd had a weird obsession with control so if I asked for something he took pleasure on saying no. The race began at Oberstdorf, Germany on Sat 3th, Stage one was a gentle 27.2 K with 1806 of elevation gain and 1496 of elevation lost finishing in the town of Hirschegg, Austria. I felt great that day, running hills has never been my strength and that day was no exception when my Bernd saw me run uphill for the first time he had the look of a man who just saw his girlfriend for the first time without her Victoria Secret's push up bra, a bit disappointed. But on the downhill, we caught up and finish a strong 31st team, now since I have run with some of the people on the race and know they are the best in the world, I knew that finishing 31st was a dream.

Stage 2 was a grueling 53.2K with 2481M of elevation gain and 2913M of elevation loss, I felt OK but for some reason, I wasn't as fast as the day before, my legs were tired but on a long day especially so early on the race slowing down wasn't too bad, it ended in Schruns, Austria.

Stage 3 was delayed due to bad weather and the stage was re-routed but still was 43K long; I had a hard time with the wind the rain. Many people would quit this day, including Spain's elite mountaineer Edurne Pasaban. We arrived cold and tired in Switzerland by the end of stage 3. We have been staying at small hotels away from the other competitors, just us, Bernd and his best friend who was crewing for us and I, I couldn't stand him anymore. The excitement of the race was now over and the reality that we still had 5 more days of these was starting to weigh in, Bernd was unhappy as well and he was no holding back.

Stage 4 was 39.9K long with 2339M of elevation gain and 27M of elevation loss, the weather was milder but I felt tired and my stomach hurt like somebody punched me hard, it hurt just to breathe, I stayed behind with a group and that's where I realized that a lot of people were feeling the same, some of the people on the back had done TransAlps before and place quite well but for some reason, a lot of us feel sluggish and incredibly tired. I was talking to a couple of American guys and they both now on their own, after fighting with their team members, slow but on their own. I tasted freedom, "You mean I can do that?" they say sure, a lot of teams had now split for many reasons. My teammate caught up to me and I mention that we could do that, I said, "I know you been unhappy and you were talking about how hard it was to go slow since you are used to running fast, I have a solution, we can become solo and we go our own pace!" this is what I said, I swear that you would have thought that I said, " You know Bernd, the guys and I were noticing how small your feet are, and you know what they say!" All the passive aggressiveness was now gone and it was a full-blown argument. He flipped. Now, I usually keep details like this out of my posts. I had a similar incident while climbing, is the very nature of doing something physically demanding and having different personalities causes frictions every time. I have thought about the incident many times, It is not the argument is the words are spoken while angry that matter at the end. He called me a liar and a pretender, that stung, that if he had known that I was such a terrible climber as well as a slow runner he would never have asked me to come, I didn't want to run the race with a stranger, I said no for about 6 months, repeatedly telling him that there were many better runners than me, but he didn't want to hear it," you have endurance, that's all that matters" he said. Eventually, I said yes, after all, it was TransAlps race and I have always wanted to run it. So no, fuck you Bernd, you do not get to treat me like that. Later I found that he had heard about me through an article at Runner's World magazine, unknown to me. The article refers to me as an elite ultrarunner, that's why I shun the word athlete when talking about me, I am average at best and I don't mind it one bit. I am average on a not so average group, the ultrarunners. I didn't take it lying down, the old me would have tried to smooth it over and try to get thought, now I didn't put up with it one bit. Eventually, I told him that it was possible to finish as a team but he could not say a single word to me during the race and definitely never after. Advice to anybody, in an argument, stick to the issue; this is not the time to tell the person about things that annoy you about their personalities or physical aspect. We arrived In Scuol, Switzerland second last and I moved to camp with the other runners, the race organizers heard about him treating me like that and offer me a free camping area with other racers and left him to stay at the hotels he had secured for us.

Stage 5 was a short day, 6K but vertical, the nice thing was that we not only got to sleep in a bit, we also stayed in the same town for a couple of nights, but it was also nice to have some time to sightseeing. It was a great day for Bernd; he was able to run hard as he had wanted, I felt better now that I was able to sleep and eat when I wanted. TransAlps organizers and volunteers are among the best I have seen. They accommodated our needs fast and without a hassle, not easily done when you have such a large group but it always felt like a local 5K to me, not like the large elaborate event like it was. The next few stages where my favorite, I was now feeling stronger and healthier, it still hurt to breathe deeply but it was not as painful. I started to take Ginko Biloba, something that I use when I mountaineer, supposedly it helps with altitude.

Stage 6 was 37K and 1332M elevation gain and 1474 of elevation loss, we were now running up one mountain, the past stages we had to run up two or three, and the downhill was dreamy, I have always loved running downhill, is my favorite, is like dancing, by now Bernd was starting to feel fatigued, and I was feeling better, I could see the face of disappointed when I caught up to him quickly, the downhill was 16K, we later try to joke that he was actually begging for an uphill so I could slow down. This stage was also the most beautiful, we entered Italy though a canyon. These are the moment where I am reminded why I do it, not the version of nonrunners, the addiction, the runners high, so many times I have wished for runners high, no luck, mostly is painful but if you let go and relax then something happens, after so many days of being in pain and having everything hurt, then magically it doesn't hurt as much anymore. The body is a wonderful machine, it will adapt to the changes and excel at it, we don't stop exercising because we are too old, we grow old because we stop exercising.

Stage 7 was the stage that I feared the most, we had to climb to over 3000M that day, I hardly slept fearing timing out. We started in Mals at 8am as usual. That day more people quit than the other days, the leading female ladies, Team Salomon, quit because of injuries I was told, also many people simply couldn't face one more long day and simply walked away, there are never right or wrongs, we all reach different breaking points. But likely for me It was not mine yet. You have no idea how it felt to stand on top of that big mountain with plenty of time to spare, and nothing but downhill ahead, I caught up to Bernd running fast all the way to Sanders.

 With stage 7 behind and only stage 8 to finish, I felt pretty confident about finishing as long as we didn't fall and break anything. At only 30K and 1700, it was a fast day, by now the pain was completely gone and I could take a full breath, no more painful shallow breaths. The climb went fast and stayed with my partner most of the time or not far behind, by now I was observing other people around me to figure out the best way to go up and realized that the best runners were hunched over when climbing, I became the Hunchback of Notre Dame and climbed faster than I had, finally, I was getting a hold of things and it was my last day, the excitement, the beauty of the mountain, I ran the hardest I have run in a while, I guess you can say I experience the runners high, I was 100% taken by that moment, nothing else mattered, not the early struggles, the pain, nothing, I felt completely taken by that moment. That day ended up being the best we had done as a team. I think we all operated on a high, in spite of passing over 200 runners on the last 18K we still crossed the finish line 38th mixed team. I didn't care one bit, I was happy to be there, to have done. Bernd was happy, I had ran him into submission; finally, he had a bit of what he had been searching on a partner. I can't help if he felt disappointed if he looked at me and realized, that he was capable of doing the same things that I had done, that I was not extraordinary or special. I didn't feel regret or embarrassment, yes, he could do it, the only difference between him and me was that I had not waiting for anybody to teach me that or berated people along the way. You know when people said that they hate certain painter's work because it looks like something they could do? Well, you didn't and that's the difference. That what I teach my kids, the world belongs to the once that dare, talent is nothing if you are unwilling to do the work. Everybody wants to learn a new language, very few people are willing to do what's necessary to learn it, I speak three languages only because I am not afraid of making a fool of myself and I am willing to work hard. I could show you lots of pictures of the race but there is one that I love the most, the one that will stay with me. Is the face of the last person to cross the finish line, the last person to complete the race, you can see the sweepers behind her, celebrating her, I stood there watching arrive, you could see she was using every ounce of energy and courage to continue, I saw her the day I got sick, she was struggling, a lot of us struggled one time or another, for her, the struggle was daily but she continued, I had face a day where I didn't know if I could do it and it was scary, she did the race every day unowning is she was going to finish yet she choose to continue and give her best anyway. I stood there yelling, "You are amazing" and I meant it. It's a shame that some people have a narrow definition of success. How could I she be disappointed in anything? Sure I came motivated and excited to train after all I want to see my best, what that is will not be up to me, if I go to my next race and I am that woman I hope you will know that I will feel nothing more than proud. Go and take chances, you can spend the rest of your life waiting for the right moment but maybe the right moment is now. Fear can hold you back if you let it paralyze you or it could be the force that drives you, I can tell you that I fear more not trying that not succeeding.

Sunday, September 25, 2011

Are You Ready?.

If anybody ever asked what would be my most important personality trait it would be that I am incredibly naïve. I really believe that things are possible, even when confronted with the hard fact of why I will never succeed as long as I can picture it clearly in my mind then it is possible. Time and time I have succeed but most important time and time I have failed too. Is then when being naïve had helped me tremendously, when that happens I never hear, they are right, I hear, "I was so close! Next time for sure" I recently went out on a date, sure I been asked out before since Charlie and I broke up but this is the first time I actually went to my closet to find my " date" clothes, which btw, they smelled funky like they been on a box under my bed 'cause they were. It was somebody I have known for a very long time, back when I was in sales and wore nice suits and expensive jewelry. We never really took the next step; even then I knew that our priorities were not the same. He is a very successful man, he had been married once and it helped him realized that kids was not what he wanted, sort of George Clooney. We sat there, at the restaurant, from the distance, maybe things hadn't changed much but looking closely I have changed dramatically. He was distracted by one thing, my funky bracelets, gone is the Tag Heuer, replaced by a functional Timex Ironman and red bracelet. The read bracelet I wear is a symbol that remind me of climbing Aconcagua, one of the guides was wearing a simple red thread around his left wrist, after a few days of being stuck on a tiny tent together, I finally asked why, he told me that his girlfriend was a very superstitious person, that this was his first job as an assistant guide, he had been a porter for 5 years prior and finally was promoted, his girlfriend had put it on to ward off jealousy and envy since the other porters were going to resent him for sure, he told me he thought it was all silly but he didn't want to hurt her feelings. I am not superstitious, I lean more towards science, but I told him to take it that I meant that she cares, let her love him. Last year everyone seemed to go wrong, my sister Muñeca is very superstitious and was telling me all the things I needed to do to, I jokingly said that as things continue to go wrong, I was willing to dance with a chicken under the moonlight, *and while you are at it to put the red thread*, she found a red thread on her sawing kit, as she was putting it around my arm I realized that she truly wished me a better life. I have had it ever since, I bought a more durable one in Spain on a recent trip, one for each of my sisters and one for me. Oprah and her friends might have their marching diamond rings, my sisters Muñeca, Lourdes and I have matching red bracelets. I after telling him my story I realized that nothing had changed, we were still not right for each other, "Your kids will be gone in a few years, can you imagine the trips we can take?" I told him that it would be more likely that I would then sell everything and be a dirtbag so I can do the things that I love the most every day, trail run, climb and live a life of service. That was a few days ago, today, I went out on the perfect date, a lot of sweating and little clothing. His name is trailrunning and he makes my hear race! When I run I felt strong, free, happy. We all get lonely sometimes, but if I date or choose to be with somebody it will be because he is right for me not because I am lonely.

Updated note: Boy this post stung a lot. I just recently divorced again but after I finished reading the post I realized that it's okay to be alone.

Monday, December 12, 2011

Running Home; A Journey To End Violence

I haven't posted in such a long time. Somewhere down the line things became so complicated. I like the way my life is right now but I also miss the simplicity of what running used to mean to me, so I am going back to the basics again. I created Running Home A Journey To End Violence, a project that will take me from my house in Delta, BC where I live to Mazatlan Mexico where I was born. I decided it was time to write the book I been meaning to write. I wanted to go to Everest before I did that, I was so focused on making it happen. A lot of people that knew about my desire to climb have always been worry about the dangers, I have never been afraid, I know that if somebody tells me it can't be done is only because they can't picture it themselves. We all fear something, and my fears aren't mountains, I respect them, but I don't fear them. Then I realized what my fear was, standing up to my past so I couldn't delay writing anymore. I started writing it a few months ago and I became almost paralyzed, is hard reading my journals again, I keep them because I will not deny who I am. I am so much different than the woman of those pages, but to write the book I had to take myself back to those times, it's not easy, the only thing that helps me get through it is to know that I am not there anymore.

Friday, December 30, 2011

"Go Confidently in the Direction of Your Dreams. Live the Life you Have Imagined." Henry David Thoreau

I was recently looking thought Craig's List for sports equipment and I was shocked to find tons of stuff. Most of the headlines read "hardly used" so as the New Year approaches a lot of you will be making their resolutions. I been thinking a lot about what makes someone quit. I don't make New Year resolutions; I am of the mentality that as soon as I realize I need to work on something or change something right then is the right time. How many times have I heard the " I will quit smoking after

New Year's/my vacation/ my birthday" I just think to myself, why?. However, If you are making resolutions and considering making some health changes here are some tips.

1.Start small. As an endurance athlete, this might sound hypocritical but my 'small' might not be 'your' small. All journeys start with a single step. I often see beginners take on too much and that adds to disappointment and quitting because you are setting yourself to fail. If you are a beginner establishing a routine is the most important, be realistic about how much time and effort you can commit and go for it. I have a daunting goal ahead of me but I broke it into smaller tasks and then applied it. I started with establishing running without a day off first, then increased my distance then added the heavy pack. If you are thinking of bettering your time, start by adding speed training to your routine on what you think your body can handle safely, once or twice and don't worry if you don't hit your target every time, you will hit your desired pace once, then twice and so forth. The most important here is that you are trying to change your behavior and mentality, no runner to runner, slow runner to faster runner, couch potato to gym goer.

2.Stop making excuses. It hard for everybody and sure sometimes it's harder for you at that moment more than for anybody else but is that the real reason why you are not doing it? My past success in overcoming challenges is that I spend more time trying to figure out what I contribute to the problem than what others did, not about assigning blame, it might not have been my fault but what did I do that contributed to the outcome? I can't control others but I have control over my actions and thoughts. Sure I have been the victim of unfair circumstances that I had little control of it but I took ownership 100% on how I reacted to it and how much I let it affected me. Sometimes it will be hard or impossible because of injuries or commitments but that is never the reason to quit. When it becomes hard to train because of circumstances I focus on the other things that I need like planning the logistics of my quest or getting ahead on my responsibilities. So when the window of opportunities opens again I am ready! Stop looking around to find excuses for why you can't do it and start spending time focusing on how you can make it happen. Remember that you become better at whatever you spend the most energy on, and if the energy is spent on making up excuses you will just become better at finding more excuses. I remember the first time I was criticized for running ultras way back when I started, somebody was telling me about a conversation of somebody who was trash-talking about me " Who does she think she is?" she has only been running for a few months. My friend Nadia was upset until she noticed I was smiling, she was puzzled " is fabulous" I said "A few months ago everybody took pity in me, nobody wanted my life and now somebody wants my life!" Why were people so upset? Because when someone around you doesn't follow the pattern of making excuses then it becomes harder for you to do it. They are faced with the painful truth that if I can do it so can they. Stop making excuses and go for the life you want. Be the person that shows those around you that it can be done. When you find yourself at rock bottom learn to rock climb.

3. Commit fully. This is a big one. I see lots of new runners or people at the gym at the beginning of the year and just fade away next few months. Why? Anything worth having requires effort. Like a marriage, at the beginning is all butterflies and excitement then it turns into responsibility and doing someone's laundry, but is all on what you focus on. When I decide I want something I embrace all aspects of it since they are all integral parts of the whole project. The moment you decided to take charge of your health you didn't say " I will get healthy until it gets too hard or boring" It Is exciting to start something because everybody is supportive and excited for you too. " Go for it" "100% behind you" In no time things change when it starts affecting your old life, all of a sudden you are not cooking all 3 meals from scratch or changing the sheets every two days or meeting your friends for a drink every Thursday. I took a long break last year, I was getting pressure from everywhere and continuing at the pace I had been going was not possible. Both of my kids needed me home, Karl because of his condition, teachers struggled to find the right plan for him and needed my full attention as he adapted to his new school, Hans' grades started to plummet so I needed to take charge, while I knew that his lower grades where more about the social distractions about a particular video game, I swear you can see a pattern of lower grades every time Call Of Duty releases a new edition I was being blamed for it. "You focus on saving the world more than

them!" First of all I don't give up much to conversations like that, I want my kids to be givers, not takers. If my son Hans ever told me I was favoring sons for spending so much time with his brother I would tell him he should be on his knees thanking God every night it wasn't him who is going blind because the odds were just as high. What bother me is not that it was true, but what if he thought so? Hans heard some family members say that and at one point he voiced that same opinion when I called him on his lack of effort. I spent a year and a half watching SNL with both of my boys and making 100ths of waffles for sleepovers until Hans had no excuse for bringing C's home then he had no choice but to admit what I knew. " You are right mom, I haven't had the best attitude towards learning lately and blaming you was the easiest way of justifying it". Through it all I never lost my commitment towards my goals, I simply had to exercise patience, deal with setbacks as they came and maybe had to modify my plans a bit. I wish you much success in the next year and all others to come; there is nothing more rewarding than taking control of one's life. I am known as an incredibly stubborn person and that has cost me some friends or relationships but if somebody doesn't respect your decisions they shouldn't be in your life anyway. it's not selfishness, people that play emotional blackmail should be in your life. I surrounded myself with people better than me not because I want them to take care of me but to learn and grow. In my life, I am the president and CEO of my destiny. Passion can't be stopped or ignored, just go out there and shine and the rest will follow.

Friday, January 20, 2012

Final Running home Preparations.

I am still getting ready for Running Home, things are going as scheduled. The beauty of being able to just run from my house unsupported gives me the freedom that If I don't feel my kids are ready for me to go yet, I can just postpone until they are comfortable with my decision. Training had been going well until two weeks ago, I was showing signs of overtraining. After two weeks finally, I felt whole again. The hardest part is writing the book, I have had to walk away several times. It is strange and difficult since I have to be emotionally involved in the writing to make it truthful and make justice to it but also emotionally absent to criticize the style and organize the content around the thousand memories floating around my head. The best way I can organize my memories is by choosing the stories of the audience I hope will one day read my story. I was at the Doctors yesterday, I was there to make sure that my fatigue was not due to something more serious such as anemia. I had my doubts but I need to make sure I am at top of my fitness before I embark on a 2600 mile quest. The Doctor listens to my request, asked me to fill a questionnaire and left me in the room. As soon as I saw the form I recognized it. It was to assessed depression. He came back and told him my symptoms where strictly physical not emotional. He apologized but clarified that most people that suffer from extreme fatigue are mostly from depression. I explained with as much detail the reasons why it couldn't be. Only a person who has been there could know. Like a wine connoisseur would explain the differences in grapes from one region to another to a novice. After I explained how I had no problem enjoying my life, hanging out with my family, watching Mexican soaps with my sister or driving across town to taste the best hot chocolate ever. I just felt tired after running for only two hours. He seemed horrified that I wanted to ever run more than two hours! but agreed that people who are experiencing depression felt no more pleasure or desire on the things once gave them joy and I just seemed irritated that I couldn't do more. After my visit, it became clearer. The people that I want to read my story are those who are experiencing pain. Not to reinforce their notion that life is unfair, quite the contrary it's to make someone that is about to lose home that even though life is unfair, sometimes all you need is the courage to claim the destiny that was meant for you. The book idea only came in full force when I was talking to my sister Muñeca that I had decided to talk about my past, she was horrified knowing I was opening myself to criticism and victim blaming, I jokingly said, I know, it will be easier to run home physically that mentally revisiting home, and that's how the idea came about! My journey is about violence because my life has been marked with terrible violence but not talking about it doesn't erase the past, quite the contrary, violence only thrives in silence. It's not lost in me that my son is the same age I was when my father died and my mom became single mom, maybe this is the universe telling me to wake up and to fight to break the cycle. Karl's condition makes him a target for all kinds of abuse because he is vulnerable, from bullying to domestic violence and that is something I will fight until the end of my days. I hope to speak about my life so I don't have to talk about that part of my life ever again.

Sunday, February 19, 2012

"Oh The Places You Will Go. You Can Get So Confused That You'll Start In To The Race Down Long Wiggled Roads At a Break-Necking Pace and Grind On For Miles Across Weirdish Wild Space, Headed, I Fear, Toward a Most Useless Place. The Waiting Place..." Dr. Seuss

Time goes by painfully slow when you are waiting. As a single mother, I understand that there are a lot of things that I don't have much control, that doesn't make it easier for me to control my frustrations when I am sidelined because of an injury or scheduling conflict. To prepare me to take off for two and a half months off there is a long list of things that need to be checked off. Importance over urgency, always. And also the things that are necessary but give me no joy. So the last few months my life has been consumed with boring but necessary tasks of making sure my house runs as smoothly as possible for my mom to take over while I am gone. A pleasant side effect that performing endless mind-numbing tasks such as laundry is that it makes me yearn for an open road and adventure. After all, you are never going to find a bumper sticker that reads " I will rather be organizing my closet" The reverse will be true after my run to Mexico I will savor the normalcy of being at home if only for a short while. The hardest part now is being present in my current life, to be a mother, a sister, an actress on a TV Show. I am physically here but mentally I have to make a conscious decision to be part of my life. My pack is ready to go and I take it out of my closet every day and reorganize the contents every day. A form of meditation that allows me to then participate in my current life. The difference between an addiction and a passion is how it affects your personal life. A passion makes you a better person and an addiction feeds your insecurities. Is that understanding that makes me appreciate the other part of my life, knowing my kids support what I do make me want to be a better mother, yes, sometimes I need to have long conversations with my youngest about his fears about my safety. Fear is all relative, safety is an illusion. Fear is not the same as danger, fear is the perception of danger, danger is real risk coming at you. So if your fear usually comes after you think " what if" then is not real, I don't need to teach you about danger, you'll recognize it when it's staring at you. I do agree that some sports or activities carry more risks because are impossible to eliminate risk of 100% but I have done my best to prepare for the what ifs and then go for it anyway. I am ready and excited to start, I have everything I need and have no desire to buy any fancy equipment, it will be just me and a beautiful road : The US 101 Route. So if you run into me and like my friends say, you will know exactly the moment when we know you have lost me, is the look in my face that tells you that I am already gone, taking in all the beauty and challenges that I am sure to conquer.

Sunday, March 25, 2012

Running Home- Final preparations

It is almost time to go! I have a few weeks until I start my run home. I am very excited but also full of nervousness. Almost like being pregnant, you can't wait to have the baby then when you are due to give birth you start asking yourself questions like " Am I ready?". I got home to an empty house, my kids were off with their dad to Miami. It was nice to be able to just focus on the details of Running Home, I got a new tarp tent so is very light. Is madness figuring out where to be since I can't run on interstate highways, I have to avoid Interstate 5 and some bridges. I have gotten the preparation to the point where I can sleep at night, not awaking every 2 hours panicking because I am not sure how to go across the Washington- Oregon border. The next most important thing is lightening my pack, hygiene is vital but not appearances so no deodorant. Safety is important so yes to technology no to extra clothing, reverse and wear. I am sure I would go thought it over and over it before it is ready but I am getting there. I haven't been training since I ran Modesto Marathon last Sunday, my hip feels better but the lack of training was a bit hard on my confidence after all training hard is what allows me to feel that I can run all the way to

Mazatlan. Whenever I am starting to lack confidence I tell myself the same thing I tell my kids when they say " I am never going to be better" or " I am not good at this". It takes 10,000 hours to archive excellence on anything. I read an article about this somewhere, can't remember where but what the article talked about some scientist that had done the research to figure out if being great at something is nature or nurture and they figure out that is nurture, nature takes care of the type of talent such as Olympic marathoner vs a 3:10 marathoner but nature can't do anything of you don't nurture it. When I tell my kids that, it makes sense, they automatically know they are just being impatient, have they really tried for at least 10,000 hours before deciding they are never going to be any better? I am just excited now for the opportunity to get that much closer to my better self. What I am most excited and proud about Running Home is that is simple yet it touches on what is important, we all can make it from Vancouver BC to Mazatlan, Mexico, it might take some 5 years and others only a month what matters is that we all can. I will be scraping by on my run by surviving on very little. I don't have sponsors but that okay, I wanted to show everyone that in the age of fancy sponsorships, adventure is what you make of, don't get me wrong, I have a long list of adventures that I need funds for but right now I wanted the simplicity of creating a project that wasn't going to be shelved until I had the funds. The one thing I am most grateful for is the amazing support of my family, without their support it would have to be impossible to dream as big as I do. I might not talk to you before I go, I need to focus on what's in front of me and spending time with my family. My brother Carlos in Mexico will be once more managing my social networking when I can't. This is truly an amazing opportunity, I can't tell you how excited is to be going back home. Until then, don't settle for anything before deciding if this is the best you can do. "Every day is a journey, and the journey itself is home." Matsuo Basho Updated Post:

I made it all the way to Mazatlan Mexico in 78 days. From Vancouver to the US/ Mexico border I ran every mile, mostly unsupported. In Mexico I ran about 50% of the distance some areas too dangerous even with protection from the government. I released the book Running Home to a lot of controversy, about 70% of my family don't want to talk to me anymore because I spoke about my grandfather and that the reason why I stopped witting publicly for so long.

Thursday, May 30, 2013

The Road Less Traveled

The last week I have broken down crying for no apparent reason in the oddest places, in my driveway, on a bathroom stall just before my swim. I assumed it had to do with all the training I been doing and the energy that it takes to coordinate the massive effort that it is to pull intense workout out hours on top of all of the other very important and time-consuming responsibilities I have like, raising two very different teens and work. I finally figure out what it was when I pulled my sons' travel itinerary for his upcoming trip to Toronto to do the training and ultimately bring his guide dog home. Then and there the overwhelming feeling came rushing. No matter how much I tell myself this is not because is any indication that Karl is getting worse, Is just for independence, it just tears me apart. I still hate he is affected by his condition, as much as I did the first time I head the diagnosis. Karl is one of the bravest people I have known and he is also the sweetest. I feel the last few weeks it's like we are back to the beginning and I am fighting ignorance and discrimination when some places wouldn't allow him with his dog. Eventually, the gym apologized and is allowing him to bring his guide dog with him, but only when I threaten to sue them and take the story to the press. Luckily Karl was never aware of it but it made me realized that this fight is far from over and he still has a lot of discrimination to overcome. I know that once more, Karl will come home with his dog and make me feel that everything is OK by taking everything with the positive attitude he always has. Throw in the fact that I also speaking in LA about Running Home and you have a ticking bomb. I still hate the fact that that story exists but I don't hate it as much as the fact that is still happening. I just watched the news about the rescue of the three women that were held captive. The joy of the families, the horror of the public when they realized that such a monster was living near them, then the further victimizing of the brave young girls, " the door was left unlocked in a couple of occasions and they didn't escape?" Every time I hear that it breaks my heart that we are still liberating abusers of any responsibility by placing blame on victims, let me make this clear, nobody deserves or wants that. Something else bothers me, what are we doing to prevent this from happening to anybody else? Is not true that we don't know this is happening, this is happening right now but we close our eyes to the obvious. I am not saying that these young women had it easier but how is that different than the thousands of girls that fall prey to prostitution because of lack of social support and abuse. I am not going to go over the debate between prostitution vs sex work, because either way th eons affected are the women performing the job. To ensure that is clearly a choice it will be to eliminate the vulnerabilities that forces so many women and girls to that life. Losing sleep is part of reaching that place in your heart that says "enough" I refuse to stay silent any more. My book seemed to touch a lot of people deeply and I make no apologies, if you think is a painful reading detail account of being victimized, try living it. I will never be OK, I have learned to not only survive and thrive considering my past but make no mistake, there will not a single day pass that something will take me to the deep pain I felt, the fear and the shame that I was forced upon me. Luckily, I have worked hard in building dreams where once nightmares lived. My frustrations are from being unable to accept limitations from others, or myself, all I know is that I don't have to accept that the cure for blindness will not be here in time for my son or that human trafficking is such a difficult and complex problem than single individual fighting to end it will not have a significant impact. Nobody has the right to tell me what my hopes and dreams have to be. In the world I am working towards, my son Karl can see perfectly the face of the woman he will fall in love with and I will never read that another child or woman disappeared. I made a commitment to my son that day we sat down on my front steps when he was 11 years old that I was going to support him though whatever he chose in life for him. After that day, I embarked on a journey and there is no turning back.

Tuesday, August 6, 2013
"When Words are Both True and Kind, They Can Change the World". Buddha

I ran Tijuana's marathon this past weekend. International Network of Hearts (INH) invited me to join them since they were the featured charity of the run. I was looking forward to finally meeting one of my heroes. My boyfriend Kevin Compayre and I arrived the day before to a full schedule that included catching up with some of my childhood friends, picking up the race package and meetings with the entire team of my next project Be Relentless, I will be breaking the current Guinness record for the world Longest triathlon. You are probably wondering a couple of things right now, can it be done? And/or why? As much as I love to run, I love adventure more. It's getting tough to join the races that I want to do, they fill fast and some are by invitation only. I love that the ultrarunning scene has gone mainstream, after all, that is part of being part of the social network community to share my experiences and inspire others to try new things. The disadvantages are of course is that then I am scrambling with everybody else to run races. So it is time to find a new sport in the extreme adventure scene. If there is one thing that separates me from others isn't talent or ability but that my brain sees things differently. Most people get discouraged when they see odds like one in a million chances, I think I will be the ONE!. When I heard the struggles of Alma, the director of INH I knew it was time for a new project to raise funds for her shelter and awareness about human trafficking. I open up about my history of abuse and violence, even as a survivor of human trafficking, something that until now I have not shared because I am already fighting for the right to tell my story about childhood trauma I just didn't want to open and other door to my pain but then I heard Marisol's story of her incredible journey I spent many sleepless nights wondering ,Why is my life better and not Marisol's? Our lives would have probably been parallel, I knew that I could never make sense of things, there are is no meaning behind tragedies like that, the only thing I could do was to make something positive out of it. Marisol was sold as a young girl to a man that took her to the USA, having a very sick mother she willingly followed him thinking that she was going there to work to pay for her mother's medical bills but ended up being sold over and over again for sex as well as being abused by her captor on a regular bases. What breaks my heart is when Marisol talks about going to prison being one of her happiest days, the day she was finally freed from the horrors of her slavery and it was the day she went to prison for a crime her captor committed. Marisol spent 17 years behind bars still deprived of her freedom but compared to the prison she had lived it was paradise. It's being two years since she finally regained her freedom fully, having her sentence reversed and declared innocent with the help of a Catholic nun that advocated for her. Finally meeting her after the marathon, her first in freedom, she ran in prison to keep sane. Our run together was incredibly powerful and symbolic for her but bittersweet for me, I am happy she is finally free from the horror she lived but I also know that it's difficult to escape the nightmares. My biggest pain is that even though she was a victim, and forced into that lifestyle, she has limited options not because of her abilities but because of our society. The stigma will follow her forever, she will relive the shame and humiliation that sex crimes bring, sex crimes aren't about sex, they are about taking your dignity away, trying to destroy the very core of human existence. " You could have escaped, obviously you liked it" was one of the comments she heard recently. I admire Marisol's strength, her ability to handle everything so positive and with class. Sitting there across her I felt the closeness that comes with being able to be yourself, to be accepted and understood. I like meeting other survivors, I feel less alone, yes, even after all these years and my thousands social media friends, I still feel lonely sometimes. The loneliness that one feels when you are silenced and lose your identity because society doesn't wants to acknowledge your feelings. "I know what happened to you but I don't want to hear about it". The shame that a statement like that brings, makes us feel like there is something wrong with us. Marisol and I took turns telling out worse moments like we needed to purge our souls even for a second. Marisol is the strong one, I am the lucky one. Even though all my pain, I had the support of my family, that was always the source of my strength, I don't know if I had not given up if I had been in her shoes. So doing a documentary to hopefully influence a chance is something that at least lets me sleep a bit better a night. Compared to the difficult journey she still has ahead of her, my Guinness World Record is a walk in the park in comparison. I will be following the trafficking route from Cancun to Washington DC passing through towns to empower the community, to have each one declare, not in my neighborhood, the most powerful neighborhood watch program. I have faith in humanity, I have faith that Marisol will have plenty of opportunities ahead of her, that she will be celebrated as the amazing survivor she is, a proof that goodness does succeed against evil and that one day she would not only live an abundant life but she also finds a person that would look into her eyes and say, " You are worthy". Kevin and I just started dating, is too soon to tell but so far it's going really well. What's different this time is that all the cards are on the table. I don't want to make excuses when something triggers me anymore. I want a relationship that allows me to be able to set firm boundaries and be respected for it. I went to visit the girls that live at INH's shelter, I want them to see me unapologetically living in the open, I don't want to be invisible anymore. I want to take as much space as possible. I am so much more than the worse things that ever happen to me. I been so busy trying to piece myself back together thinking that I was broken, but I was just supposed to make the most beautiful mosaic of these moments of my life. I still head to a trail when I need to listen to my soul. I love adventure but it was never about adventure or running, It was about finding the courage to dream of doing something so daring and crazy in the midst of the pain.

Update

So much has changed since my last entry but so many things remain the same. I broke the Guinness World Record for the Longest triathlon May 4, 2014, swimming 152.1 kilometers, cycling 3692.2 kilometers and running 1138.7 kilometers almost tripling the old record and spoke publicly about surviving sexual violence and human trafficking in Washington

DC soon after at a United Nations-sponsored event then #MeToo movement happened. I have spent the last few years speaking on behalf of victims of sexual violence all over the world more than I have ran races because I thought that's what the world needed of me. In 2015 Kevin and I exchanged vows in Tijuana and the same girls from the International Network of Hearts shelter stood as bridesmaids. In many ways it seemed my world had changed for the better. My son Karl had just graduated from Emily Carr Bachelor Of Art's visual arts program and Hans was attending New York city's The New School studying business. It seem that I finally made it to the finish line. I was no longer a single mother, my kids left the nest and I was now a wife again. Then my world imploded February 3, 2019 when I got injured at The Yukon Ultra 400 mile race and become unable to run. Within months I went into a deep depression as my marriage crumbled under the pressure of my unhappiness. My husband didn't make me unhappy, it was my own sense of failure that broke us, falsely believing that I had failed him by going to the Arctic Circle instead of focusing on my marriage. I take full responsibility of all the unhappiness that followed. Somehow the beliefs that I wanted to free myself from were the same ones that brought me down. Love is not sacrificing ourselves until there is nothing left of us to love. I lost myself in the belief that was what my marriage and the world needed from me as an activist. The sense of shame that followed started to seep through into the other parts of my life but now I know this for sure. I will continue to speak up about issues that affect those around me. We made progress on awareness about gender-based violence (GBV) but it became relegated to marches and keynote speeches. Complacency is what's stopping us from succeeding and I am not ready to quit the fight against GBV or to hang my running shoes yet. In an incredible twist, I am back at home in Canada with my two sons in self-isolation mothering them like the old times and the only time I am spending outside is on an remote trail to avoid contagion. I spent the last year trying to understand what happened and the same journals you are reading now it's what served as clues. I need adventure, it's not a frivolous endeavor. I need to Run Wild, it's who I am and what makes me feel alive. I don't know about you but I am ready for what's to come. If you think my life is extraordinary until now, you haven't seen anything yet.

Sincerely A Mexican Running Wild.

About the Author

Norma Bastidas is an author, adventurer and Women's Rights activist that when not in an adventure splits her time between the USA and Canada. Her next book Trigger Warning will be released in 2022.

About the A Mexican Running Wild Bookcover.

Cover photo courtesy of Tourism Sinaloa. Backcover arctic photos courtesy of Claudia Katz Photography. Be Relentless finish photo courtesy of iempathize. Running Home photos courtesy of Jerry Gamez. Cover design by Hans Christie.

Made in the USA
San Bernardino, CA
07 May 2020

71266215R00212